Cultural Processes of Inequality

Cultural Processes of Inequality

A Sociological Perspective

Amanda Udis-Kessler

ANTHEM PRESS

Anthem Press
An imprint of Wimbledon Publishing Company
www.anthempress.com

This edition first published in UK and USA 2025
by ANTHEM PRESS
75–76 Blackfriars Road, London SE1 8HA, UK
or PO Box 9779, London SW19 7ZG, UK
and
244 Madison Ave #116, New York, NY 10016, USA

First published in the UK and USA by Anthem Press in 2024

British Library Cataloguing-in-Publication Data
A catalogue record for this book is available from the British Library.

Library of Congress Control Number: 2025932582
A catalog record for this book has been requested.

ISBN-13: 978-1-83999-545-3 (Pbk)
ISBN-10: 1-83999-545-9 (Pbk)

This title is also available as an e-book.

I dedicate this book to sociologists Eve Spanger, who trained me, and Tim Haney, whom I trained. I am forever grateful to these two wildly smart, passionately committed advocates of human well-being. *La lucha continua*.

CONTENTS

LIST OF FIGURES

ACKNOWLEDGMENTS

The acknowledgments section of any book is often the book's most sociological component, demonstrating as it does that we build society together, experience society together, and change society together. I'm grateful for the many people who have helped me think through and write down these ideas that, at the end of the day, are about changing our societies for the better. There are too many of you to name, but here, in alphabetical order, are some of the most important contributors. Some of you encouraged me. Some of you beta read chapters. Some of you provided other kinds of guidance or offered endorsements at early stages. Deep thanks to all of you:

Dr. Elizabeth Armstrong, Dr. Helen Bishop, Dr. Warren Blumenfeld, Conie Borchardt, John Brooking, Dr. Liliana Carrizo, Justin Cook, Dr. Helen Daly, Dr. Nancy DiTomaso, Deb Donley, Mari Franklin, Dr. Tim Haney, Maggie Jusell, Dr. Janet Lincoln, Chris Lombardi, Dr. Phoebe Lostroh, Dr. Bill Marsiglio, Jean McIntosh, Dr. Vanessa Munoz, Dr. Gail Murphy-Geiss, Dr. Nancy Naples, Dr. C. J. Pascoe, Dr. Fran Pilch, Jessy Randall, Dr. Eve Spangler, Rev. Deborah Tinsley, Dr. James Vela-McConnell, and Chelsea Witt.

To whoever should be listed above and is not, I apologize and thank you.

My gratitude also to the staff at Anthem Press, particularly Mario Rosair and Jebaslin Hephzibah. Your predecessors patiently kept inviting me to write a book for Anthem for years. I hope I've done right by you.

This year marks the 30th anniversary of the first college course I taught. It was called "Inequality in America." Deep gratitude to my students over the years. I hope you learned as much from me as I learned from you.

Now, let's all go change society together—for the better.

EPIGRAPHS

[I]nequality is not the result of mysterious forces. We can see how resources are transmitted in families; how skills and self-confidence are nurtured (or not) in schools; how people gain access to (or are excluded from) the networks through which information and opportunities are obtained; how gatekeepers and bosses make decisions about employees […] how rules of the game are made, interpreted, and enforced. Behind every unequal outcome there is a process that can be analyzed by answering *How?* Questions. If we understand these processes, we're in a better position to try to change them. (Schwalbe 2020: 12–13)

Girls and women may be down-ranked or deprived relative to more or less anything that people typically value—material goods, social status, moral reputation, and intellectual credentials, among other realms of human achievement, esteem, pride, and so on. This may happen in numerous ways: condescending, mansplaining, moralizing, blaming, punishing, silencing, lampooning, satirizing, sexualizing, belittling, caricaturizing, exploiting, erasing, and evincing pointed indifference. (Manne 2018: 30)

White people know very well one thing; it's the only thing they have to know. […] They know they would not like to be Black here. (James Baldwin; Westerfeld 2021)

The idea that some lives matter less [than others] is the root of all that is wrong with the world. (Farmer n.d.)

The dividing lines of us and them shift and change, but the *processes* endure. (Wills 2008: viii, italics in original)

INTRODUCTION

On the first day of the semester, I walked into my Sociology of Inequality course and told the students to design a new society from scratch. They had complete control over every aspect of the society. The only criterion? They had to make sure that the society was socially, politically, and economically divided by hair color. They were to make it crystal clear that dark-haired people were the valued members of society while fair-haired people counted for nothing. Their assignment was to generate as many strategies as they could to send this message. They could set institutional policies, develop popular culture materials, create laws, limit social interactions, or do anything else that occurred to them. The students bent over their notebooks.

Half an hour later, all four blackboards in the room were full, and my arm was tired from writing down nearly a hundred suggestions. The students' ideas covered every major social institution, every form of popular culture known to humankind in 2005, and a wide range of interpersonal interactions. They figured out how to make fair-haired people feel inadequate in any social setting, whether dark-haired people were present or not. The students made sure dark-haired people would never be held accountable for their mistreatment of fair-haired people. The students even struggled with how to treat redheads; were they valued or devalued? (Most students went with "devalued.")

We looked at the four blackboards and everyone took a breath. I told them that they had done a great job and added, "Congratulations—now you understand how racism and sexism work in the United States." I then handed out a pile of statistics and class went on from there.

I had students complete this exercise on the first day of courses on racism, sexism, heterosexism, and inequality more generally. Year in and year out, it never failed.

At some level, we know more about how systemic inequality works than we think. While the students were always creative, their creativity was fueled by real-life examples: newspaper stories, movies, and conversations they had with friends and family. At the same time, as each course continued after that first day, I noticed the same problem. Students struggled to see how different forms of inequality, such as sexism and racism, were similar to one another. The challenge was not in finding individual examples of both, which students could always do, but in making sense of what different forms of inequality had in common once their specific histories were taken into account. I like to think that *Cultural Processes of Inequality* had its genesis in that discrepancy.

Since you're reading this book, you probably already care about racism, sexism, or other forms of systemic inequality. You may know from your personal experiences or in other ways about the harm inequality causes, the lives it shortens, and the joy it strips away.[1] You may recognize that inequality robs everyone in society of the gifts that members of devalued groups could offer (or could offer more abundantly). Perhaps you have wondered whether inequality makes large-scale problems such as global climate change worse. (It does.[2])

Caring about inequality is the crucial first step in addressing it; understanding how it works is the second. Until we recognize the processes that keep inequality in place, we will not be able to work effectively against those processes. Fortunately, there are a wide variety of superb resources on the history of inequality in its various forms,[3] as well as thoughtful accounts of how institutional inequality works as a system.[4] This book focuses on a less-discussed aspect of systemic inequality: the cultural processes by which inequality is produced and reproduced, often by well-intended people.

---

1 The literature on physical and mental impacts of racism, sexism, and heterosexism is extensive. See, for example, Bailey et al. 2017; Dallas 2018; English et al. 2020; Flores et al. 2018; Goosby et al. 2018; Green et al. 2020; Harnois and Bastos 2018; Mahowald et al. 2020; Miller 2020; Ozier et al. 2019; Rooney 2021; Sima 2023; Simons et al. 2018; Stacey et al. 2022; Trevor Project 2022; Umberson 2017; What We Know 2019; Zeiders et al. 2018.

2 Paul 2022.

3 Useful resources on the history of racism in the United States include Abrams et al. 2020; Anderson 2018a; Daniels 2020; Goldstone 2020; and Holder and Koppelman 2022 on voter suppression; Branch and Jackson 2020; Katznelson 2005; Rothstein 2017; Taylor 2019 on segregation; and Medwed 2021 on the death penalty.

4 See, for example, Acker 1990; Anderson 2010, Chapter 1; Bonilla-Silva 1996; Golash-Boza 2016; Ray 2019; Tilly 1998; and Udis-Kessler 2008, Chapter 7.

Why Cultural Processes?

As sociologist Michael Schwalbe points out,

> The behavior that reproduces inequality is, like all behavior, a result of the meanings people learn to give to things and of how they perceive and interpret their circumstances. Understanding the reproduction of inequality thus requires looking at what these meanings, perceptions, and interpretations are. We also need to look at where these ways of making sense come from and whose interests they serve. What we may discover is that inequality is held in place, on a routine basis, less by what is done to people's bodies than by what is done to their minds.[5]

Writing specifically about racism, sociologist Erik Withers observes that whiteness "is accomplished—in part—through […] worldviews, values, frames, repertoires, narratives, and symbolic boundaries, which together serve to maintain racial oppression and normalize an imbalanced racial hierarchy."[6]

Similarly, sociologist Penny Edgell and her collaborators observe that, "Drawing symbolic boundaries is not a benign practice; rather, it is associated with willingness to draw social boundaries that support material and political inequality."[7]

When these sociologists lift up the importance of meanings, perceptions, interpretations, worldviews, and symbolic boundaries to the maintenance of inequality, they are pointing specifically to the importance of *cultural* elements and processes as a key component of inequality. Such elements and processes deserve their own attention, especially because they play out across multiple kinds of systemic inequality—in fact, I would argue, across all forms of inequality.

We often think about inequality in terms of institutional practices, such as discrimination: how exactly are people treated unequally? Alternately, we may consider the impact a form of inequality has on members of a devalued group: the financial penalties they pay, the limited life options they experience, or the violence they suffer. These are all extremely important components of inequality, about which many other people have written.

In this book, I consider instead how cultural processes work across different forms of inequality. Many of these processes have the effect of either drawing

5 Schwalbe 2015: 113.
6 Withers 2017: 1.
7 Edgell et al. 2020: 309.

or reinforcing what Edgell and her collaborators call "symbolic boundaries." These symbolic boundaries, in turn, have the effect of legitimating social, political, or economic boundaries by defining members of devalued groups as unworthy of positive treatment. Once we believe that certain people do not deserve the same good things that we would want for ourselves, it's easy for us to mistreat them or to do nothing while others mistreat them. Symbolic boundaries thus turn into social, political, or economic boundaries through a kind of moral transformation. Some people are deemed part of the "moral community" of those who must be treated well while others are defined as outside of that community. This book explores the cultural processes that inform this moral transformation.

Sociologists, anthropologists, and others who study human social life have a lot to say about what culture is and is not.[8] I take a fairly straightforward approach to culture in this book. As I note again in Chapter 2, I'm defining culture as shared understandings—those ideas, beliefs, and values that we hold in common which enable us to make sense of the world collectively. Language, symbols, and stories are thus part of culture. Culture also includes the shared assumptions underlying our common ideas, beliefs, and values. Finally, culture includes the norms, rules, and laws that emerge from those shared understandings.

While the examples in this book are limited to anti-Black racism, sexism, and heterosexism in the United States (because those are the forms of inequality about which I know the most), the power of a "cultural processes" approach to inequality is that it can be used to make sense of any and every form of systemic inequality. The examples will be different but the processes are the same.

For example, when sociologist Robert Merton first wrote about moral alchemy (covered in Chapter 4), his main example involved anti-Semitism. Islamophobia relies on assumptions about Muslim dangerousness that would be familiar to anyone who knows about US anti-Black racism. Women and Black/Indigenous/People of Color (BIPOC) people are not the only ones presumed to be incompetent; ageism and ableism guarantee that the same presumptions are made about older people and those with disabilities. The "world built for men" described in Chapter 6 is also a world built for able-bodied people. While I touch on transphobia only briefly in the book, many of the mechanisms that disempower women and Black people similarly disempower trans people, perhaps especially the lack of credibility afforded them.

---

8 See, for example, Patterson 2014; Swidler 1986.

Introducing Myself

All people are human beings, with universally shared situations and needs.[9] All people are also individuals, with unique life histories and perspectives. Finally, all people belong to valued or devalued social groups; most of us belong to at least one valued group and at least one devalued group.

If my self-description here focuses on some of the valued and devalued groups to which I belong, it's not because my individuality or my humanity don't matter. It's because both my individuality and my humanity are impacted deeply by those group identities. For example, in a racist society, my whiteness makes it easier for me to get my basic human needs met, to pursue my individual passions,[10] and to avoid dangers that could hurt or kill me. At the same time, being female and queer in a sexist, heterosexist society cuts into my joy, adds fear to my days, and otherwise interferes with my well-being.[11]

The first moment in my life that eventually led to my writing this book happened while I was in college. I came out as bisexual in high school and immediately faced jarring and painful heterosexism, so by my college years, I was a committed activist and could talk for hours about how heterosexism worked and why it was so harmful.

One day, I attended a college protest against racism and had an insight while listening to a speaker. I realized that some of my struggles with heterosexism were similar to struggles people of color (a common term then) had with racism. Many of the details were different but both racism and heterosexism were built on what I now call bad-faith treatment (described in Chapter 3) driven by what I now describe as cultural processes of inequality (Chapters 4–8). Recognizing this fact forced me to ask whether I benefitted from racism just as heterosexual people benefitted from heterosexism. For the first time, I had to confront the fact that I had what would soon come to be called white privilege even as I paid a price for being queer. That insight came to me more than 30 years ago, but it has shaped my life ever since.

---

9 We are all embodied. We all have emotions. We all need to connect with other people. We all need to make sense of the world. We share a number of other attributes in common. This is actually a topic about which I've written another book (Udis-Kessler 2024).

10 My personal passions include sociology, progressive religion, writing, songwriting and composing, cats, British baking shows, and selected series of Star Trek. I also have every professional recording of the musical *Godspell* ever released in English.

11 There are also things I love about being female and queer, to be sure. These are positive identities for me, not just difficult ones.

I'll share a few personal stories over the course of the book, but the last thing I want you to know for now is that I am deeply committed to human well-being, and as much as possible to the well-being of all people. Flourishing makes my heart sing, while suffering makes my heart break. I yearn unashamedly for a society in which every last person gets to flourish. My intellectual and creative projects, the antiracism trainings I offer, and the activism in which I still sometimes engage are all motivated by that yearning.

The Plan of the Book

In Chapter 1, I introduce the idea of "mattering," which involves having your well-being prioritized when it is in competition (or apparent competition) with the well-being of other people. I discuss racial segregation in the United States as an example of how systemic inequality can work when the desires of one social group matter more than the desires of another group. I then provide examples of ways in which the comfort, education, rights, health, and lives of members of valued groups are prioritized. I introduce the concept of moral exclusion and conclude with an example of how society values sexual assaulters more than the women they assault.

In Chapter 2, I introduce the concepts of power-to and power-over, and then describe three important ways of thinking sociologically about power: decision-making power in institutional contexts, cultural power as the ability to influence meaning systems, and individual power as enhanced credibility. I conclude with a discussion of why it matters that members of valued groups are so often in power.

In Chapter 3, I present the idea of good-faith assumptions and treatment as the granting of the benefit of the doubt, and bad-faith assumptions and treatment as the withholding of the benefit of the doubt. Systemic inequality can be understood as granting or withholding the benefit of the doubt based on valued or devalued group membership, along with the resulting good-faith or bad-faith treatment. I then revisit the concept of moral exclusion from Chapter 1, indicating its ties to bad-faith assumptions and treatment.

I next discuss systemic discrimination as a form of institutional bad-faith treatment, noting research on housing discrimination, hiring discrimination, and racial discrimination in the criminal justice system. I conclude by reimagining the idea of privilege in a way that moves beyond individualistic "privilege lists" to posit privilege as the many systematic outcomes of good-faith treatment based on receiving the benefit of the doubt. Organizing existing privilege lists (across white privilege, male privilege, and heterosexual privilege) into themes suggests larger social patterns connected to differential granting or withholding of the benefit of the doubt, which in turn sets up the main topics of the rest of the book.

In Chapter 4, I discuss Robert Merton's concept of moral alchemy as a kind of granting or withholding of the benefit of the doubt. I then cover false equivalencies as a kind of reverse moral alchemy.

In Chapter 5, I focus on three kinds of meta-assumptions into which good-faith and bad-faith assumptions often fall: competence/incompetence, trustworthiness/suspicion, and innocence/guilt. I then discuss the sociological concept of self-fulfilling prophecies, showing how self-fulfilling prophecies emerge from good-faith and bad-faith assumptions that lead to good-faith and bad-faith actions. I conclude the chapter by introducing the idea of good-faith and bad-faith cycles.

In Chapter 6, I discuss ways in which visibility and invisibility receive positive and negative valence such that members of valued groups benefit from visibility in some contexts and from invisibility in others, while members of devalued groups suffer from both negative visibility and negative invisibility.

In Chapter 7, I discuss the distinction between being defined as "having" a problem and "being" a problem. I then address how devalued groups are held responsible for dealing with problematic situations caused by valued groups. I conclude by considering victim-blaming as an example of bad-faith assumptions and treatment.

Chapters 4–7 covered cultural processes of inequality individually; in Chapter 8, I provide several examples of how the processes work in tandem, discussing women's pain, rape myths, antiabortion discourse and laws, racialized school discipline, racial profiling in "white space," and police targeting people for "driving while Black."

Sometimes members of devalued groups collude in their own devaluation. In Chapter 9, I focus on cultural processes that help explain why collusion might take place. These include the power of socialization and the ways in which inequality shapes our subjectivity, as well as how cultural power (discussed in Chapter 2) is connected with ideology. I close with a discussion of internalized oppression.

In Chapter 10, I suggest specific ways in which we can work against the cultural processes of inequality discussed throughout the book. I also provide concrete guidance about how individuals in valued groups can work toward building a good-faith society in which all people might receive the benefit of the doubt.

Each chapter ends with discussion questions.

The Appendix provides a brief introduction to sociology for students and others who may be encountering it for the first time. In it, I explain what sociology is, indicate the range of topics sociologists study, introduce the sociological imagination, and describe several core sociological insights. These include the social construction of reality, the relationship between individuals and society, human interdependence, the importance of the taken-for-granted, and how sociologists understand freedom and its limits. I close with some thoughts on how sociology can be a force for equality.

Some Caveats

Because this book focuses on cultural processes of inequality rather than on any one form of inequality in detail, it is illustrative rather than exhaustive. I could use many more examples than I do but that would take up more space without necessarily adding much insight. I could cover a wider variety of types of inequality but since the cultural processes work similarly across different forms, I'm hoping you can extrapolate from my examples to situations related to whatever form of inequality concerns you the most. Alternatively, I could try to cover anti-Black racism, sexism, and heterosexism more thoroughly, but such coverage, though important, is beyond the goal of this book.[12]

Both the examples and research cited are overwhelmingly US-centered. Because the processes described in the book are so broad, I hope that readers in other countries will be able to come up with parallel examples from within their own societies.

While the book includes many examples of intersectionality, the ways in which different forms of inequality interact with one another in the lives of people with multiple devalued identities,[13] there is not an explicit discussion of how intersectionality works or why it is important. Similarly, the book does not address directly the complexities of privilege and disadvantage among people with a mix of valued and devalued identities.[14] These are important topics, but also beyond my goal here.

---

12 The bibliography includes many resources about how anti-Black racism, sexism, and heterosexism work in the United States.

13 Examples of intersectionality mentioned in the book include the gendered pay gap, discussed in Chapter 5; as researcher Rakesh Kochhar (2023) points out, in 2022, white women typically earned 83 cents for every dollar earned by white men, while Black women typically earned 70 cents. On a different topic, the Human Rights Campaign Foundation (2023) notes that anti-trans violence disproportionately affects BIPOC trans women; since 2013, Black trans women have represented 63 percent of all known trans female victims, and over half of known trans female victims in 2022 were Black.

14 White women can, of course, perpetuate racism while suffering from sexism, just as heterosexual Black people can perpetuate heterosexism while suffering from racism. We need to be able to hold complexities such as these in our minds while working for an end to all forms of inequality.

Class inequality is a central facet of life across the world, both as it flows from neoliberal capitalism[15] and as it intersects with other forms of inequality. However, in a book that focuses on cultural rather than structural aspects of inequality, it is difficult to address most of the ways in which class inequality plays out within and across societies. While class inequality has important cultural components,[16] focusing on them alone without covering the other ways in which class inequality works risks being potentially misleading. I have therefore reluctantly decided not to address class inequality in this book.

Finally, any discussion of sexism that focuses only on women who were assigned female at birth is incomplete. Because this book uses examples of sexism to elucidate cultural processes of inequality rather than seeking to provide an exhaustive account of sexism, I have elected to use the term "women" without elaboration except when specifically discussing trans women. Cultural processes of sexism affect nonbinary and genderqueer people as well as those assigned female at birth, and certainly affect trans women in tandem with transphobia and cissexism. A more exhaustive coverage of antiabortion discourse and laws would refer to "pregnant people" and "people who can get pregnant" rather than "women." I hope that others will extend the ideas in this book more fully to the many women and other people whose experiences of inequality are not covered here.

Potential Discomfort Ahead!

If you have not studied inequality from a sociological perspective before, you may find this book uncomfortable in places. It may unearth assumptions you

---

15 Harvey 2005.

16 See, for example, historian Nancy Isenberg's (2016) study of poor whites in the United States or work on how the poor are blamed for their poverty (Greenbaum 2015; Katz 2013). Sociologist Elizabeth Seale (2023: 7) points out that, "People in poverty are often characterized as dependent, lazy, fraudulent, criminal, violent, untrustworthy, unintelligent, dirty, loud, addicted, unmotivated, passive, bigoted, and ignorant." Criminologists Jeffrey Reiman and Paul Leighton (2020) demonstrate how the criminal justice system grants wealthy people the benefit of the doubt. Sociologist Lauren Rivera (2015) similarly shows how wealthy students are defined as "good fits" for elite jobs. More broadly, as sociologist Michèle Lamont (2023: 69–70) points out, "economic inequality is often deeply rooted in identity-based discrimination and injustice. A major reason that Black people in the United States have accumulated less wealth than their white peers, for example, is that they were systematically excluded from homeownership through redlining, discrimination on the part of banks, and other explicitly racist practices. But these hurtful actions were always motivated by cultural beliefs about this group; identity is and always has been a basis for hateful attacks."

did not know you had, and it will certainly push you to examine the ways in which you take inequality for granted. If you tend to see the world individualistically, as so many people in countries like the United States do, the focus on cultural *systems* may feel awkward or seem wrongheaded. If you find yourself uncomfortable with my claims or the evidence I provide, I can only ask you to wrestle with your discomfort rather than letting it drive you away from the book or the class in which you are reading the book. Discomfort is not the same as danger; indeed, discomfort is often a good thing, a sign of learning taking place. I wish you productive wrestling with any discomfort you experience while reading this book.

Let's get started.

Chapter 1

MATTERING: INEQUALITY AS DIFFERENTIAL VALUATION

> The U.S. Supreme Court has been very busy lately making clear which kinds of people it truly values. By striking down *Roe vs. Wade*, the justices showed us how much they value the opinions of women who want a say in their own health care. By striking down affirmative action, they showed us how much they value White over Black and Brown students. [...] And today they essentially legalized the unequal treatment of LGBTQ people [by permitting religion-based discrimination against them].[1]

> The reversal of *Roe v. Wade* by the Supreme Court in 2022 affects negatively not only the health and well-being of women across all classes, but also their sense that they matter and are perceived as fully independent and competent citizens by their government.[2]

How much we matter to society turns out to matter a lot to us. It matters for our happiness, our well-being, and the opportunities we will have in life. And how much we matter has a lot to do with whether we belong to socially valued groups or not. For example, men tend to matter more than women, white people more than members of Black/Indigenous/People of Color (BIPOC) communities, heterosexual people more than lesbian/gay/bisexual people, and cisgender people more than trans people. And this difference in mattering is at the heart of all forms of systemic inequality, which turns out to be a matter (so to speak) of valuing some people more than others and enshrining that difference in valuation through differential treatment.

But don't take my word for that. Let's consider some evidence. We'll start with racial segregation in the United States, a powerful example of what happens when the desire of white people to live in white-only neighborhoods matters

---

1 Broome 2023.
2 Lamont 2023: 46; italics in the original.

more than the desire of Black people to live in integrated neighborhoods.[3] Historical studies of segregation[4] demonstrate that Black people did not choose to live in segregated neighborhoods; rather, white people systematically forced Black people into housing segregation by refusing to rent or sell to them or to live in the same neighborhoods, a refusal supported by both the federal government and private citizens, and involving strategies ranging from lying to legal discrimination to violence.

But segregation is not just a matter of history; it continues today and it continues to harm Black people and others living in the racially segregated neighborhoods abandoned by white people. Those in such neighborhoods have to contend with economic struggles, political disempowerment, limited access to important resources, and dangers not faced by others. Their challenges include the following:

- Lower home values that contribute in turn to diminished wealth accumulation opportunities and the racial wealth gap, with houses in White neighborhoods worth between 2.3 and 3.7 times more than houses in Black neighborhoods, even holding most variables (home size, home quality, and neighborhood characteristics) constant.
- Underfunded schools (because school funding draws from property taxes), leading to unequal educational opportunities and lower rates of high school and college graduation for Black students.
- Limited access to job networks and job opportunities, leading to lower median household income.
- Less access to high-quality food, which impacts obesity rates.
- Less access to health-care and fitness services and to medical resources including doctors and hospitals, which leads to poorer medical care.
- Less access to financial services along with higher charges to open and maintain checking accounts.
- More predatory alternative finance establishments (check cashing, payday lenders, pawn shops).
- Neighborhood disinvestment by developers and municipal organizations, including lower-quality housing options and crumbling physical infrastructure.
- Environmental toxins including but not limited to air pollution and lead in buildings; such toxins contribute to poor health outcomes including

---

3 For simplicity's sake, I only discuss Black segregation here. Segregation affects members of all Black/Indigenous/People of Color (BIPOC) communities, to differing degrees and in different ways.
4 Katznelson 2005; Rothstein 2017.

higher infant mortality rates; greater rates of illnesses such as asthma, cancer, diabetes, cardiovascular disease, tuberculosis, and hypertension; and a shorter life expectancy.

- The mental health challenges of living in underinvested neighborhoods with fewer resources and less economic capital.
- Underinvestment in basic traffic safety measures (streetlights, crosswalks, sidewalks), leading to more pedestrian and bicyclist deaths.
- Policing based on racist assumptions about danger and criminality that targets innocent people while failing to provide the level of professional support that white neighborhoods can generally expect.
- Less access to political influence, including the targeting of segregated neighborhoods to restrict voting access.[5]

These harms and limitations combine to keep neighborhoods largely segregated over time, meaning that racial segregation is reproduced from generation to generation.[6] White people continue to reap the benefits and members of BIPOC communities continue to pay the price. Not mattering, it turns out, has a substantial impact on our lives: how long they are, how good they are, and whether we get the chance to pursue our dreams and become the kinds of people we want to be.

Racial segregation is a stark example of some people mattering more than others, but there are many other examples of what mattering more and mattering less can look like. In this chapter, I consider examples that help us understand whose comfort matters, whose education matters, whose rights matter, whose health matters, and whose life matters (and whose does not). I draw on academic and other research to surface important gaps in mattering. I also focus briefly on the particular example of valuing men accused of rape more than the women who accuse them. I conclude the chapter by discussing the idea of moral exclusion, a concept that helps us understand why we tolerate such systemic differences in mattering, and by introducing the importance of power in studying inequality.

---

5 Anderson 2010, 2017; Bailey et al. 2017, 2021; Faber and Friedline 2020; Fleischmann and Franklin 2017; Garcia 2020; Harris and Curtis 2018: 200–203; Howell and Korver-Glenn 2018; Institute for Policy Studies 2018; Korver-Glenn 2021: 5–6; Krysan and Crowder 2017: 4–5; Lee 2019, 2021; Menendian et al. 2021; Nardone et al. 2020; Perry et al. 2018; Quillian 2014; Richardson et al. 2020; Roithmayr 2014; Rugh 2020; Singletary 2020; Susaneck 2023.

6 Gentrification complicates this pattern, but does so in ways that continue to benefit whites at the expense of BIPOC communities.

Whose Comfort Matters?

> A far, far too common response to #MeToo has been to bemoan
> that men feel less comfortable in their workplaces, which springs first
> of all from a habit of not just valuing male comfort more but centering
> attention on it. [...] Comfort itself is often invoked as though it were
> a right of the powerful.[7]

Comfort and discomfort can take many forms. Here, I touch on dress codes
for girls in school; attempts to censor teaching about racism and about lesbian/
gay/bisexual/trans/queer (LGBTQ) communities and issues; and book bans.
I also briefly address gender and race differences in pain treatment.

Girls are often subject to dress codes in school in situations where boys
have no such restrictions. Dress codes limit girls' freedom and comfort and
may mean that their education is interrupted if they are sent out of class
to change what they are wearing because their clothing does not comply
with the code. What purpose do these dress codes serve? Education
professors Torrie Edwards and Catherine Marshall[8] claim the codes assure
that heterosexual boys are not too distracted by the girls to focus on their
work, meaning that straight male comfort is more important than female
comfort in educational settings. Interestingly, in these situations, there is no
apparent concern about heterosexual girls getting distracted by what the boys
wear, nor is there any concern about the comfort of same-sex-attracted people
or any acknowledgment of gender beyond the male–female binary.

White discomfort with acknowledging the reality and impact of historic
and current racism explains many recent challenges to teaching about racism,
usually framed as challenges specifically to "critical race theory."[9] Since
January 2021, as of this writing, 44 states have introduced bills or taken other
steps that would restrict teaching critical race theory or limit how teachers
can discuss racism and sexism, according to an *Education Week* analysis.
Eighteen states have imposed these bans and restrictions legally or in other
ways. As sociologist Victor Ray points out:

> These laws have been forwarded under the pretext that these works
> make white kids uncomfortable, and discomfort is to be avoided.
> But America's history is disturbing, and a healthy society would be
> disturbed. Banning discussions of structural racism is an unforgivably

7 Solnit 2019: 7.
8 Edwards and Marshall 2020.
9 Schwartz 2023.

cruel *type of structural racism* designed to deny marginalized people both the affirmation that comes from learning their stories matter and the conceptual tools that help them understand and alter their position.[10]

White discomfort is thus important enough to restrict teaching about racism and even to pass laws against such teaching. The discomfort of BIPOC students (either with racism more broadly or with having their history and experiences censored) does not matter.

Similarly, as of September 2023, 11 US states had state laws censoring discussions of LGBTQ people or issues in school, popularly referred to as "Don't Say Gay or Trans" laws, while five other states required parental notification of LGBTQ-inclusive curricula and allowed parents to opt their children out. In 2023, 42 of 50 states introduced such bills. Such laws are clearly a response to the discomfort of some heterosexual people with homosexuality as a topic or with LGBTQ people; the discomfort that such laws cause LGBTQ people does not matter to the people proposing and enforcing the laws.[11]

Beyond laws limiting topics that can be covered in class, book bans are a common way to keep children from encountering the experiences, history, or insights of certain groups of people. Almost 2,600 unique book titles were challenged in 2022, with almost 1,300 attempts to restrict library materials.[12] Between July and December 2022, 30 percent of the books challenged or banned had BIPOC characters or discussed race and racism while 26 percent had LGBTQ characters or themes.

One Texas state representative compiled a list of almost a thousand books that potentially violate a law barring the teaching of material that could cause a student to feel "discomfort, guilt, anguish, or any other form of psychological distress on account of the individual's race or sex." It's important to recognize that this law has not been used to ban racist or heterosexist books that might make BIPOC or LGBTQ people uncomfortable—only to ban books about BIPOC and LGBTQ people and issues that might make some white and/or heterosexual people uncomfortable. As of 2023, the most common themes of books targeted for removal were race, history, sexual orientation, and gender. Unsurprisingly, BIPOC and LGBTQ children who live in states where such censorship or bans are in effect report experiencing discomfort and fear at these restrictions.[13]

---

10 Ray 2022: 127–128; italics in the original.
11 Movement Advancement Project 2023b, 2023f.
12 Beacon Press n.d.
13 Blow 2023; Haupt 2022; PEN America 2023; Winter 2022.

Understanding whose physical comfort matters is as important as understanding whose emotional comfort matters. Research shows that women and members of BIPOC communities are more likely to have their pain dismissed and less likely to receive adequate medical treatment for pain:

- Black children with appendicitis were significantly less likely than white children to receive any pain medication if they reported moderate pain and significantly less likely to receive opioids if they reported severe pain.
- Teenage girls were significantly more likely than teenage boys to report that a physician dismissed their report of chronic or recurrent pain.
- Two studies of emergency department visits for adults (18–55 years old) with chest pain showed that men were seen significantly more quickly than women and were significantly more likely to be evaluated for possible heart attacks and admitted to the hospital for treatment; members of BIPOC communities also waited significantly longer to be evaluated by a doctor and were less likely to be seen by a doctor at any point in their visit.
- An analysis of 981 emergency room visits found that women with acute abdominal pain were up to 25 percent less likely than men to be treated with opioid painkillers.
- An Oregon study found that Black patients were 40 percent less likely than white patients to receive pain medication from Emergency Medical Technicians (EMTs) and paramedics.
- A review of a national emergency services database over three years found that Black patients experiencing fractures, burns, or penetrating injuries were less likely to receive pain medication from emergency medical transport staff than members of other racial groups.
- Finally, one study examined racial–ethnic disparities in opioid prescription at emergency department visits. Among adults (18–65 years old), Blacks reporting back and abdominal pain were less likely than whites with the same symptoms to receive opioid prescriptions when discharged from the emergency room.[14]

These studies suggest that being white and male improves the odds of having one's reports of pain taken seriously and receiving appropriate treatment for the pain. (I cover women's pain more extensively in Chapter 8.)

---

14 Banco et al. 2022; Bever 2022; Foden-Vencil 2019; Goyal et al. 2015; Hewes et al. 2018; Igler et al. 2017; Singhal et al. 2016.

Whose Education Matters?

Learning is deeply important for people. We learn because we have to and we want to, for competence and joy, to become more knowledgeable and capable. Learning is an important way in which we exercise our agency in the world and choose who we want to be. Anything that interferes systemically with learning limits our life options and sends messages that we are unable to learn or unworthy of being given the opportunity.

The censoring of materials on BIPOC and LGBTQ lives and history interferes with learning, of course, as do book bans. Clearly, the education of BIPOC and LGBTQ students matters as little as their comfort for those doing the censoring and banning. Moreover, and equally clearly, dress codes for girls that center boys' comfort send a message that boys' education is more important than girls' education.

As noted earlier, racial segregation leads to deep and profound inequalities in educational experiences and access because public school funding systems rely on local property taxes which are based on home values. The wealthiest students receive the best education in schools with access to the greatest number and quality of resources. Wealthy neighborhoods with large property tax bases get well-funded public schools; poor neighborhoods get poorly funded schools. In 2018, the highest-spending districts spent nearly ten times more per student than the lowest-spending districts. This wealth is not racially neutral; because of the economics of racial segregation, nonwhite districts received about $1800 less per student on average than districts serving the fewest BIPOC students in 2018. Moreover, 86 percent of children attending districts with majority Black student populations had funding gaps that lessened their access to resources in 2020.[15]

Racially segregated schools attended by BIPOC students are associated with the following:

- More teacher turnover
- Lower teacher quality
- Less experienced teachers
- Fewer teachers with advanced degrees
- Fewer special education teachers
- Lower teacher salaries
- Larger class sizes
- Fewer extracurricular offerings

---

15 Century Foundation 2020; Graves and Goodman 2022: 168; Raikes and Darling-Hammond 2019.

- Poorer facilities
- Fewer classroom resources such as up-to-date textbooks and computers, musical instruments, and science labs
- Fewer arts offerings
- Less access to advanced courses and gifted and talented courses, especially in STEM (science, technology, engineering, and mathematics)
- Lower math and reading achievement percentiles compared to state averages
- Harsher disciplinary climates
- More chronic absences
- Higher school suspension rates
- Lower test scores
- Lower high school retention rates
- Lower high school graduation rates
- Lower college graduation rates[16]

While racism and class inequality play important roles in limiting educational access and opportunities, heterosexism can also have a negative impact. A review of research found that homophobic bullying leads to negative educational outcomes, while a national survey of LGBTQ US Americans found that 21 percent of respondents reported experiencing harassment or discrimination at school. About a third reported that the discrimination had a moderate or significant negative impact on their school environment, especially trans and BIPOC respondents.[17]

A 2021 national survey of LGBTQ students[18] found that 68 percent of respondents reported feeling unsafe in school because of their sexual orientation, gender identity, and/or gender expression. A third (32.2 percent) missed at least one entire day of school in the month before completing the survey because they felt unsafe or uncomfortable; 11.3 percent missed four or more days during the same period. Almost all students (97 percent) heard "gay" used in a negative way and almost all students who heard this reported feeling distressed by the language. Almost as many students (95.1 percent) heard the phrase "no homo" at school and 63.3 percent heard it frequently or often. Nine-tenths (89.9 percent) heard other types of homophobic language, such as reference to "dykes" or "faggots." Students were not the only offenders;

---

16 Cashin 2021: 159; Garcia 2020; Graves and Goodman 2022; Harris and Curtis 2018: 200–203; Menendian et al. 2021; Owens 2020; Owens and Candipan 2019; Tatum 2017.
17 Mahowald et al. 2020; Moyano and Sánchez-Fuentes 2020.
18 GLSEN 2022.

58 percent of respondents reported hearing such language from their teachers or school staff, and 72 percent reported hearing negative remarks about gender expression from teachers and school staff. Three-quarters of students (76.1 percent) experienced in-person harassment and a third (31.2 percent) experienced physical harassment (of whom more than a third were physically assaulted).

Homophobic and transphobic treatment from other students and from school faculty and staff send a clear message that neither the education nor the broader well-being of LGBTQ students matters, just as the educational outcomes of racial segregation coupled with property tax-based funding tell us that neither the education nor the broader well-being of BIPOC students matters.

Whose Rights Matter?

> Recognition is conferred in different ways. At the broadest level, it is a matter of which groups are granted political rights by societal consensus— the right to vote, to representation, to access public resources (like public education, or medical care), to economic autonomy, and more.[19]

> The thing about rights is they're not actually supposed to be voted on. That's why they're called rights.[20]

In the United States, we tend to think of rights as fundamental and nonnegotiable; even those of us who are not history buffs remember that the Declaration of Independence mentions "certain unalienable rights" that should guarantee everyone access to "life, liberty, and the pursuit of happiness." When we consider both laws on the books and the enforcement of those laws, we must admit that some people's rights matter more than others.

For example, in 2017, Supreme Court Justice Ruth Bader Ginsburg observed, "I would like to be able to take out my pocket Constitution and say that the equal citizenship of men and women is a fundamental tenet of our society like free speech." Six years later, the blocking of the Equal Rights Amendment in Congress means that women are still not guaranteed equal rights under the constitution.[21]

Indeed, the Supreme Court's Decision overturning Roe v. Wade stripped people who can become pregnant of reproductive rights they had previously had under the law, the first Supreme Court decision to do so. As the dissenting

---

19 Lamont 2023: 63.
20 Maddow n.d.
21 Jackson 2023; Salam 2019.

Justices observed, "Whatever the exact scope of the coming laws, one result of today's decision is certain: the curtailment of women's rights, and of their status as free and equal citizens. [...] [F]rom the very moment of fertilization, a woman has no rights to speak of. A state can force her to bring a pregnancy to term, even at the steepest personal and familial costs."[22]

In recent years, hundreds of state bills limiting LGBTQ rights have been introduced. As of the end of 2022, 13 states had signed anti-LGBTQ bills into law and 23 other states had introduced them. The bills censored in-school discussion of LGBTQ issues and people, banned or censored drag shows, limited access to books by and about LGBTQ people, and weakened civil rights laws by allowing employers, businesses, and hospitals to turn away LGBTQ people or refuse them equal treatment.[23]

As of September 2023, two states had passed targeted religious exemptions allowing private businesses to deny services to married same-sex couples, nine states had passed targeted religious exemptions allowing medical professionals to decline to serve LGBTQ clients, and 13 states permitted state-licensed child welfare agencies to refuse to place or provide services to children and families, including LGBTQ families and same-sex couples if doing so was against their religious beliefs. In addition, two states passed laws that permit state and local officials to decline to marry couples whose marriage they disapprove. A federal judge ruled in 2021 that for-profit businesses whose owners have "sincerely held religious beliefs" do not have to abide by LGBTQ discrimination claims, allowing for-profit businesses and others to refuse to hire LGBTQ people and to fire them for these identities. More recently, the Supreme Court sided with a web designer who said she had a First Amendment right to refuse to provide services for same-sex marriages.[24]

Almost a hundred laws have been passed limiting the rights of trans people alone. These laws have included

- bans on trans youth participation in school sports,
- restrictions on trans people using single-sex facilities such as bathrooms and locker rooms,
- restrictions on access to accurately gendered identification documents,
- laws requiring teachers to "out" trans students to their parents, and

---

22 Traister 2022.
23 Brainstetter 2023; Center for American Progress 2022; Hamilton 2022; Human Rights Campaign 2022, 2023; Ogles 2023; Shin et al. 2023.
24 Breslin 2021; Liptak and VanSickle 2023; Movement Advancement Project 2023c.

- broad religious exemptions that allow people to discriminate against trans people on the basis of their religious values in arenas such as child welfare services and health care.

Twenty-one states ban best practice medication and surgical care for trans youth and another state bans best practice surgical care. Five states make it a felony crime to provide best practice medical care for trans youth. In addition, medical centers offering gender-affirming care have had funding blocked and insurance coverage for gender-affirming procedures has been blocked.[25]

No one, needless to say, is introducing (let alone passing) laws to restrict heterosexual or cisgender rights, in any of these areas or in any other realms.

Voting suppression

Voting suppression provides a particularly clear example of the rights of BIPOC communities not mattering.[26] When a community is unable to vote, one of its most important ways of impacting society and protecting itself is stripped away; the message such communities receive is that neither their rights nor their well-being matter.

In 2013, the Supreme Court struck down key provisions of the Voting Rights Act of 1965, which had been enacted specifically to combat racist voter suppression. Since 2013, many states have changed their election laws, policies, and practices in ways that have the effect of suppressing the vote in BIPOC communities. A 2015 national study found that states with high turnout of voters of color in 2012 were expected to see more than three additional restrictive proposals every two years on average. In 2021, Republican legislatures in 19 states passed 34 laws that restricted access to voting. State lawmakers in 32 states pre-filed or introduced 150 restrictive voting bills during the 2023 legislative session alone.[27]

Voter suppression takes many forms, including "racialized redistricting, voter ID laws, proof of citizenship, voter restriction hurdles, reduction of days for early and absentee voting, felony disenfranchisement, purging of voter rolls, [and] preemption laws." Other practices include elimination of same-day voter registration or otherwise making it harder to register to vote,

---

25 Movement Advancement Project 2023a, 2023d, 2023e.
26 It's worth noting that strict voter identification requirements may also target trans voters (Movement Advancement Project 2023g).
27 Brennan Center for Justice 2023; Institute for Policy Studies 2018: 26; Portillo et al. 2020; Scientific American Editorial Staff 2022.

restricting access to voting by mail, closing polling places, voter intimidation, and refusing to count ballots from majority-Black counties. As noted earlier, racial segregation makes it easier for voter suppression efforts to target particular communities. Research indicates that restricting early voting disproportionately impacts voting in BIPOC communities, which rely more on early voting than heavily white communities. Similarly, BIPOC communities are disproportionately impacted by polling place closures (often concentrated in Black communities) and the banning of ballot drop boxes (now banned in 11 states).[28]

Strict voter identification laws also suppress the BIPOC vote. County-level turnout data across the country has shown that the racial turnout gap grew in states that enacted such laws, with the white–Black turnout gap nearly doubling in primary elections. Data from multiple elections collected by the Cooperative Congressional Election Study found that Black turnout in primaries was 4.6 percentage points lower in states with strict voter ID laws than in other states; a study of nationally representative data from the Current Population Survey across nine election years showed that strict voter ID policies could reduce the probability of self-reported voting by up to four percentage points, enough to change the outcome of a national election.[29]

Multiple studies have found racial disparities in voting wait times, with residents of largely or entirely Black neighborhoods waiting longer to vote across multiple elections. During the 2020 general election, Blacks were four times more likely than whites to report that they did not vote because they left a line that was too long.[30]

Laws, policies, and practices that effectively keep members of BIPOC communities from voting not only disempower members of those communities; they also make it more likely that their chosen candidates and issues will lose at the ballot—and, at least as important, that candidates favored by those who support voter suppression will win and go on to support both voter suppression and other racist policies. Two presidential examples are particularly instructive. African American Studies professor Carol Anderson[31] points out that voter suppression in Florida impacted the 2000 presidential election substantially. More than half (53 percent) of invalidated

28 Anderson 2018a; Brennan Center for Justice 2022a, 2022b; Hamilton 2018; Institute for Policy Studies 2018: 25; Movement Advancement Project 2023g; Portillo et al. 2020; Ray 2022: 52.

29 Brennan Center for Justice 2022a; Darrah-Okike et al. 2021; Hajnal et al. 2017; Institute for Policy Studies 2018: 26–27.

30 Chen et al. 2019; Klain et al. 2020; Mellman 2021.

31 Anderson 2018b.

ballots were cast by Black voters, and Blacks were ten times as likely as whites to have a vote rejected. George W. Bush won the state of Florida by 537 votes; Anderson points to later research that revealed multiple forms of voter suppression in the state, including faulty voting machines, purged voter rolls that targeted BIPOC communities, locked gates at polling places that should have been open, and piles of ballots from Black districts left uncounted.

Anderson also notes that in 2016, the first general election after the Supreme Court struck down key provisions in the Voting Rights Act, voter suppression across the country led to a drop in Black voter turnout of 7 percent across more than 30 states, significant enough to have changed the outcome of the Presidential election. A study of voter suppression in the state of Wisconsin[32] concluded that Donald Trump's winning the state could be traced to the drop in Black voter turnout.

Whose Health Matters?

Among its other harms, racial segregation makes it easy to target BIPOC communities for the kinds of environmental hazards that no white person would choose to experience. Black neighborhoods, especially those that are economically poorer and that have been segregated over generations are far more likely to

- contain or be close to trash incinerators, industrial waste dumps, Superfund sites, bus depots, lead smelters, petrochemical plants, and refineries;
- expose residents to high levels of fine particulate matter pollution (often from cars, trucks, buses, coal plants, and other industrial sources), leading to higher rates of asthma and cancer and to higher COVID-19 mortality rates;
- expose children to lead, mercury, arsenic, and other industrial chemicals known or strongly suspected to lower intelligence;
- be hotter in the summer, due to having fewer trees and parks, which can increase the risk of heat-related deaths; and
- put residents at greater risk for poor outcomes from COVID-19 as a result of these health challenges coupled with such neighborhoods having less well-resourced hospitals.[33]

---

32 Berman 2017.
33 Asch and Werner 2021; Cashin 2021: 154–155; Fernandez and Williams 2022; Hoffman et al. 2020; Jbaily et al. 2022; Kodros et al. 2022; Lane et al. 2022; Misir 2022; Richardson et al. 2020; Tessum et al. 2021; Washington 2019; Wilson 2020; Wu et al. 2020; Zhong and Popovich 2022.

Lead exposure in particular has been linked to IQ reductions, increased infant mortality, anxiety and depression, anemia, heart disorders, reduced kidney function, hypertension, and learning and behavioral difficulties.[34]

Whose Life Matters?

The health hazards of racial segregation cut lives short as well as simply causing harm, but other evidence also shows clearly the extent to which Black lives matter less than white lives in the United States. Within the criminal justice system alone, we can point to police killings of Black people and the racialized use of the death penalty.

Research on racial disparities in killings by police officers shows the following:

- Black people are between 2.5 and 2.9 times more likely than white people to be killed by police.
- Police are more likely to use both lethal and nonlethal force against Black people than against white people, and are more likely to shoot Black suspects than white suspects.
- Black men and women face a higher lifetime risk of being killed by police than white men and women do, with Black men facing a risk 2.5 times higher than that faced by white men.
- The degree of state-level structural racism (based on segregation, economic disparity, employment disparity, incarceration gap, and educational attainment gap) is a significant predictor of disparities in police shooting rates of victims not known to be armed. For every ten-point increase in the state racism index, the black–white disparity ratio of police shooting rates of people not known to be armed increased by 24 percent.[35]

As journalist Michael Harriot[36] has documented, Black people can be killed by police officers for (among other things) walking, running, driving, turning their backs to officers, facing officers, not complying with an order, complying with an order, standing up, lying down, carrying a firearm legally, carrying anything that could possibly be misinterpreted to be a firearm, looking at an officer, and breathing.

---

34 Washington 2019.
35 Edwards et al. 2019; Kovera 2019; Mapping Police Violence 2023; Mesic et al. 2018; Washington Post 2023.
36 Harriot 2018.

Death penalty data and experimental research on sentencing values similarly show a lack of regard for Black lives compared to white ones, especially when we consider whose murder is likely to result in a death penalty sentence and an actual execution:

- Of defendants actually executed since 1976, 55.6 percent were white and 34.2 percent were Black, meaning that whites were underrepresented compared to their percentage in society (about 61.6 percent of US Americans), while Blacks were overrepresented compared to their percentage in society (14.2 percent).[37]
- In an experimental study, participants who were told that life without parole was the maximum sentence for a triple murder were equally likely to convict white and Black defendants. When the death penalty was an option, 80 percent of respondents convicted African American defendants but only 55 percent convicted white defendants.
- Killers of Black people rarely receive death sentences and white killers of Black people almost never receive death sentences. Three-quarters of murder victims whose killers were executed since 1976 were white; during this period, 21 white defendants who had killed Black people were executed while 304 Black defendants who had killed white people were executed. A separate study found that defendants who killed a white person were 17 times more likely to have been executed than defendants who killed a Black person.[38]

Valuing Sexual Assaulters More than Assault Survivors

College athlete Brock Turner faced 14 years in prison for sexually assaulting Chanel Miller while she was unconscious. He received three years' probation and six months in jail, of which he ultimately served only three months. His role in the rape was never in question, nor was the harm it caused Miller, who later wrote:

I am a human being who has been irreversibly hurt, my life was put on hold for over a year, waiting to figure out if I was worth something.

37 United States Census Bureau 2021. One might argue that perhaps Black people are more likely to commit murder than white people, or to commit more heinous murders. Extensive evidence of racial discrimination in the criminal justice system more broadly, discussed in Chapter 3, suggests that racism plays at least some role in the overrepresentation of Black people executed; Bryan Stevenson's book *Just Mercy* (2014) provides a detailed look at how this racism can play out.
38 Balko 2020; Death Penalty Information Center 2023; Glaser et al. 2015; Phillips and Marceau 2020.

My independence, natural joy, gentleness, and steady lifestyle I had been enjoying became distorted beyond recognition. I became closed off, angry, self-deprecating, tired, irritable, empty. The isolation at times was unbearable. You cannot give me back the life I had before that night.[39]

Why was Turner let off so easily? Why was he not held accountable for the harm he caused? Law professor Deborah Tuerkheimer's study of why we "doubt accusers and protect abusers" provides an answer. As Tuerkheimer writes,

It turns out our care is distributed unevenly and predictably: the suffering of [a sexual] abuser who could face accountability for his misdeeds matters far more than the suffering of his victim. The disparity between inadequate regard for survivors and excessive regard for offenders reflects what I call the *care gap*.[40]

Thus, the credibility of the accuser's claim and the accused's denial is not simply a socially neutral matter but has to do with mattering—specifically with whose suffering matters.[41] While it is understandable that Turner's relatives should be supportive of him, the lack of concern shown for Miller in their statements to the judge is stunning:

- "His life will never be the one that he dreamed about and worked so hard to achieve. That is a steep price to pay for 20 minutes of action out of his 20 plus years of life."
- "A series of alcohol-fueled decisions that he made within an hour timespan will define him for the rest of his life. Goodbye to NCAA championships. Goodbye to the Olympics. Goodbye to becoming an orthopedic surgeon. Goodbye to life as he knew it."[42]

More disturbing is the judge's ultimate sentence, which reflected the same values expressed by Turner's father and sister. As Miller later wrote, "The judge had given Brock something that would never be extended to me: empathy. My pain was never more valuable than his potential."[43]

---

39 Tuerkheimer 2021: 165–167; see also Manne 2018: 196–205 and Manne 2020: 36–49.
40 Tuerkheimer 2021: 135; italics in the original.
41 Tuerkheimer 2021: 137.
42 Turner's father and sister, respectively; Tuerkheimer 2021: 166.
43 Tuerkheimer 2021: 167.

Tuerkheimer describes a similar dynamic in Christine Blasey Ford's testimony against Brett Kavanaugh at his Supreme Court confirmation hearings. We have yet to explore how and why so many people believe those accused of sexual assault rather than believing the accuser, or why so many people are more sympathetic toward the accused. I address this topic in Chapter 8 (once we have a better understanding of the cultural processes at play), but the examples of Turner and Kavanaugh are not anomalous, even if they are extreme in some ways. They are examples, however dramatic, of a larger pattern that Miller captured accurately: the man's potential matters more than the woman's pain.

Moral Exclusion

The findings I've presented thus far might not be surprising. Both racial segregation and voter suppression have been with us for generations. Police have killed members of BIPOC communities for decades with virtually no accountability, though that has begun to change recently. Laws restricting women's rights and the rights of LGBTQ people are nothing new, though recent decades have seen major changes in both public acceptance of and the freedoms enjoyed by both groups (along with backlashes).

Precisely because these differences in mattering are part of our history, culture, and institutions, it may not occur to us to ask how it comes to be that anyone finds systemic inequality morally acceptable. Even if racism, sexism, and heterosexism are a deep part of our history, why are they still present? Why do any of us tolerate them? Why does our society perpetuate them?

There are many answers, but one that is both important and underappreciated involves a concept that I will introduce with a personal story.

For as long as I've lived in Colorado Springs, Colorado, the politically progressive bumper stickers on my car have been vandalized and the Democratic campaign signs in my yard have been stolen. In recent years, I've attended a church that flies Black Lives Matter and LGBTQ Pride flags, which are also regularly stolen or vandalized. This is sad and frustrating, but sociologically fascinating.

Why fascinating? Because Colorado Springs has a strong libertarian streak and private property is highly valued. Most residents don't want to pay for public services; they want control over their money and over what happens to anything they own. Yet somehow, my private properties—my car, my campaign signs—are not quite so respected by local conservatives, who think nothing of damaging or stealing them.

Colorado Springs also has one of the largest conservative religious communities in the country and is the location of massive Evangelical churches such as New Life Church as well as many conservative parachurch organizations such as Focus on the Family. Some people refer to the city as the "Evangelical Vatican." One would think, in so religious a city, that church property would be virtually sacrosanct and yet my church's flags are targeted regularly.

Is this simple hypocrisy? No, it's a double standard, and one that underlies every form of systemic inequality from racism to sexism, from heterosexism to Islamophobia, and from ableism to ageism. If we understand this double standard, we begin to grasp how inequality works because the double standard is not about what we consider valuable but rather about who is valued and who is not.

Social psychologist Susan Opotow[44] refers to this double standard as "moral exclusion." By "moral exclusion" Opotow means the processes and practices by which some people are socially defined as undeserving of moral treatment. As she puts it,

> Moral exclusion occurs when individuals or groups are perceived as outside the boundary [within] which moral values, rules, and considerations of fairness apply. Those who are morally excluded are perceived as nonentities, expendable, or undeserving. Consequently, harming or exploiting them appears to be appropriate, acceptable, or just.[45]

My Colorado Springs experiences suggest that for some conservatives, private property is only inviolable if it belongs to people who share their political values. The Black Lives Matter bumper sticker on my car signals to such conservatives that I fall outside their moral community of those whose private property must be respected. Therefore, my car, though undeniably my private property, is open to vandalism because my political values place me outside of the set of people understood by these conservatives as the "moral community." They can believe in the sanctity of private property and simultaneously believe that my private property is open for desecration because I am, as Opotow might put it, "undeserving" of having my private property respected. The same point could be made about my church: by flying the flags it does, it advertises a politically progressive identity that renders it undeserving of having its property rights respected.

---

44 Opotow 1990, 2011; Opotow et al. 2005.
45 Opotow 1990: 1.

Another recent example of moral exclusion comes to us from a parents group suing a school over a curriculum that teaches kindness and compassion. According to news coverage of the lawsuit, one protesting parent stated that, "Not every human is deserving of my child's empathy."[46] A clearer example of moral exclusion could hardly be imagined.

Moral exclusion is at the heart of all forms of systemic inequality. In 1857, the US Supreme Court found in the Dred Scott case that people legally classified as Black had "no rights a white man must respect."[47] Despite the US Declaration of Independence claiming that all people had "certain inalienable rights," the Supreme Court found Black people to fall outside the category of those entitled to rights. This decision suggests that the Supreme Court did not understand Black people to be people in the fullest sense of the word; it also indicates that Black people were open to any kind of harm or exploitation that white people might inflict on them and that they had no legal protection against such harm.

Critical legal theorist Elise Boddie provides a more recent example of racist moral exclusion in the United States, focused on safety rather than rights:

> [T]here is a high likelihood that when general references are made to public safety, they do not include Black people. 'Safety' is raced as White, as is 'the public.' Because Black people are stereotyped as dangerous, they are functionally excluded from the body politic. Thus, their safety is not a matter of public concern.[48]

Indeed, we might think of racial segregation as an example of spatialized moral exclusion, in which many white people tolerate the harms and human devaluation of segregation because they already believe at some level that members of BIPOC communities do not deserve the same opportunities that they, as white people, take for granted for themselves. Once a group of people has been morally excluded, excluding them geographically is not that difficult.

In a sense, the rest of this book represents an elaboration on the idea of moral exclusion as it works in contexts of racism, sexism, and heterosexism. The concept itself does not explain what Opotow refers to as the "processes and practices" by which people exclude others or even the assumptions

---

46 Clarke 2023.
47 Ray 2022: 72.
48 Boddie 2022: 496.

underlying those processes,[49] but it provides a baseline to help us understand the logic of systemic inequality. Racial segregation would not be morally acceptable to white people were it not for racist moral exclusion. The pain of (primarily female) rape survivors would not be so unimportant to men were it not for sexist moral exclusion. Laws restricting the rights of LGBTQ people and the bullying of LGBTQ people in schools would be anathema to heterosexual and cisgender people absent the heterosexist moral exclusion implying that LGBTQ people deserve whatever bad treatment they get—or at least do not deserve the good treatment that heterosexual and cisgender people take for granted. As for the "processes and practices" by which moral exclusion actually works, those are the focus of Chapters 3 through 8 of this book.

Thinking Sociologically about Systemic Inequality: The Importance of Power

Before we turn to those processes and practices, we need to consider one other issue. Racial segregation, for example, is a large-scale phenomenon involving many different individuals and institutions including the government, the housing market, the health-care system, and multiple industries; segregation takes place both across space and over time. To say that racial segregation is an example of spatialized moral exclusion, as I have above, begs two questions: who exactly is doing the moral excluding, and what enables them to succeed at it?

Does systemic inequality simply come down to the actions of large numbers of individuals? If so, how is it that all of those actions work in tandem to produce widespread, systemic segregation? Alternately, should we say that large-scale institutions such as the federal government practice moral exclusion? This solution sounds more sociologically appealing, but it misses the point that large-scale institutions are not entities in themselves; they are made up of groups of people acting collectively while (for the most part) holding the same values, following the same rules, and pursuing the same goals. In this way, the federal government and all other institutions are like board games, as the sociologist Allan Johnson has pointed out:

> If no one plays Monopoly, it is just a bunch of stuff in a box with rules written inside the cover. And if no one plays 'Toyota Motor Company,"

---

49 Opotow (1990) provides examples of these processes, some of which I also discuss in this book.

it is just a bunch of factories and offices and equipment and rules and accounts written on paper and stored in computers.[50]

People have to play "federal government" to make the federal government happen. And people have to play "federal government" in racist ways to make the federal government support racial segregation. This point means that it is *people* doing the moral excluding: individual judges empathizing with rapists rather than rape survivors, particular police officers killing Black people, and specific teachers saying homophobic things in classrooms. This observation is not incorrect, but it seems incomplete; it appears to miss how extensive and well-coordinated systemic inequality is. It also does not explain how an interaction between two individuals can be so unequal, such that one of them can say or do things that reproduce systemic inequality even beyond the specific interaction. We need a way of understanding what individuals have to do with larger social structures and forces: organizations, institutions, and culture. To understand that set of relationships, we have to think about power: what it is, what it does, and how it works. I consider power and its relationship to inequality in Chapter 2.

Discussion Questions

1. What are some ways in which the social groups to which we belong matter for how our lives go, according to the examples in this chapter? What other examples can you think of that involve race, gender, or sexuality? What examples can you think of involving other forms of inequality?
2. Consider the different challenges faced by people living in racially segregated, majority-BIPOC neighborhoods. How might these challenges build on each other to make it harder for an individual to escape segregation? How might the combination of these challenges contribute to segregation continuing over time and across generations?
3. The chapter discusses findings suggesting that some people's comfort, education, rights, health, and lives matter more than that of others. Can you think of other situations in which one group's comfort comes at another group's expense or where the education of some people is prioritized over the education of others (for example)? Beyond comfort, education, rights, health, and life, what evidence do you see that some people's well-being matters more than others in ways that suggest (or contribute to) systemic inequality?

---

50 Johnson 2014a: 15–16.

4. Law professor Deborah Tuerkheimer refers to a "care gap" in explaining why so many people are more sympathetic toward accused sexual offenders than toward their accusers, meaning that those people care more about the (potential) suffering of the accused than about the (existing, documented) suffering of the accuser. Can you think of any other examples of such a "care gap?" Whose suffering receives the most sympathy across society? Whose suffering receives the least?

5. Social psychologist Susan Opotow observes that "[t]hose who are morally excluded are perceived as nonentities, expendable, or undeserving. Consequently, harming or exploiting them appears to be appropriate, acceptable, or just." Can you think of examples of moral exclusion involving forms of inequality other than racism, sexism, and heterosexism? Have you yourself ever been morally excluded? If so, what was that experience like?

Chapter 2

POWER AND SYSTEMIC INEQUALITY

Introducing Power

> And part of being Black and being a woman in this country is that, even when you're very successful, you just don't control the terms of your success. My success is always limited by how well other people can imagine the possibility of me.[1]

> At the end of the day, aren't 'systemic' problems—systemic racism, poverty, misogyny—made up of untold individual decisions motivated by real or imagined self-interest?[2]

I still remember waking up with a knot in my stomach on June 26, 2015. The US Supreme Court was due to announce its findings in *Obergefell v. Hodges*, and I hoped my same-sex marriage would still be legal in an hour. That day brought good news for my household and many other households. Almost exactly seven years later (June 24, 2022), I woke up with a knot in my stomach again for a different reason: it seemed clear that the Supreme Court was about to overturn *Roe v. Wade* and, in so doing, take rights away from women and make a lot of lives harder. Sure enough, an hour later, rights that allowed women to flourish had been stripped of their national protection and were soon overturned in many states. And indeed, another year later (June 30, 2023), the Supreme Court ruled, in *303 Creative LLC v. Elenis*, that it was legal to discriminate against same-sex couples in the marketplace if the discrimination was based on sincerely held religious beliefs.

These three rulings are a useful place to begin considering how power works as well as its relationship with systemic inequality. The rulings have two lessons for us: first, some people have the capacity to impact other people's lives, for good or for ill, in ways that are built into our society and accepted by most if not all people. Second, while this point is not immediately

---

1 Tressie McMillan Cottom, cited in Klein 2021.
2 Desmond 2023: 42.

obvious to some people, heterosexuals and men, rarely, if ever have to worry about their rights (as heterosexuals or as men) being up for a public vote, about Congressional legislation that might overturn those rights or about a Supreme Court decision that might strip those rights. Power is socially defined, unequally distributed, and differentially enforced, such that some people wind up determining other people's opportunities and enhancing or limiting other people's well-being. People with power not only get to matter themselves, but they get to decide who else matters, how much, and with what outcomes.

As I mentioned at the end of Chapter 1, we need a way of thinking about the relationship between individuals and society as a whole that holds together two seemingly contradictory facts. Only individuals can discriminate and morally exclude (neither "institutions" nor "culture" can act, only the people who make up the institutions and live out the culture), yet some individuals seem to have more ability than others to impact other people and even to impact society more broadly with their words and actions. That ability to impact other people is power, and this chapter describes how power works sociologically as well as the implications of how differentially it is distributed. In the absence of power, individual words and actions have individual consequences. In the presence of power, individual words and actions can have systemic, even society-wide consequences, as with the Supreme Court rulings with which I started the chapter. What, then, is power?

We can think of power as capacity or "power-to": the ability to say something, do something, accomplish something, or create something. "Power-to" is connected to agency and freedom: as long as someone is not completely physically or mentally disabled and as long as they have at least some liberty to do what they want they have access to this capacity.[3] We tend to take "power-to" for granted unless we face restrictions (for example, physical, legal, or political) that keep us from being able to say or do what we want; otherwise, we go about our lives, pursue our interests, and strive to achieve our goals. If power-to were the only kind of power there was, we would not have systemic inequality.

---

3 Of course, the freedom to say what you want (for example) does not necessarily mean freedom from the consequences of what you say. If what you say hurts someone else, you may be held accountable; if what you say is controversial, you may face pushback in ways that range from the informal to the legal. Neither of those facts means that you do not have freedom, simply that others may have freedom to respond in ways you do not like.

However, power-to is accompanied, and often restricted, by "power-over." If I have power over you, I have the capacity to help you or harm you, to enable you or constrain you, or to enhance or limit your freedom. If I have power over you, I can grant you access to resources, experiences, or opportunities, or I can withhold those resources, experiences, or opportunities from you. I have the power to treat you well or badly, to leave you alone or make your life harder. I have the power, in fact, to empower you or disempower you; my "power-over" you can either support or limit your "power-to" do something. I can use my "power-over" as "power-with" and empower you by sharing my power, or I can hoard my power. If I have power over you, my assumptions about you, my decisions about you, and my actions toward you can impact your life or well-being substantially, for good or for ill.

More power means expanded options. When we have power to live our own lives as we want, our personal options are greater. When we have power over others, our ability to expand or restrict their power is greater. When other people have power over us, their options about how to treat us are expanded, and how they actually treat us may, again, either expand or limit our power. Whoever has power over others in a particular situation is likely to win or get their way in the case of a conflict; as mentioned in Chapter 1, we have racial segregation because white people wanted it, members of BIPOC communities did not, and white people had more power.

"Power-over" tends to take one or more of three forms: institutional decision-making power, cultural power, and individual power.

Institutional Decision-Making Power

I define inequality in organizations as systematic disparities between participants in power and control over goals, resources and outcomes; workplace decisions such as how to organize work; opportunities for promotion and interesting work; security in employment and benefits; pay and other monetary rewards; respect; and pleasure in work and work relations.[4]

Our lives are impacted by the decisions that others make in the context of institutional positions that they hold. A college professor, a loan officer at a bank, and a police officer on patrol do not merely act as individuals; they act on behalf of the institutions they represent, and they are authorized by those institutions to act in certain ways and make certain decisions as part of their roles. Moreover, precisely because they make their decisions on behalf

---

4 Acker 2006: 443.

of the institution, most people outside the situation will accept the decisions they make as legitimate—whether those decisions empower or disempower others, help them, or harm them.[5]

College professors have the power to "enforce rules, assign tasks, judge student work, and give grades."[6] A loan officer is empowered to grant or deny a mortgage loan and has control over how good the terms of the loan are. A police officer can decide whose car to pull over and whose car to leave alone. Similarly, a doctor can prescribe pain medicine for someone (or not, as we saw in Chapter 1). A judge or a magistrate can decide what sentence to give someone convicted of a crime. In the workplace, supervisors have the power to "enforce rules, assign tasks, judge employee work, and decide about pay and promotions."[7] In these examples, the college professor, the loan officer, and the others are still individuals and yet they have power that goes beyond individual capacity or "power-to"; they have "power-over," specifically power over what happens to other people.

On a day-to-day basis, what looks like a simple interaction between two people can have profound implications for the life of the person who is empowered or disempowered, granted or denied access, encouraged or treated suspiciously. A mortgage loan approval may help someone escape poverty; a mortgage loan denial may contribute to that person staying in a difficult or even dangerous housing situation. The student defined as "really smart" and encouraged by a teacher (or many teachers) may find doors opening that others don't encounter, while the student identified as "a problem" by the teacher may face extra discipline and be shunted into the school-to-prison pipeline. The woman identified as a "potential leader" by her workplace supervisor will have more opportunities than the woman who was encouraged to leave because she "just wasn't quite the right fit for us."

Even interactions that don't take place can make a positive difference when the interaction would have led to discomfort or harm. The shopper

---

5 When sociologists talk about institutions, we usually mean large-scale institutions such as the family, education, religion, the economy, the government (including the military and the criminal justice system), the health-care system, the media, the arts, and sports. Most individuals don't interact with large-scale institutions but rather with specific organizations. For example, we interact with the health-care system by going to see a specific doctor, visiting a particular emergency room, or getting a consultation with an individual specialist at a given location. I use the term "institution" in this section because institutional decision-making authority is larger than any one organization, even though the decisions are made in specific organizations.

6 Schwalbe 2020: 7.

7 Schwalbe 2020: 8.

not followed by a security guard, the driver not pulled over by a police officer, the teenager not shot by a vigilante, and the woman not harassed on the street all get to go about their days untroubled—or at least, untroubled by the fear, humiliation, legal trouble, physical harm, or even death that can follow these kinds of encounters.

So far, I've discussed institutional decision-making power as a matter of a single interaction between two individuals, but there are three points to remember that help bridge the gap between a single interaction and the larger social patterns that make up systemic inequality in all its forms.

First, such interactions don't happen to members of devalued groups only once in their lives. A woman harassed on the street has likely been harassed multiple times in various settings with differing degrees of danger. Someone who faces suspicion from a security guard for "shopping while Black" has likely faced suspicion from plenty of security guards, police officers, and others. A student identified by one teacher as being "a problem" may well have been identified similarly by prior teachers. Moreover, because systemic inequality crosses institutions, people face racism, sexism, and other forms of inequality in school, on the street, in the workforce, while trying to access health care and in other contexts; each new encounter with institutional decision-making power that ends in poor treatment makes life harder, exacerbates stress, and deepens the message that the person doesn't matter—that their comfort, education, rights, or life are not important.

Second, the effects of these interactions on the individuals who contend with them ripple out into the lives of those they love and those who love them. For every child whose education does not matter, there are family members and friends who suffer along with them. For every LGBTQ person whose rights are rejected, there are others whose hearts break. For every person whose life is treated carelessly, there are families, neighborhoods, and religious communities left to grieve and to fear for themselves.

Third, institutional decision-making power is never about a single interaction; every day, millions of college professors, bank loan officers, police officers, doctors, judges, supervisors, and others with institutional decision-making power are making decisions and acting on those decisions across towns, cities, states, and countries. Moreover, to the extent that professors at different universities, supervisors at different companies, and police officers in different cities (for example) share beliefs, practices, rules, or laws, they will tend to make similar decisions about who to treat well or badly, who should have access to resources, opportunities, or experiences and who should not, who is trustworthy, and who might be dangerous.

Of course, not all forms of institutional decision-making power come down to a single interaction between two people. The Supreme Court rulings with which I started the chapter have substantial implications for the empowerment, joy, well-being, and lives of many people. When a state legislature passes a law to restrict teaching about racism or LGBTQ lives (or to restrict voting rights), when a school board bans books, or when the Federal Housing Authority restricts its insurance of home mortgages to properties in white-only neighborhoods, individuals or groups of people are using institutional decision-making power to widespread effect. Similarly, a university admissions office decides who to admit, an employer chooses who to hire, and the editorial board of a newspaper decides which stories to print. These individuals and groups are often making their decisions behind closed doors, out of view of—and unaccountable to—the public. The effects of their decisions can be as substantial as decisions made in an interactional context, if not more so.

Institutional power and discretion

Often, people acting in their institutional capacities have some flexibility in the decisions they make; they are not restricted to a single option but can choose how to respond or what to do based on their understanding of the situation. Institutional decision-makers thus have the discretion to share or withhold social, cultural, political, or economic resources. It's up to them whether to restrict, punish, or target people or to choose not to do so. This point is important because a decision-maker's interpretation of a situation may be informed by assumptions of which they may not even be aware, such as those discussed later in the book. Researchers have studied the role of discretion in a number of decision-making contexts; examples from the criminal justice system include

- whether police officers respond to a sexual assault claim in which an assailant is identified by pursuing the suspect and making an arrest or not,
- which neighborhoods police target, who they stop and search in those neighborhoods, and the grounds on which they stop them,
- whether prosecutors press initial charges and how they handle the plea-bargaining process, and
- whether defense attorneys decide that a defendant is "'worthy' of their time and resources."[8]

---

8 Berdejó 2018: 1197–1198; Boddie 2022; Campbell et al. 2022; Tasca et al. 2012; Van Cleve 2016: 13; Venema 2016.

Similarly, as sociologist Elizabeth Korver-Glenn points out in her study of housing market racism in Houston, Texas:

> [M]ortgage bankers depended on the routine of *racialized discretion* when they interpreted mortgage borrower and property risk. They gave White borrowers and homes in White neighborhoods the benefit of the doubt, assuming they were the least risky and most valuable. By contrast, they cast shadows of doubt on borrowers of color and homes in neighborhoods of color. [...] Racialized discretion has consequences for whether and under what circumstances mortgage loans are approved.[9]

What Korver-Glenn refers to as "racialized discretion" shows up when white teachers refer Black kindergarten students with high test scores to gifted programs less often than they refer white students; when medical professionals require drug tests for pregnant patients who are Black but not for those who are white; and when a golf course calls the police on a group of five Black women for "golfing too slowly" despite the group behind them not having any complaints about their speed (and despite no white golfers facing the same accusation).[10]

Cultural Power

Let's say that I know a man named Bart, who tells me that women are not acceptable as pastors in God's eyes. If Bart is just a man who lives on my street, I might be skeptical of his claim; why should I believe him in particular? However, if Bart is Bart Barber, the current President of the Southern Baptist Convention (as of October 2023), I might respond differently. If I'm a Southern Baptist myself, I don't experience the claim as coming from Bart the individual; I experience it as coming from my church, which I understand to have a legitimate understanding of the truth in these matters. Even if I am not a Southern Baptist, and even if I personally think women should get to be pastors, I might grudgingly admit that Bart comes by his beliefs legitimately—that's just what he was taught to think—and I might further grudgingly admit that Bart has a right to encourage others in his tradition to believe as he does.

Bart Barber, of course, has decision-making power in his position as President of the Southern Baptist Convention; he can play a role in making

---

9 Korver-Glenn 2021: 18; italics in the original.
10 Grissom and Redding 2016; Marco and DelValle 2018; McCabe 2022: 165.

sure that women are not ordained as pastors in the denomination and in expelling congregations from the denomination for ordaining women. Bart, however, also has another kind of power in the situation, a power that is related to decision-making power but is also distinct from it. Bart has cultural power—as do all people in institutional contexts who shape how we make sense of society.

By culture, I simply mean shared understandings—those ideas, beliefs, and values that we hold in common, the shared assumptions underlying them, and the norms, rules, and laws that emerge from those shared understandings.[11] Not everyone shares exactly the same understandings, and subgroups in any country may disagree sharply about certain social or political realities, but some understandings are shared so broadly that, while not universal, they inform the thinking of most if not all people in a society.

Cultural power is the ability to influence how people make sense of the world around them, to convince others that certain ideas, beliefs, or values are right or wrong, good or bad, too obvious to mention or totally inconceivable. Those with cultural power define what (and who) is worthy and unworthy, what (and who) is cool and hopelessly uncool, who is part of our moral community and who is not. Those with cultural power set the agenda, define the problems, and control which solutions are plausible and actionable.

Cultural power is complicated because, when we are young, many individuals have an impact on how we encounter the world. Our beliefs, values, perspectives, and opinions are influenced by our parents, our older siblings if we have any, our friends, our teachers, religious leaders if we are part of a religion, and any other adult whose worldview makes an impression on us. Even after we are old enough to start thinking for ourselves, we may pay extra attention to social media influencers and other publicly visible people, such as performers and athletes who speak out about issues unrelated to their art or sport. If this is the only way we think about cultural power, we may understand it as mostly about individual people or individual interactions.

If we think back to the Southern Baptist example, however, we will recognize that cultural power also works through institutions. I discussed earlier how we accept the *decisions* of those acting on behalf of institutions

---

11 We commonly talk about "popular culture," meaning TV, movies, magazines, and perhaps social media. Alternately, we may be referring to the arts when we use the term "culture." I mean something much broader here. Certainly, our shared understandings take form in the arts and we see them in all kinds of mass communication as well, but I'm also thinking of ways of making sense of the world that inform our day-to-day actions even when they are not made manifest in publications, music, or other forms of what we usually call "culture."

because they are representing those institutions. In the same way, we are likely to accept the *interpretations, accounts, and claims* of people acting on behalf of an institution if we accept that institution as legitimate.

In fact, many of those interactions we had as children in which we learned how to make sense of the world were not just individual interactions; they took place in the context of larger institutions (the family, the education system, or religion) that are dedicated in part precisely to teaching us values, ideas, beliefs, and perspectives. Just as the professor who has the decision-making power to control our grade has that power as part of an educational organization, the pastor who tells us that homosexuality is an abomination before God is authorized to do so by virtue of being part of a religion.

Those with cultural power can use it in three different ways. They can tell us what (or who) is right or good or patriotic or moral, in which case we are likely to take their claim seriously unless we already have a good reason to find it problematic. They can tell us that a particular perspective, idea, or value is incorrect or otherwise problematic (often by suggesting that it comes from someone untrustworthy), in which case we are unlikely to take that perspective, idea, or value seriously (again, unless we already have a reason to find it compelling). Alternately, those with cultural power can refuse to raise certain ideas or perspectives entirely, meaning that we may not even think of those ideas or consider those perspectives unless we come upon them somewhere else. In all three cases, cultural power involves control over information, whether that control involves supporting an idea or claim, opposing an idea or claim, or suppressing an idea or claim. Controlling information makes it possible for those with cultural power to shape our beliefs, values, ideas, and ideals, and thus to influence what we want, what we fear, and what we think is reasonable—or ridiculous.[12]

Just as not all decision-making power involves face-to-face interactions, not all cultural power involves learning lessons through conversations with people we know. News media, for example, shape our perceptions through coverage of particular stories (minimal or extensive), avoidance of certain perspectives or topics, and the positive or negative tone with which a story is treated. News media can also misrepresent reality, as when racially biased coverage of crime[13] leads white US Americans to believe that Black

---

12 As British sociologist Steven Lukes (2005; 27) has pointed out, someone "may exercise power over [someone else by] influencing, shaping, or determining [their] very wants. Indeed, is it not the supreme exercise of power to get [someone] to have the desires you want them to have[?]."

13 Equal Justice Initiative 2021.

people are more likely than whites to be criminals. Reporters, news show anchors, and others who control the news can mislead us into believing things that are not true and fearing people who are not harmful.

Similarly, fictional and nonfictional crime shows on TV (*Law and Order: SVU, Snapped*) often portray sexual assault in ways that perpetuate rape myths, such as the idea that sexual assault is usually committed by strangers when in reality most sexual assault is committed by people who know the victim.[14] As we will see in Chapter 8, this particular rape myth makes police officers, juries, and other decision-makers less likely to treat a situation as rape when the accuser knew the accused. In such cases, the extent to which these myths are reproduced in popular media can have an effect, however indirect, on the ability of women to have their accounts of rape taken seriously and to have the assailant be held accountable. This example is also helpful in showing how people with cultural power can influence the perspectives of people with institutional decision-making power, informing the decisions they ultimately make.

In Chapter 1, I mentioned research showing that Black patients are less likely than white patients to receive pain medication in situations involving Emergency Medical Technicians (EMTs) and emergency rooms (ERs). This is, on the face of it, a simple example of decision-making power at work. Why, however, are the EMTs and ER doctors less likely to give Black patients pain medication? Why would they assume that two people reporting the same level and type of pain should be treated differently? Research suggests that many medical professionals believe that Black people feel less pain than white people,[15] a false belief that they learned at some point from an individual or information source they found trustworthy. Somewhere along the line, someone with cultural power encountered misinformation about race and pain and passed it along; now that misinformation may be impacting the decisions of those EMTs and ER doctors.

There is one last way in which cultural power and institutional decision-making power intersect. As already noted, most people treat the decisions of institutionally authorized decision-makers as legitimate in most cases. Why? Why should sitting behind a bank desk, wearing a badge, holding a professorship, or wearing a clergy robe (for example) justify someone's actions? Here, too, cultural power is at play. We learned from trustworthy sources that people in these roles have the authority to share or withhold

---

14 Merkin and James 2020. I normally prefer the term "survivor" but believe "victim" is clearer in this context.

15 Hoffman et al. 2016.

resources, to treat people well or badly, and to find someone benign or suspicious. The very legitimacy we grant institutional decision-makers is a result of cultural power impacting us. The fact that we rarely think about this point shows how taken-for-granted the workings of cultural power can be.

Individual Power

> In a modern society, who is allowed to speak with authority is a political act. Of course, all U.S. citizens are allowed to speak. [...] But not all of us are presumed by the publics to which we belong to have the right to speak authoritatively. Speech becomes [persuasive] only when the one speaking can make a legitimate claim to some form of authority. It can be moral authority or legal authority or rational authority. At every turn, black women have been categorically excluded from being expert performers of persuasive speech acts in the public that adjudicates our humanity.[16]

In Chapter 1, I referred to the gendered and racial pain treatment gap, particularly the research showing that men and white people are more likely than women and Black people to receive medication when they report pain. Journalist Maya Dusenbery (2019) argues that the gendered pain treatment gap is based on a prior "trust gap" in which medical professionals do not believe women's accounts of their health problems, instead often interpreting the women's problems as "stress" or psychological disorders.[17] From the perspective of these doctors, Dusenbery writes, "women are not very accurate judges of when something is really, truly wrong in their bodies."[18]

The pain gap is only one example of the ways in which women are not allowed to be experts on their own experiences.[19] As trans activist Julia Serrano has noted, "we tend to take men at their word, while viewing women's self-accounts and motives as questionable."[20]

During my doctoral research on the struggle over lesbian/gay inclusion in the United Methodist Church, I found that heterosexual conservatives

---

16 Cottom 2019: 19–20.
17 Once, the evening after an extensive sinus surgery, I called the (male) surgeon because I was concerned that something was wrong. He responded by asking me if I was "stwessed"—and yes, he did pronounce it that way.
18 Dusenbery 2019: 4.
19 This gendered "trust gap" impacts abortion policy, as we see later in this chapter and more fully in Chapter 8.
20 Serano 2020: 51.

in the church similarly treated lesbian/gay Methodists' accounts of their religious and spiritual experiences with suspicion, distrust, and hostility.[21] Because openly lesbian/gay/bisexual people have often been defined as inherently immoral on the basis of their sexuality (regardless of how morally exemplary their individual lives might be), it is not surprising that they might then be understood to be untrustworthy in making other claims about themselves. The recent attacks on trans rights in the United States can be understood as a parallel mistrust of trans people and a belief that they are not the experts on their own lives, bodies, needs, and well-being.

There is a kind of power in knowing that one can tell their story and trust that other people will hear it and pay attention to it. This power includes the experience of having one's ideas and contributions taken seriously, but it goes beyond that experience; it includes being understood as an expert on one's own life and being treated as a reliable narrator about oneself. It is not the same as institutional decision-making power, nor is it identical to cultural power. I call it "individual power," for lack of a better term. Individual power, however, is not simply a matter of who has more charisma or who is a better storyteller or public speaker. As the examples above indicate, individual power is granted more readily to members of socially valued groups. When it comes to pain, men are thought to be more believable than women, and white people are more believable than Black people. When it comes to spirituality or leading a moral life, heterosexuals are thought to be more believable than lesbians and gay men. When it comes to one's gendered identity, cisgender people are thought to be more believable than trans people.

Individual power, in short, is about *credibility*: some people are more credible than others. Sociologist Howard Becker referred to this phenomenon as the "hierarchy of credibility," or, as sociologist Victor Ray puts it, "our propensity to believe those with greater power or higher status."[22]

Feminist philosophers have offered useful insights about the gendered nature of credibility in sexist societies. Miranda Fricker, for example, draws a distinction between a "credibility excess" associated with men and a "credibility deficit" associated with women, in which men are seen as more competent and trustworthy in whatever they say, while women are seen as less competent and trustworthy.[23] Deborah Tuerkheimer, whose work

---

21 See, for example, Udis-Kessler 2008: 104.

22 Becker 1967: 241; Ray 2022: 85.

23 Fricker 2007: 17; see also Manne 2018: 185–187. Similarly, sociologist Elijah Anderson (2022, Chapter 3) writes about the "deficit of credibility" attributed to Black people.

we encountered in Chapter 1, refers to the same phenomenon as "credibility discounting," which she contrasts with "credibility inflation":

> Once you have a name for it, you see credibility discounting everywhere. It's not isolated or idiosyncratic—it's patterned and predictable. It happens in the workplace, when [women's] contributions are treated with disrespect. In medical settings, when [women's] description of symptoms [are] cast aside as untrue or unimportant. In the course of salary negotiations, when [women's] requests are dismissed as unseemly posturing. In the classroom, when the value of [women's] insights is minimized. In intimate relationships, when [women are] somehow held responsible for the conduct of [men].[24]

Tuerkheimer's examples point to situations in which people differ on how to interpret a situation or in which people make competing claims about what to do or whom to believe. The person with more individual power in the situation will win the competition: their version, account, opinion, or viewpoint will count for more than that of the other person in the eyes of society. If the disagreement is between a man and a woman, the man's version will count for more in a sexist society. If the disagreement is between a white person and a Black person, the white person's version will count for more in a racist society. The same pattern exists for all other forms of systemic inequality.

When a white person makes a racist joke and a person from a BIPOC community complains about the joke, other white people are likely to grant the joke-maker more credibility than the person complaining, to downplay the importance of the racism ("it's just a joke"), or to discredit the complainer ("don't you have a sense of humor?"). When a man harasses a woman in the street, at least some people (especially, but not only, other men) will say that she should be flattered by the attention rather than feeling dehumanized or threatened. In such situations, the racist joke-maker and the harasser are let off the hook rather than being held accountable while the person harmed by the interaction is blamed.[25]

Who's In Power and Why It Matters

[I]f you're female, of color, or in some other way on the outside of [power], when you look upward in all kinds of power structures you don't see

---

24 Tuerkheimer 2021: 9–10.
25 I cover victim-blaming in more depth in Chapter 7.

people like you. Your interests are not represented where power is wielded and rewards are distributed.[26]

Some people matter more than others, and some people have more power than others, and these two facts are related. Those with power, especially cultural power and institutional decision-making power, can use that power in ways that impact who matters. As discussed earlier, medical professionals have decision-making power over making pain medications available, power they can use in racist and sexist ways such that women and Black people receive less medication for their pain—because their pain matters less. Legislators can change voting laws in ways that suppress the BIPOC vote and can change education laws in ways that restrict teaching about racism, heterosexism, and the lives of BIPOC and LGBTQ people. They change these laws because they already believe that BIPOC rights matter less and that the comfort of BIPOC and LGBTQ people matters less.

People with more power can use that power to benefit groups to which they belong, as we see with the examples of segregation and voter suppression. In both cases, white individuals with decision-making power may have benefited themselves but they also benefited white people as a group. Segregation allows white people to keep their resources in white areas and "enables officeholders to make decisions that disadvantage segregated communities without being accountable to them."[27] While the details of racial segregation are complicated, the principle is simple: white people were (and still are) in most positions of power and Black people were (and still often are) excluded from the moral community as defined by white people. Once members of a valued group dominate in positions of decision-making and cultural power, systemic inequality is more likely to continue over time and across space than it is to be overturned.

Who, then, is in power? Overwhelmingly, white men—who are overrepresented in Congress and other political leadership positions,[28] the police (especially in urban areas),[29] corporate leadership,[30] higher education,

---

26 Johnson 2006: 95.

27 Anderson 2010: 2.; Korver-Glenn 2021: 6.

28 As of 2023, 100 percent of US Presidents have been male and all but one have been white. Women make up 51 percent of the US population but only 28 percent of Congress (Schaeffer 2023).

29 For example, white men represent 30 percent of the US population but 90 percent of sheriffs across the country (Reflective Democracy Campaign 2020).

30 As of January 2023, women held 8.2 percent of CEO positions at Dow Jones S&P 500 companies ("Women CEOs of the S&P 500" 2023).

the clergy, and creative and financial leadership in the film and TV industries and media organizations more broadly.[31] These institutions (and others in which whites, men, and white men are overrepresented) have a tremendous amount of decision-making and cultural power that impacts the lives and well-being of members of BIPOC communities and white women.

One particularly telling example of how concentrated power can impact the lives of those who matter less comes from the recent overturning of *Roe v. Wade* and the subsequent restriction of the reproductive rights of people who can get pregnant. As researcher Diana Greene Foster points out,

> [Abortion access] is about women's control over their financial security, health, and bodily integrity, ability to care for their existing children, prospects for healthy relationships, and their plans for the future. It is about women's control over their own lives.[32]

A 2022 analysis indicated that 21 US states had "trigger laws" that would ban abortion once *Roe v. Wade* was overturned. In all 21 states, more than half of the Republican legislators supporting the bans were white men; in 15 states, more than 80 percent of the legislators were white men, and 70 percent of prosecutors who were empowered to bring criminal charges against pregnant people for seeking abortions were white men.[33] In other words, the people making legal (and ultimately, in some cases, criminal) decisions about pregnant people's lives, controlling what they could do with their bodies, were overwhelmingly men. In contrast, no serious efforts have been made to regulate what men do with their bodies despite the fact that male participation is essential to pregnancy.

---

31 American Association of University Women n.d.; Keating and Uhrmacher 2020; Lauzen, 2022, 2023a, 2023c; Newman 2022: 99–100; "Ordination of Women" n.d.; Reflective Democracy Campaign 2020; Schaeffer 2023; Sieghart 2021: 179; Smith et al. 2023; "Women CEOs of the S&P 500" 2023.

32 Foster 2020: 313. People of good conscience can disagree about the morality of abortion, but research such as Dr. Foster's makes it clear that abortion access enables women to flourish in ways that they cannot when abortion access is restricted. Chapter 8 discusses ways in which antiabortion discourse is based on the moral exclusion of women. I also recognize that some people who do not identify as women, such as trans men, can get pregnant. I use the term "women" for simplicity's sake; a fuller discussion would use a phrase such as "women and others who can get pregnant."

33 More broadly, 79 percent of Republican state legislators were white men in 2022, despite Republican white men making up about 16 percent of the US population (Reflective Democracy Campaign 2022).

How thoughtful or knowledgeable are these Republican politicians about pregnant people's bodies, needs, or desires? One such politician was asked whether a law to make abortion illegal from the moment of conception (and punishable by 99 years in prison) had an exception to allow incest survivors to obtain abortions. He responded, "Yes, until she knows she's pregnant." Another Republican congressman argued that abortion was unnecessary because "no one forces anyone to have sex," raising the question of whether he was unaware that incest and rape can result in pregnancy. Perhaps the most telling answer comes from Ohio Representative Jim Buchy, a strong opponent of abortion access, who was once asked why a woman might want an abortion. According to the reporter interviewing him, Buchy paused for a few seconds, then replied,

> Well, there's probably a lot of re—I d—I d—I'm not a woman. [Laughs] So I'm thinking now if I'm a woman why would I want to get—some of it has to do with economics. A lot of it has to do with economics. I don't know—I've never—it's, it's a question I've never even thought about.

Answers such as these are why it matters who is in power.[34]

Thinking Sociologically about Systemic Inequality: The Benefit of the Doubt

Thus far, we have considered some of the differences in mattering that can make people's lives better or worse. We have also explored some of the ways that power works, as well as how power matters for systemic inequality. It's now time to turn to systemic inequality more directly, particularly to the cultural processes that keep it going on a day-to-day basis. Both decision-making power and cultural power play out through uncountable numbers of decisions and actions that take place over time and across space in patterned ways. What, however, drives those decisions and actions? What assumptions underlie them? What's going on when someone acts in a way that reproduces systemic inequality? We begin to answer these questions in Chapter 3.

Discussion Questions

1. Consider the distinction between "power-to" and "power-over" discussed at the beginning of this chapter. Where do you see both kinds of power

---

34 Valenti 2019; CarolinaForward 2022; Bland 2016.

operating in your own life? Who has power over you? How do you know? How have their decisions impacted your life?

2. Can you come up with some examples of institutional decision-making power beyond the ones mentioned in this chapter? If possible, think of an example in which you or someone you know benefitted from, or was harmed by, institutional decision-making power.

3. Why does discretion matter so much for institutional decision-making power, according to the author? What role does discretion play in the examples you came up with in answering Question 2?

4. Why is cultural power so important? How have people with cultural power shaped how you see the world? Can you identify a moment in which you learned something important that influenced your thinking? If so, whose cultural power was at work in that influence?

5. The chapter identifies individual power with credibility and believability. Can you think of a time when you had to decide between two competing accounts of a situation? Whose account did you find more credible? Why? Looking back, could race, gender, sexuality, or another social identity have played a role?

6. Why does who's in power matter? The author used the example of abortion access; can you think of another example of one group using power to limit the rights or power of another group? Try to come up with an example that has not been discussed in the book yet, perhaps even an example from your own life.

Chapter 3

THE BENEFIT OF THE DOUBT

[…] how could I have forgotten the first lessons I'd ever learned as a Black person in America, about what [white people] see when they see us? About how quick so many white people could be to assume the worst of us […][1]

I moved to Colorado Springs, Colorado, in 2003, and promptly got my first speeding ticket ever. I was driving 40 mph, which I noticed right after I drove past the 30-mph sign. Then I heard the siren.

The (white) police officer was very polite. He could see that I was nervous and apologized for having to write me a ticket. As he left, he waved and yelled, "Drive safe now!" Throughout the interaction, he was gentle and friendly. His final words felt more like a kindness than an instruction. I still remember how light his voice was. He wasn't worried or concerned or afraid. He did not see me as a problem.

To this day, that is the only speeding ticket I've ever received. Not that I haven't driven above the speed limit. I do so regularly. And not that I haven't sped in front of marked police cars. I have, on multiple occasions. But somehow, my speeding is never an issue. Every time I speed past a police officer, they decide that I am not a problem. They give me the benefit of the doubt.

On November 22, 2014, a 12-year-old Black boy playing alone in a park and causing no harm to anybody was seen as a problem and denied the benefit of the doubt. Police officer Timothy Loehmann shot Tamir Rice to death for the "crime" of playing with an Airsoft gun in a park while being 12 years old and Black.[2] The 911 responder appears to have asked twice whether Tamir was Black or white before deciding whether to send police. Loehmann fired within two seconds of arriving on the scene.[3]

---

1 McGhee 2021: xiv.
2 Airsoft guns fire nonlethal plastic pellets.
3 BBC editorial staff 2014; Dearden 2014; Ferrell 2014; Fitzsimmons 2014; Izadi and Holley 2014.

Loehmann, it turned out, had been deemed "an emotionally unstable recruit and unfit for duty" in a prior position as a police officer and supervisors had sought to terminate him for lying and insubordination. He had not revealed this to the Cleveland police, and they never reviewed his previous personnel file before hiring him. In 2015, a grand jury declined to bring criminal charges against Loehmann for killing Rice; a year later, the City of Cleveland settled with Rice's family for $6 million, and in 2017, the Cleveland Police Department fired Loehmann—not for killing Rice but for having lied about his prior record on his job application for the police force.[4]

Had Tamir been white, the responder would likely not have dispatched police officers; white boys play with guns all the time. Had Loehmann waited two minutes rather than two seconds before firing, he would have seen that Tamir did not pose a threat. Had the Cleveland PD checked Loehmann's personnel file before hiring him, he would not (I hope) have been on the force there in the first place. But instead, Tamir joined the long list of Black people, before him and since, who were deemed a problem, denied the benefit of the doubt, and killed by police officers and vigilantes.

Tamir Rice's death may seem unrelated to my experience with the untroubled officer who gave me a ticket, and it may seem even less related to the times I have sped past police officers without being stopped. I think there's an important connection, however, and in this chapter, I begin to suggest the nature of that connection. I introduce the idea of good-faith and bad-faith assumptions and treatment, the cultural linchpin of systemic inequality that rests on who receives, and who is denied, the benefit of the doubt.

"The benefit of the doubt" does not sound like a sociological concept; people use the phrase all the time in normal conversation. This simple concept, however, can help us make sense of systemic inequality, individual (and institutional) discrimination, and that overused but under-theorized term, privilege.

The Benefit of the Doubt: Good-Faith and Bad-Faith Assumptions and Treatment

We've already seen how systemic inequality involves some people mattering more than others, and we've considered what power, mattering, and well-being have to do with each other. What we need now is an understanding of

---

4 Chung 2022; Mai-Duc 2014.

the *impulse* underlying differential treatment of people based on the groups they belong to.

When decision-makers use their discretion to treat someone well, this treatment is likely based on positive assumptions about the person. Similarly, when a decision-maker treats someone badly, this treatment is likely based on negative assumptions about that person. We might call the positive assumptions "good-faith assumptions" and the negative assumptions "bad-faith assumptions," and we might similarly speak of good-faith treatment and bad-faith treatment.[5]

Good-faith and bad-faith assumptions and treatment come down to whether we give someone the benefit of the doubt or not. When we give someone the benefit of the doubt, we assume the best about that person and expect the best from them in a context where we don't know them personally and don't know what they are like as an individual. Giving someone the benefit of the doubt is a matter of both assumptions and treatment: we presume that this is a good person and we treat them accordingly—in good faith.

Similarly, when we withhold the benefit of the doubt from someone, we assume the worst about them and expect the worst from them, absent any evidence about what they are actually like. Presuming that someone is a bad person and treating them accordingly is a presumption, and an act, of bad faith.

Since good-faith and bad-faith treatment start with assumptions, it's important to name some common good-faith and bad-faith assumptions. Good-faith assumptions include expecting someone to be competent, whether at their job or at whatever else they choose to do: to be successful. We may expect them to be intelligent, hardworking,[6] trustworthy, moral, financially stable,

---

5 If you've taken a philosophy course you may have heard the terms "good faith" and "bad faith" as used by the philosopher Jean-Paul Sartre. I am using the terms differently here. Moreover, the word "faith" in this context has nothing to do with religion or spirituality, but refers instead to trust—specifically, trust (or lack of trust) in another person.

6 It's important to recognize that the expectation that people are either "hardworking" or "lazy" (or fall somewhere in between) includes many other problematic assumptions about physical and mental ability and indeed about the value of labor in a capitalist society that values people only for the work they do, not for their simply being human beings. The expectation is thus both ableist and classist. I am including this expectation in my list, even with these caveats, because my experience is that it is a common expectation that should not be ignored but should, rather, be understood as problematic. Thanks to Chris Lombardi for pointing out this issue.

and a positive contributor to society. We may expect them to be rational and reasonable, and we may assume that what they want for themselves is also rational and reasonable; they are appropriately self-interested to the same degree that we are appropriately self-interested. We presume that their values and actions will fall within the bounds of what we consider normal and that we will find them unproblematic. Finally, we presume that they are harmless.

To the extent that we hold most or all of these good-faith *descriptive* assumptions about someone, we are also likely to hold certain good-faith *evaluative* assumptions about them: to find them worthy of respect, to believe that they are deserving of good-faith treatment. We include them in the moral community, the group of people who ought to be treated ethically.

Bad-faith assumptions include expecting someone to be incompetent and a failure. We may expect them to be unintelligent, lazy, untrustworthy, immoral, financially unstable or insecure, and a detriment to society. We may expect them to be irrational or unreasonable, perhaps finding them overly emotional or "hysterical" or "too angry"; we may think of them as wanting "special rights," "special treatment," "privileges," or "entitlements." We may interpret their actions as abnormal or extreme, marking them as problematic. We may expect them to prove dangerous to us or others. To the extent that we hold most or all of these bad-faith descriptive assumptions about someone, we may find them unworthy of our respect and feel that they do not deserve to be treated in good faith. We exclude them from the moral community and find it ethically unproblematic when we or others treat them badly.

Undoubtedly, you know people who always give their best and people who don't, people you can trust and people you can't, people who are good at what they do and people with fewer skills. When you think about those people and what you know about them, you're not making good-faith or bad-faith assumptions; you are drawing on evidence that you have collected over time. We learn what kind of person someone is by interacting with them. The closer we are to them, the better we know their strengths and weaknesses, their successes and failures. The problem with good-faith and bad-faith assumptions is precisely that they are *assumptions*; they are not based on evidence about what a person is really like.

These assumptions become even more problematic when they inform whether we give someone the benefit of the doubt or not. For example, we may wind up assuming the worst about someone and treating them badly when they have done nothing to deserve bad treatment. It might be that if we knew the person, we would recognize that they are competent, moral, and harmless, but in the absence of that information, we treat them as incompetent, morally suspect, and potentially dangerous. Similarly, we may give someone the benefit of the doubt only to find out later that they are untrustworthy or violent.

Good faith and bad faith have a kind of inertia once they are in place. If I assume that someone is trustworthy, it takes a change of understanding, a reorientation, for me to start seeing them as untrustworthy. Perhaps you've encountered a news story about a mass shooting in which the neighbors of the killer were shocked that the "nice young man" next door could kill people. The neighbors had made good-faith assumptions about someone who, it turned out, did not deserve them. Similarly, once I assume that someone is untrustworthy, I may have a hard time accepting that I was wrong and that they are actually trustworthy.

The above discussion of good-faith and bad-faith treatment focuses on our response to individuals, and indeed we sometimes give people the benefit of the doubt or withhold it for reasons having to do with what they seem like as an individual. More often, however, our good-faith and bad-faith assumptions and treatment have to do with the social groups to which people belong. If someone perceives me or thinks about me in the context of a socially valued group to which I belong, I will receive the benefit of the doubt. People will be inclined to view me positively and to support my gaining access to society's resources, opportunities, and valued experiences. People will not be inclined to view me with suspicion or to think poorly of me. People will be inclined to see my well-being as mattering because I am understood to be a part of their moral community.

If, on the other hand, someone perceives me in the context of a socially devalued group to which I belong, they may be suspicious of me, not expect much from me, and act as though my well-being does not matter because I'm not understood as part of their moral community. They may, in short, deny me the benefit of the doubt.[7]

Systemic Inequality and the Benefit of the Doubt

Sociologist Elizabeth Korver-Glenn, mentioned in Chapter 2, carried out an extensive study of housing developers, real estate agents, mortgage brokers, and appraisers in Houston, Texas. She was interested in how the routine words and actions of housing market professionals reproduced racial segregation.

---

7 Since all of us have multiple identities in terms of gender, race, sexuality, and so on, our real-life experiences of good-faith or bad-faith treatment will depend on which of our identities is most germane in a particular moment. For example, I may receive the benefit of the doubt as a white person or be denied the benefit of the doubt as a queer person, depending on the context.

These housing market professionals had decision-making power in that they could (for example) choose to show a home in a particular neighborhood or not, or to approve a particular mortgage loan or not. The professionals also had some cultural power since their values and assumptions could influence the decisions of prospective homebuyers.

Many of the white professionals Korver-Glenn studied used what she called a "racist market rubric" in which they described Black people as "undesirable as neighbors," "occupationally inferior to whites," and "financially unstable and not knowledgeable about [the] U.S. financial system." The white professionals also described Black neighborhoods as "unsafe or dangerous."[8] These assumptions informed how housing market professionals interacted with white and Black clients, as well as how those interactions led to housing decisions that continued to build on already existing patterns of segregation. Moreover, the "racist market rubric" of the white housing professionals was not based primarily on experience or evidence but rather on stereotypes of Black people and Black neighborhoods, meaning that the rubric represented an elaborate set of bad-faith assumptions that informed bad-faith treatment of Black homebuyers.

Good-faith and bad-faith assumptions and treatment play an important role in how even well-intentioned people can act in ways that keep racism, sexism, heterosexism, and other forms of inequality in place. Korver-Glenn's study shows how bad faith produces and reproduces racism in the housing market. Tamir Rice's death shows bad faith at work in a police shooting.

To really understand how inequality works, however, we also need to take good-faith assumptions and practices into account. For example, every time I speed past a police car and the officer ignores me because I'm white (and therefore presumably not carrying drugs, guns, or stolen money), I receive the benefit of the doubt. While I can't know for sure, the officer's failure to pull me over may be based on their good-faith assumption that though I am definitely speeding, I am not a criminal, dangerous or otherwise problematic.

This noninteraction, this failure to ticket me for speeding, has implications for the officers, for me, and for how racism works more broadly, so it's worth considering why a police stop that didn't happen can still be important.

I don't use or sell illegal drugs, but what if I did? I have to admit that I would be pretty likely to get away with it if I sold drugs, given how many times I have sped past police cars and not been pulled over. Each time an officer decides to give me the benefit of the doubt and not pull me over for speeding, the officer

---

8 Korver-Glenn 2021: 10–11.

does not learn whether their assumption about my innocence (or the broader innocence of white people) is correct. In that sense, it doesn't matter whether I do or don't have drugs in my car if I never get pulled over. Each police failure to ticket me for speeding demonstrates the officer's assumption of my innocence while reinforcing that assumption in the officer's mind.

Each police failure to ticket me for speeding also confirms that I have tremendous freedom to break the law without being held accountable. This is an example of white privilege, one that I might not be aware of if I were not already committed to thinking about how racism plays out in my life and how I benefit from it. Since those of us who are white do not need to understand how racism benefits us in order to survive in society, we may not think consciously about the fact that we can get away with a lot without being held accountable and that we benefit from this situation.

Moreover, the experience of being trusted by police officers makes it easier for me to trust them back. I am not hounded or harassed by police officers when I'm not doing anything wrong, as so many BIPOC people are; I'm not even stopped when they have a legitimate reason to stop me. Since I don't experience the police as oppressive or racist, I could potentially think of the police as a force for good in society and might not understand why so many BIPOC people fear and resent them. If I felt this way, I might come to think of BIPOC fear and resentment of the police as unreasonable, and might even assume that if the police pull over BIPOC drivers more often, they must have a legitimate reason to do so. That I could potentially have this thought even as I am aware that police officers really ought to pull me over when I speed speaks to the human capacity to hold conflicting ideas at the same time, as well as to the complexities of systemic inequality.

Every time a particular officer does not pull me over for speeding, there are assumptions at work in the officer's mind and in my mind, and there are consequences for both of us. The implications, however, go beyond two individuals because racism and other forms of systemic inequality are reinforced daily through millions of individual decisions and nondecisions exactly like this one, situations in which someone is given the benefit of the doubt or not, based on the valued or devalued identities they hold, with consequences for all involved.

Some of these decisions are about policing someone's behavior; do we let someone go about their business or do we investigate what they are doing and perhaps intervene with a judgmental comment, a warning, an arrest, or even an attack? Some of these decisions are about whether to provide resources to someone or not, as with Korver-Glenn's housing market professionals. Some of these decisions are about whether we find the rape survivor or accused rapist more credible, or whether lawmakers believe LGBTQ kids should be able to learn about LGBTQ history in school even if it makes some parents uncomfortable. The decisions span all aspects of our lives and impact us in a wide variety of ways, and they tend to build on each other and reinforce each other over time.

What these decisions have in common is that members of valued social groups—white people, men, heterosexuals, and especially white heterosexual men—tend to be met with good-faith assumptions over and over again, assumptions which translate into good-faith treatment. Assuming the best of someone makes it easy to treat them as competent, credible, moral, and harmless. Similarly, members of devalued social groups (including members of BIPOC communities, women, LGBTQ people, and people with more than one of these identities) are met with bad-faith assumptions over and over again, and the bad-faith assumptions tend to translate into bad-faith treatment. Assuming the worst of someone makes it easy to treat them as incompetent, without credibility, immoral, and potentially dangerous. Good faith and bad faith can operate in the smallest of interactions as well as broadly across institutions and societies.

Bad Faith and Moral Exclusion

As I've already implied, bad-faith assumptions and treatment are bound up with moral exclusion, the process by which a society treats some of its members as outside the boundary within which morality applies. Once someone is identified as falling within the moral community, most people will believe that they deserve fair treatment and will treat them fairly. Such a person's claims to justice, dignity, and respect will be taken seriously because they have been identified as the sort of person who has a right to justice, dignity, and respect. Their account of their own life will be taken seriously because people defined as within the moral community are understood to be experts on their own lives. Most people will understand that a person within the moral community wants freedom to live as they wish and will support that person's freedom just as they would advocate for their own freedom.

In contrast, once someone has been identified as falling outside the moral community, many people will not treat them fairly because such a person is not seen as inherently deserving of fair treatment. People may be suspicious of such a person's demands for justice, dignity, and respect, seeing those demands as a call for "special rights" or "entitlements." People won't find such a person's account of their own life compelling and may not believe them when they say (if female) that they were raped or (if Black) that they weren't doing anything wrong or (if lesbian, gay, or bisexual) that they are not "grooming" heterosexual children to "make them gay."

Bad-faith assumptions → Moral exclusion → Bad-faith treatment

Figure 1. From bad-faith assumptions to bad-faith treatment.

Once someone is defined as falling outside the moral community, that person's need for freedom and autonomy is seen as less important than the values or assumptions of those within the moral community, even if those values and assumptions lead to restricting the person's freedom. If restricting someone's freedom harms that person, others will likely find a way to blame the person for the harm they have experienced. They may tell a pregnant teenager that "she should have kept her legs shut" (without holding the man involved accountable) or tell a gay man fired from his job for sharing that he just married his husband that "he shouldn't have flaunted it" (without blaming his supervisor for discrimination).

Bad-faith assumptions thus fuel and justify moral exclusion, which in turn makes it easier to legitimize bad-faith treatment, as shown in Figure 1.

Good-faith assumptions, in contrast, can justify moral inclusion, and once we see someone as part of our moral community, it is easier to give them the benefit of the doubt, as shown in Figure 2.

This relationship between bad faith, withholding the benefit of the doubt, and moral exclusion plays a role in all forms of systemic social inequality, as does the relationship between good faith, granting the benefit of the doubt, and moral inclusion. We see the relationship in acts of fear and violence; in cultural messages about who matters, who's worthy, and who counts; in institutional discrimination; and in the internalized oppression suffered by members of devalued groups.

Institutional Good Faith and Bad Faith

When Timothy Loehmann shot Tamir Rice, he did so not as a private citizen but as a representative of the Cleveland Police Department. His uniform and badge protected and, to some people, justified his actions in a way that most private citizens cannot expect. Similarly, all those officers failing to pull me over for speeding chose this inaction on behalf of the Colorado Springs Police Department. Individuals can hold good-faith or bad-faith assumptions

Good-faith assumptions → Moral inclusion → Good-faith treatment

Figure 2. From good-faith assumptions to good-faith treatment.

about others and may act on them, but institutional good faith and bad faith play a far more important, and far broader, role in creating and recreating systemic inequality.

As discussed in Chapter 2, one of the many ways that institutions shape our lives is by granting some people the legitimate authority to make decisions about other people's lives that will enhance or diminish the well-being of those people. When someone has institutional decision-making power, other people will often accept the decisions they make as appropriate because they are acting on behalf of the institutions they represent. Someone with decision-making power may wear a badge, run a company, serve as a politician, be ordained as a member of the clergy, sit behind a bank desk, teach a class, or otherwise have access to social, cultural, political, or economic resources that they can share, restrict, or divide up as they see fit.

Moreover, people with decision-making power often have substantial discretion over the choices they make; a police officer can choose to pull over a speeding driver or can choose not to, and most of the time, most people will not question either the officer's freedom to decide what to do or the decision the officer ultimately makes. Similarly, most police officers who kill Black people are not held accountable and do not face any legal or criminal consequences; this lack of accountability and consequences come in part from public perceptions that the officers were within their rights to act as they did and should be given the benefit of the doubt about the action they chose.

The range of actions available to people with institutional decision-making power, along with the discretion they have over which action to choose, combine to enable them to grant or withhold the benefit of the doubt in a wide variety of ways. For example, police officers decide which driver to leave alone and which one to stop while security guards decide which shopper to trust and which one to follow on the assumption that they are shoplifting. Organizational rules and laws can be selectively enforced such that some employees are monitored and punished for minor offenses whereas other employees get away with whatever they want. Teachers pay more positive attention to students for whom they have higher expectations, while paying more negative attention to students they perceive as potential troublemakers and paying less attention to students they perceive as having less potential to succeed.[9] The Supreme Court and state governments can make voting or obtaining an abortion easier or harder for people.

---

9 Chapter 6 addresses issues of visibility, invisibility, and attention in more detail.

Institutional good-faith and bad-faith treatment often comes down to either granting someone access to valued resources, benefits, experiences, and opportunities or withholding that access from them. When such access is withheld based on someone's race, gender, sexuality, or other socially devalued identity, we call it "discrimination."

Discrimination as Systemic Institutional Bad Faith

Journalist Mary Ann Sieghart tells the story of Boston author Catherine Nichols. With the support of accomplished writer friends, Nichols sent cover letters and the beginning of her first novel to 50 literary agents, receiving only rejections. Two of the 50 agents were willing to review the full manuscript but would not guarantee that they would represent her. Finally, on a hunch, Nichols sent the same materials to a number of additional agents with a single change: using a male name instead of her own. Sieghart reports what happened next:

> She sent off the first submission and before she had even drafted the second, she received a reply saying, "Delighted. Excited. Please send the manuscript." To the six queries she sent on the first day, she received five instant replies. Three asked for the manuscript and two were warm rejections, praising ["George's"] 'exciting' project. [...] [Nichols] decided to approach fifty agents under the male name. [...] She got seventeen positive replies compared with [the original] two. [...] One agent, who had rejected her as Catherine, not only asked to read George's book, but wanted to send it to a more senior colleague.[10]

Without intending to carry out a study of sexist discrimination in the fiction publishing industry, Catherine Nichols demonstrated what institutional good faith and bad faith look like in the simplest of ways: sending identical materials with only the gender of the name changed and receiving differential treatment that cannot be explained except by sexism on the part of the literary agents. "George" was more than eight times more likely than Catherine to receive a positive response to the same piece of writing.

Another such story involves a 2021 home appraisal in Baltimore, Maryland, in which the homeowners were denied a refinancing loan because the appraisal came in too low. The family in question was Black. They then "whitened" the house, removing any evidence that a Black family lived there

---

10 Sieghart 2021: 22–23.

and adding photos of white friends along with artwork in which white people were featured prominently. A white male colleague of the husband met the appraiser and pretended to be the homeowner. The appraisal on the home jumped from $472,000 to $750,000, and the family got their refinancing loan. They had not made any improvements on the house between the first appraisal and the second; they simply changed the appraisers' expectations about who lived there.[11]

Academic researchers have carried out more systematic and extensive versions of this kind of research, often through what are called field experiments. Sociologists Lincoln Quillian and Arnfinn Midtbøen describe how field experiments are used to study racism in hiring:

> [F]ictitious applicants from different racial or ethnic groups apply for jobs. Often field experiments use pairs of applicants, with one majority and one minority applicant applying for the same position. Some studies hire people to play applicants for jobs (in-person audit studies); others use resumes with clues, often a name, to suggest race (resume audits or correspondence studies). In both variants, applicants are given resumes that make them similar in job-relevant characteristics so that race and/or ethnicity is the only systematic difference between the [...] applicants. As a result, field experiments can confidently determine that it is perceived race rather than other factors that drives the racial gaps in outcomes.[12]

Field experiments are also used to study gender and sexuality discrimination, in hiring and other settings. For example, several business and management professors carried out an audit study of over 6500 professors in 89 academic disciplines at 259 top US universities. They invented fictional prospective students seeking to discuss research opportunities prior to applying to a doctoral program. Student names were randomly assigned to signal gender and race; the email messages were otherwise identical. The researchers found that faculty were significantly more responsive to white males than to all other categories of students, particularly in higher-paying disciplines and at private institutions. This study suggests that even before someone formally applies (for a job, to a college, or university), they can face discrimination when they first attempt to make contact.[13]

---

11 Kamin 2022a.
12 Quillian and Midtbøen 2021: 397.
13 Milkman et al. 2015.

Discrimination in housing

Recent findings related to housing discrimination (in lending and in housing rental and sales) demonstrate that when other factors are equivalent, compared to white people, Black people are

- less likely to receive a response from mortgage loan originators when requesting information,
- less likely to be approved for loans,
- more likely to receive high-cost loans (with higher annual percentage rates added),
- less likely to have units or homes recommended to them,
- less likely to be able to inspect units, and
- likely to receive a far lower appraisal estimate on their houses when trying to sell.[14]

Similarly, with other factors held equal, compared to heterosexual couples, same-sex couples are less likely to receive information about loans, less likely to be approved for loans, and more likely to be charged higher interest. Black same-sex couples face more penalties than white same-sex couples and more penalties than Black heterosexual couples.[15]

Discrimination in hiring

Research finds similar patterns in hiring discrimination. When other factors are equivalent, compared to white people, Black people are

- less likely to receive any response from potential employers,
- less likely to be offered an interview,
- less likely to receive a job offer,
- more likely to receive an offer for a low-status job, and
- more likely to receive a lower starting salary offer.[16]

Black people are also more likely to receive an interview if they "whiten" their resume.[17]

---

14 Ellis 2022; Faber 2018; Glantz and Martinez 2018; Hanson et al. 2016; Kamin 2022b; Quillian, Lee, and Honoré 2020.
15 Dillbary and Edwards 2019; Schwegman 2019; Sun and Gao 2019.
16 Gaddis 2015; Kline et al. 2021; Nunley et al. 2014; Pager et al. 2009; Quillian et al. 2017, 2020.
17 Kang et al. 2016.

Similarly, with other factors held equal, women are less likely than men, and lesbians and bisexual women are less likely than women presumed to be heterosexual, to be interviewed for positions.[18]

Racial discrimination in the criminal justice system

To understand how different aspects of discrimination reinforce and build on each other, it's helpful to pick one large-scale institution and consider the many ways differential bad-faith treatment plays out in that institution. Racism in the US criminal justice system is a particularly good example of broader bad faith:

- On average, a Black person is 3.64 times more likely to be arrested for marijuana possession than a white person, though both groups use marijuana at similar rates.
- Crack cocaine, associated with Black sellers and users, has long carried heavier criminal penalties than powder cocaine, associated with white sellers and users; for decades, five grams of crack cocaine and 500 grams of powder cocaine carried the same five-year mandatory prison sentence (a 100-to-one ratio). As of 2020, 77 percent of individuals convicted of crack cocaine offenses were Black despite historical data showing that 66 percent of crack cocaine users have been white or Hispanic.
- Black defendants are more likely than equivalent white defendants to be required to pay for bail and, for those required to pay, receive bail amounts set almost $10,000 higher than white defendants.
- During the plea-bargaining process, white defendants are 25 percent more likely than Black defendants to have their principal initial charge dropped or reduced to a lesser crime, with the outcome that white defendants who initially face felony charges are less likely than Black defendants to ultimately be convicted of a felony. White defendants initially charged with misdemeanors are more likely than Black defendants either to be convicted for crimes for which they will not be imprisoned or not to be convicted at all. Moreover, white defendants with no prior convictions receive charge reductions more often than Black defendants with no prior convictions.
- On average, Black men serve longer and more punitive sentences than white men for the same crime.
- Black people, who represent 14.2 percent of the US population, represent 47 percent of those wrongfully convicted of crimes and later exonerated.

---

18 Mishel 2016; Quadlin 2018.

Innocent Black people are 3.5 times more likely than innocent white people to be convicted of sexual assault, seven times more likely to be convicted of murder, and 12 times more likely to be convicted of drug crimes.[19]

Differential treatment of Black people and white people in the criminal justice system extends to adolescents and young adults:

• Prosecutors are more likely to charge Black juvenile offenders as adults than they are to charge white juvenile offenders as adults.
• It takes less offending for Black youth to be arrested compared to white youth. Moreover, Black youth were 71 percent more likely than white youth to be rearrested even when both groups reported engaging in equivalent amounts of criminal activity following their first arrest.[20]
• Black youths are more likely to be incarcerated than white youths in every US state, while white teenagers are less likely to be arrested than other teenagers. Unequal policing across neighborhoods plays an important role in racial arrest rates; police are more likely to intervene in criminal behavior by BIPOC youths and to ignore the same behavior when it takes place in primarily white neighborhoods.[21]
• After arrest, BIPOC teenagers are more likely than white teenagers to be detained before sentencing and to be sentenced to prison, a difference not explained by racial patterns in violent offending. BIPOC adolescents who are charged with or sentenced for property, drug, or public order offenses are much more likely to face severe consequences than white adolescents with similar charges.[22]

Journalist Radley Balko has spent years collecting and reviewing dozens of studies demonstrating racism in the criminal justice system. Sample national-level findings reported by Balko level include the following:

• Black people comprise about 12.5 percent of drug users but represent 29 percent of those arrested for drug crimes and 33 percent of those incarcerated for drug crimes.

---

19 Ahmad and Mostetler 2021; American Civil Liberties Union 2020; Arnold et al. 2018; Berdejó 2018; Congressional Research Service 2021; King 2017; Kovera 2019: 1145; The Sentencing Project 2021a; United States Census Bureau 2021.
20 Kovera 2019: 1145; Padgaonkar et al. 2020.
21 Self-report findings suggest that BIPOC teenagers and white teenagers have similar offending patterns regarding weapons possession, drug use, and getting into fights.
22 The Sentencing Project 2021b.

- A Black person who uses drugs once a month is more than seven times as likely as a white person who uses drugs once a month to be incarcerated in the federal prison system.
- After adjusting for other variables, federal prosecutors are almost twice as likely to bring charges carrying mandatory prison minimums against Black defendants as against white defendants accused of similar crimes.
- Black people are more likely than white people to be arrested for equivalent gun-related crimes, more likely than white people to get longer sentences for similar crimes, and more likely than white people to get sentencing "enhancements" (additional penalties).
- Although white and Black youths are charged with "offenses against persons" at almost identical rates (and although Black youths represent less than one-sixth of youths in the United States), 53 percent of minors transferred to adult court for this type of offense are Black.[23]

Studies of racism in the criminal justice system are particularly powerful in making visible the ways in which a network of decision-makers act across a range of processes that reinforce and exacerbate racism at different stages of the criminal justice process. We can think of the criminal justice system as a kind of conveyor belt. Black people are more likely than white people to wind up on the conveyor belt in the first place, and less likely to be able to leave the conveyor belt before it deposits them in prison. White people are more likely to avoid the conveyor belt entirely and to be able to exit it mid-process, a difference that cannot be explained by either self-reported offending or the nature of the offenses in many cases.

The studies I've mentioned provide evidence of racial-, gender-, and sexuality-based discrimination in mortgage lending, the housing rental and purchasing market, hiring across various types of employment, and (in the case of racism) the criminal justice system, showing how these institutions are venues in which systemic inequality is created and recreated on a daily basis. We can go further, however, and understand discrimination as *institutional bad faith*, a set of processes by which people with institutional decision-making authority use that authority to withhold the benefit of the doubt from certain kinds of people while granting it to other kinds of people.

When the only difference between otherwise identical resumes involves race, gender, or sexuality (for example), we can reasonably expect that some kind of race-, gender-, or sexuality-based assumptions are at work. Korver-Glenn's research on Houston housing market professionals demonstrates how

---

23 Balko 2020.

a "racist market rubric" leads to racial—and racist—bad-faith treatment. The findings summarized above show such bad-faith treatment at work more broadly, in housing, hiring, and the criminal justice system. Each home loan approved for a white person but not for a Black person in an otherwise identical circumstance suggests a difference in who receives the benefit of the doubt. Each job offered to a white person with a criminal record but not offered to an equally qualified Black person without such a record shows how good-faith and bad-faith treatment are racialized, while each plea-bargain that ends with a white person not being charged and a Black person in the same situation being charged compels us to ask whether the Black person's real crime was being Black.

Of course, discrimination against a devalued group necessarily involves discrimination in favor of the parallel valued group, which we can understand as a kind of privilege. I consider the concept of privilege next, discussing ways in which this concept could be made more useful to our understanding of systemic inequality.

Privilege as Systemic Good-Faith "Benefit of the Doubt" Treatment

Most people encounter the idea of "privilege" in one of two forms: "privilege lists" (usually white privilege lists and male privilege lists) or the phrase "check your privilege," aimed at well-meaning liberal or progressive people who don't understand how their whiteness, heterosexuality, wealth, or maleness is informing and perhaps undermining their activism.

Privilege lists have been a useful if limited way of thinking about how inequality benefits people in valued groups. Decades ago, feminist psychologist Peggy McIntosh developed a list of white privileges from which she benefited, inspired initially by her frustration that men were so unable to recognize the ways in which sexism benefited them. McIntosh's white privilege list is among the most well-known of such lists. Her examples include the following:

- I can go shopping alone most of the time, pretty well assured that I will not be followed or harassed.
- I can turn on the television or open the front page of the paper and see people of my race widely represented.
- When I am told about our national heritage or about "civilization," I am shown that people of my color made it what it is.
- Whether I use checks, credit cards, or cash, I can count on my skin color not to work against the appearance of financial reliability.

- I can swear, dress in second-hand clothes, or not answer letters, without having people attribute these choices to the bad morals, the poverty, or the illiteracy of my race.[24]

In the same essay, McIntosh reflected:

I have come to see white privilege as an invisible package of unearned assets that I can count on cashing in each day, but about which I was 'meant' to remain oblivious. White privilege is like an invisible weightless knapsack of special provisions, maps, passports, codebooks, visas, clothes, tools, and blank checks. [...] I see a pattern running through the matrix of white privilege, a pattern of assumptions that were passed on to me as a white person. There was one main piece of cultural turf; it was my own turf, and I was among those who could control the turf. My skin color was an asset for any move I was educated to want to make. I could think of myself as belonging in major ways and of making social systems work for me. [...] Whiteness protected me from many kinds of hostility, distress, and violence [...]

Since McIntosh first published this essay, academics and activists have elaborated on the idea of privilege and have generated additional privilege lists. Sociologist Allan Johnson, a heterosexual white man, tied McIntosh's idea of privilege as "unearned assets" to the ways in which being in an unprivileged group is a liability:

The existence of privilege doesn't mean I *didn't* do a good job or that I don't deserve credit for it. What it does mean is that I'm *also* getting something that other people are denied, people who are like me in every respect except for the social categories they belong to. In this sense, my access to privilege doesn't determine my outcomes, but it is definitely an *asset* that makes it more likely that whatever talent, ability, and aspirations I have will result in something good for me. In the same way, being female or [BIPOC] doesn't determine people's outcomes, but these characteristics are turned into *liabilities* that make it less likely that people's talent, ability, and aspirations will be recognized and rewarded.[25]

---

24 McIntosh 1990.
25 Johnson 2006: 21–22; italics in the original.

While McIntosh's and Johnson's insights are useful, privilege language has proved challenging to integrate into broader-scale sociological approaches to systemic inequality. Privilege lists can help people better understand how they benefit individually from inequality but the items on the lists are not necessarily related to one another or set in an analytic framework in which they make sense as part of a larger whole. I know that, as a white person, I can shop in stores without being followed by security, drive above the speed limit without being pulled over, buy "flesh-colored" bandages that look somewhat like my skin, and purchase any house that I can afford (bracketing issues of sexism and heterosexism, which might lead me to face discrimination). Knowing that I experience these benefits as a result of being white is useful and humbling, but it does not help me understand either the history or the contemporary social patterns of racism, nor does it provide guidance about how to work to dismantle racism, alone or with others.

If, however, we understand privilege as *the systematic good-faith treatment (and the freedom from systematic bad-faith treatment) that results from receiving the benefit of the doubt*, we can incorporate the idea of privilege into a broader understanding of how inequality works. Privilege is a kind of positive discrimination, or as McIntosh herself has put it, the ways in which "some people, groups, or conceptualizations are elevated, promoted, given the benefit of the doubt, trusted as responsible or sound, and considered to be extra worthy of the support and respect of the society by virtue of the good qualities associated with or attributed to them."[26] Similarly, social psychologist Robert Livingston writes,

> Being White provides a staggering amount of unearned privilege, including the luxury of being fallible—whether it's a professional mistake, a social faux pas, or a legal violation—without being condemned for eternity. It is the privilege of not constantly having a cloud of suspicion hanging over you when you haven't done anything wrong. [...] White people are given the benefit of the doubt, the freedom to make mistakes. Black people are not.[27]

Privilege here becomes a way of talking about the concrete positive outcomes of receiving the benefit of the doubt, outcomes that follow good-faith assumptions and treatment.

Reviewing privilege lists across multiple forms of inequality with this framework in mind helps us notice patterns in what otherwise appear to

---

26 Case 2013: xii.
27 Livingston 2021: 44–45.

be disparate, unrelated examples of privilege. Below, I draw on four lists that cover white privilege, male privilege, and heterosexual privilege,[28] including examples of privilege that appear on multiple lists and adding a few parallel examples. I've changed the language to avoid specifying which form of privilege is being discussed in order to show how these forms of privilege exist across different types of inequality, and I have clustered the examples and given each cluster an organizing theme.

Competence and credibility as privilege:

- People take what I say seriously, including my account of my own life, my definition of a given situation, or my opinion.
- If I gaslight someone, I am more likely than the person I am gaslighting to be believed by a third party.
- I am presumed to succeed at whatever I do; people have high expectations of me.
- I am treated as having earned my success and not understood as (for example) an "affirmative action" student or employee.
- If I have a leadership role in an organization, my presumptive competence is not questioned.

Assumption of harmlessness/innocence as privilege:

- I am trusted and am not perceived as a threat or a problem.
- I can go about my day without being policed (whether by comments from strangers or by actual interactions with the police).
- I do not face criminal justice/legal system scrutiny, and may even be able to get away with crimes more easily than members of other groups.

Positive group visibility as privilege:

- My group is culturally visible and positively represented in the media and in popular culture.
- My group is positively represented in history books and documentaries.
- Commonly used language reflects positively on my group.

Normalcy as privilege:

- Commonly used language treats my group as the norm.
- Any interests that I have by virtue of my group membership are treated as reasonable and as what any normal person would have, not as "special interests."

---

28 Johnson 2006; Killermann n.d.; McIntosh 1990; Real n.d.

- The benefits I receive are not disparaged as "entitlements."
- I fit in at my workplace; people in my group represent the norm at my job.
- Laws were written with my group's experiences and values in mind.
- Medical research has always included members of my group, both in studying diseases and in developing new drugs.

Individuality as privilege:

- I am seen as an individual, not just as a member of my group.
- My failures and weaknesses reflect only on me, not on my group.
- I am not asked to represent all members of my group.

Preferential treatment/the benefit of the doubt as privilege:

- People agree that I should pursue my desires and have an impact on the world.
- I receive positive attention and positive reinforcement in school and in other institutional settings.
- I am more likely to be hired for a job.
- In the workplace, I am more likely to be supported by people with more authority than me and to be offered greater opportunities to succeed in my job.
- I'm evaluated more positively for the same quality of work that someone in a devalued group does.
- I am more likely to get a bank loan/mortgage (probably on good financial terms).
- I will probably pay less for a car than someone from a devalued group would.
- I am more likely to be believed and treated well by health-care professionals.

Freedom from discrimination as privilege:

- I am free to live where I want, and I can assume that I will be welcome wherever I choose to live.
- I don't need to worry about sexual harassment, rape, or physical violence that target me based on my group identity.
- I don't receive unwanted attention based on my group identity.
- When I have a bad day, I don't need to wonder whether I was discriminated against based on my group identity.

Identification with or access to power/authority as privilege:

- When people create images of God in my culture, God looks like members of my group.

- My elected representatives and other people with decision-making power (and sometimes cultural power) are members of my group.
- Most people understood to be experts on topics I care about are members of my group.
- I have access to decision-making power and/or cultural power in one or more organizational contexts.
- I am entitled to dominate conversations with members of other groups.

When organized in this way, items on privilege lists provide examples of broader patterns that intersect to make up systemic inequality, largely through good-faith assumptions that lead to granting people the benefit of the doubt based on (for example) their race, gender, or sexuality:

Assumptions: Members of valued groups encounter expectations of competence, credibility, harmlessness, and innocence (and, arguably, expectations of trustworthiness); these good-faith assumptions can lead to good-faith treatment.

Positive visibility: Valued groups receive positive cultural attention; individuals from valued groups are entitled to take up disproportionate amounts of space (physically, in conversations, as an expert, in positions of authority). Members of valued groups avoid the negative invisibility of being ignored or shut out of providing input where their interests, values, or well-being are at stake.

Positive invisibility: Members of valued groups are understood as normal and treated as individuals rather than being reduced to group stereotypes, which may help them avoid institutional discrimination. Members of valued groups are also understood as unproblematic such that bad behavior (like my speeding) is ignored. Members of valued groups avoid the negative visibility of unwanted public attention, harassment, violence, or any other monitoring or policing of their bodies or actions.

Preferential treatment: Members of valued groups receive good-faith treatment in educational settings, in hiring situations, in how their work or other accomplishments are evaluated, when shopping, by criminal justice decision-makers, when interacting with the health-care system, when seeking a loan or mortgage, or in other settings where people with decision-making power grant them the benefit of the doubt.

Once set in the right framework, the individual items on privilege lists turn out to provide useful details about how the benefit of the doubt works on a day-to-day basis, helping individuals in valued groups accrue McIntosh's "unearned assets" and avoid Johnson's (unearned) "liabilities." Moreover, the role of good-faith and bad-faith assumptions and the importance of positive and negative visibility and invisibility, so evident in privilege list items, turn out to be central aspects of how the benefit of the doubt works; Chapter 5 focuses on assumptions, expectations, and self-fulfilling prophecies, while Chapter 6 explores the complexities of positive and negative "in/visibilities."

First, though, we need to consider a particular variant of the benefit of the doubt, the concept of moral alchemy as introduced by sociologist Robert Merton. Moral alchemy describes situations in which the same values, desires, or behaviors are evaluated differently depending on whether those values, desires, or behaviors come from a valued or devalued group. I discuss moral alchemy and its opposite, false equivalencies, in Chapter 4.

Discussion Questions

1. Consider the two stories that open the chapter. Have you benefited from having a socially valued identity? Have you been penalized for having a socially devalued identity? In what ways?
2. Consider the examples of good-faith and bad-faith assumptions provided in the chapter. Have you ever experienced any of these assumptions directed at you? In what situations? Can you think of any additional good-faith or bad-faith assumptions you've encountered?
3. What are some concrete ways in which you have received the benefit of the doubt, either through an action someone took or through an action someone did not take? Can you think of times when the benefit of the doubt was withheld from you? What happened? What was the experience like?
4. The author discusses discrimination in housing, hiring, and criminal justice. Can you think of examples of discrimination in other settings? How do your examples help you understand discrimination as a kind of withholding of the benefit of the doubt?
5. The author argues that privilege can be understood as "the systemic good-faith treatment (and the freedom from systemic bad-faith treatment) that results from receiving the benefit of the doubt." Does this approach to privilege help you make sense of your own experiences of privilege? Where, if at all, do you see your own life reflected in the author's organizing themes for privilege?

Chapter 4

MORAL ALCHEMY AND FALSE EQUIVALENCIES

Tennessee governor Bill Lee, the first US governor to sign into law a bill prohibiting certain kinds of drag performances, had some personal experience with drag as it turned out. Lee appeared in his own high school yearbook in drag, wearing a miniskirt, pearls, and a wig. When this information came to light, the governor's spokesperson contrasted the bill's "protection of children" from "obscene, sexualized entertainment" with "lighthearted school traditions."[1]

The spokesperson made a good attempt at defining the situations differently, but from a sociological perspective, what some people might call hypocrisy on Lee's part was really an example of what sociologist Robert Merton defined as "moral alchemy." Moral alchemy describes a situation in which a behavior that is viewed positively when a valued group engages in it is viewed negatively when a devalued group engages in it.[2] As Merton put it, "the in-group readily transmutes its own virtues into others' vices."[3] Moral alchemy comes down to the idea that members of valued groups can do no wrong and members of devalued groups can do no good—so when a member of a valued group does it, it's good, and when a member of a devalued group does it, it's wrong, as shown in Figure 3.

We find moral alchemy at work in gendered language and in sexual double standards, among other places. This chapter covers a few common examples and then considers the opposite of moral alchemy, false equivalencies.

---

1 Hesse 2023. The spokesperson also failed to mention that the cheerleaders for the Tennessee football team show enough cleavage for their performances to be eligible for definition as "obscene, sexualized entertainment" (depending on who does the defining).

2 Merton 1948: 200–202.

3 Merton 1948: 202. Merton used the term "alchemy" specifically to capture this sense in which something valued is "transmuted" or changed into something negative.

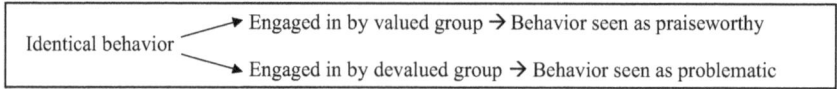

Figure 3. The logic of moral alchemy.

Justice scholar Warren Blumenfeld and social psychologist Derald Wing Sue are among those who have written about what Blumenfeld called the "double-standard language of gender," in which a man and a woman behaving the same are described differently.[4] He's "assertive," she's "bossy." He's "passionate," she's "emotional." He's "firm" while she's "stubborn." He's "good at details" but she's "picky." Successful, confident women are also called "abrasive," "strident," "shrill," "aggressive," "controlling," "pushy," and "bitchy," among other terms rarely used to describe successful, confident men.[5] One trans man reflected on how the definition of his behavior changed after his transition: "I used to be considered aggressive [as a woman]. Now I'm considered 'take charge.' People say, 'I love your take-charge attitude.'"[6]

Similarly, feminist ethicist and pastor Rebecca Peters writes about the sexual double standard in which behaviors expected of men are condemned among women:

> Women who have sex outside marriage are labeled in many ways— whore, slut, tramp, harlot, strumpet, bimbo, floozy, hussy, tart, trollop, and jezebel, to name just a few. Sexually active women who are not married are regularly described as promiscuous, loose, or fallen. Despite the increasing numbers of women who are sexually active outside marriage, these tropes still dominate popular culture and continue to influence public opinion. By contrast, male sexual promiscuity, including sex outside marriage, is alternately celebrated (Casanova, stud, ladies' man, gigolo, playboy, rake, horndog, tomcat, ladykiller, wolf, heartbreaker) or dismissed as an expected and natural aspect of male sexuality ('boys will be boys').[7]

Pregnancy and its consequences represent another arena of gendered moral alchemy. As feminist author Katha Pollitt has pointed out:

> Motherhood is the last area in which the qualities we usually value— rationality, independent thinking, consulting our own best interests,

---

4 Blumenfeld 2017; Sue 2010: 174.
5 Sieghart 2021: 98.
6 Quoted in Sieghart 2021: 43.
7 Peters 2018: 88.

planning for a better, more prosperous future, and dare I say it, pursuing happiness and dreams—are condemned as frivolity and selfishness. We certainly don't expect a man who accidentally impregnates a woman to drop everything and accept a life of difficulties and dimmed hopes in order to co-parent a baby. […] We don't like the idea that a man might be severely constrained for life by a single ejaculation. He has places to go and things to do. That a woman's life may be stunted by unwanted childbearing is not so troubling.[8]

Moral alchemy appears in other forms of inequality as well. When I was younger, homosexuality was often referred to as a "lifestyle," meaning that lesbian/gay/bisexual people got to have a "lifestyle" while heterosexual people got to have a life. Even today, many people who believe that marriage is an important goal for heterosexual couples find it to be an immoral mockery when same-sex couples engage in it.

Affirmative action represents a powerful example of race-based moral alchemy. On June 23, 2023, the Supreme Court overturned race-based affirmative action programs at two universities, setting the expectation that forms of affirmative action intended to address racism would become illegal across the country.[9] The Court, needless to say, did not address legacy admissions (university preference for children of alums), which tends to benefit white students and which is sometimes referred to as "affirmative action for whites."[10]

University admissions are, however, far from the only example of affirmative action for white people in the history of the United States. Arguably, the first example of such affirmative action was the 1790 Naturalization Act, which permitted only "free white persons" to become naturalized citizens. The 1935 Social Security Act provided a safety net for millions of (mostly white) workers while excluding agricultural workers and domestic servants, who were primarily Black, Mexican, and Asian. The Wagner Act, passed the same year, granted the power of collective bargaining to unions while permitting them to exclude BIPOC people from joining the unions. The Federal Housing Administration enabled white people to own a home while setting up a national neighborhood appraisal system that tied mortgage eligibility to race and denied mortgages to BIPOC people, with the effect of trapping BIPOC people in poor, underserved neighborhoods with housing

---

8 Pollitt 2014: 43.
9 Barnes 2023; New York Times Editorial Board 2023.
10 Gross 2019; New York Times Editorial Board 2019.

stock that did not appreciate in value (thus cementing segregation across generations). The GI Education Bill, which granted members of the armed forces access to continued education, had race-neutral language but was structured in a way that served to exclude Black veterans from its benefits. White US Americans have thus benefited from affirmative action for a very long time.[11]

When BIPOC people and white supporters protest this racial discrimination, their protests are often framed as problematic in ways that other kinds of protests are not. Criminologists Jonathan Reid and Miltonette Craig studied media coverage of Black Lives Matter protests along with protests opposing COVID-19 restrictions in six major newspapers including the *New York Times, Wall Street Journal,* and *Washington Post.* The authors found that protests involving racial justice issues were more often framed as a threat to the public interest and as "threatening" more broadly even if the protest was entirely peaceful, while protests initiated by whites were more likely to be represented by the media as "non-threatening" regardless of the actual nature of the protest. The articles generally suggested or stated outright that racial justice protests, but not white protests, required a police presence because the events were framed as violent or disorderly, a threat to the public interest in safety and property. In contrast, COVID-19-related protests were often framed by the media as part of a larger argument about getting society back to normal. About half of the articles covering mask mandate or "stay at home" protests portrayed protestors as "patriotic, passionate, and dedicated to the cause" and did not address how their perspectives might be seen as problematic in light of COVID-19 health concerns.[12]

Ultimately, examples of moral alchemy such as those discussed here show how the benefit of the doubt and moral exclusion work together to value the actions of valued groups and devalue the actions of devalued groups, even when those actions are identical.

False Equivalencies

"The law, in its majestic equality, forbids rich and poor alike to sleep under bridges, to beg in the streets, and to steal their bread."[13]

"'Why do men feel threatened by women?' I asked a male friend of mine."

"'They are afraid women will laugh at them', he said, 'undercut their world view.'"

---

11 Adelman 2003; Blakemore 2023; Katznelson 2005; Kenney 2016; Rothstein 2017.
12 Reid and Craig 2021.
13 France 1910: 95.

"Then I asked some women students, 'Why do women feel threatened by men?' 'They are afraid of being killed,' they said."[14]

If moral alchemy treats the same behavior differently depending on the social value of the people carrying out the behavior, false equivalencies err in the opposite direction by treating as equivalent two situations that are in fact different—often for reasons of inequality itself. The laws noted by author Anatole France appear to be class-neutral, but of course rich people do not need to sleep under bridges, beg in the streets, or steal bread. These laws thus punish the poor and may contribute to reproducing class inequality. Similarly, while men may feel threatened by women even as women feel threatened by men, author Margaret Atwood's comment about the distinction between the two types of fear is telling. The fear of being laughed at is not the same as the fear of being killed.

False equivalencies are thus a type of reverse moral alchemy in which differences in power, credibility, valuation, and life chances are ignored or even knowingly suppressed. Shortly after becoming Chief Justice of the Supreme Court, John Roberts wrote that, "The way to stop discrimination on the basis of race is to stop discriminating on the basis of race."[15] Given Roberts' decision about ending affirmative action, he does not appear to care about discrimination on the basis of race when it benefits white people, only when it benefits BIPOC people. Similarly, I recently saw a social media post that asked why there are no straight pride events; the post answered itself with a map of the world in which all of the countries in which it is illegal to be heterosexual (or in which people experienced violence for being heterosexual) were marked in red. No countries were marked in red.[16]

The Blue Lives Matter movement in support of police officers represents a particularly interesting example of false equivalencies, given what we know about racism in the criminal justice system. Undoubtedly, many people who support Blue Lives Matter are well intentioned and simply want to be appreciated for the work they do as police officers, or want to be in solidarity with their loved ones who are police officers. However, by calling the movement "Blue Lives Matter," these officers and their supporters are setting up a clear equivalency with the Black Lives Matter movement that, upon consideration, not only does not hold up but itself reveals racism at work.

---

14 Margaret Atwood, quoted in Griffith 2014.
15 New York Times Editorial Board 2023.
16 In fact, "straight pride" events have become increasingly common in conservative parts of the United States. They are virtually always explicitly homophobic and transphobic.

Setting "blue lives" against Black lives ignores the existence and experiences of Black police officers, some of whom report racist treatment by white officers and some of whom participate in the killing of other Black people specifically in their role as police officers. Thus, the Blue Lives Matter movement serves to render invisible both the racism experienced by Black officers and the ways in which such officers may reproduce racism themselves.[17]

Moreover, while no one is forced to be a police officer, no one chooses to be Black. The phrase "blue lives matter" is more equivalent to the phrases "firefighter lives matter," "nurse lives matter," or "English professor lives matter" than it is to "Black lives matter."[18]

While an off-duty officer out of uniform is not identifiable as a police officer, most Black people are identifiable as Black in any context where their skin is visible. Similarly, a police officer may be many things other than a police officer, and they may not all be equally impacted by the person's police officer status. In contrast, in a racist society, someone's identity as Black becomes a core aspect of who they are, touching most if not all aspects of their life to some degree.

Police officers have never faced systematic discrimination based on their being police officers; they have never been enslaved, been the target of widespread, large-scale lynching campaigns, faced a Jim Crow system, been targeted for mass incarceration, or been forced to live in segregated neighborhoods. They have never faced systematic bad-faith treatment in schools, employment discrimination, poor medical treatment, or discrimination in any other aspect of life based on their identity as police officers. The same cannot be said for Black people.

Police officers are invested with substantial institutional power, authorized to stop people and frisk them or to pull drivers over, to give tickets, and to make arrests; Black people have no such authorization unless they themselves are police officers, in which case the authorization comes from being a police officer, not from being Black.

Police officers have the legal right to do their policing wherever they see fit (though in practice they tend not to look for crime in wealthy, gated communities for a variety of reasons). In contrast, historic and current practices

---

17 Balko 2022; Lenthang et al. 2023. The framing of the struggle between LGBTQ people and "Christians" is similarly misleading, partly because so many heterosexual Christians are fully inclusive and welcoming of LGBTQ people but also because so many LGBTQ people in the United States are themselves Christians—almost half of LGBTQ people, according to a recent Gallup survey (Avery 2020).

18 Of course, every single one of these lives ought to matter; that Black lives so clearly don't matter to so many white people is why there is a Black Lives Matter movement in the first place.

of segregation and the racialization of poverty in urban areas mean that Black people are more likely to be in restricted, poorly served places that police officers can target for policing, while Black people driving or walking in "white" areas may be targeted on the basis of being seen as "out of place."[19]

Until very recently, police officers could target, harass, and kill Black people with impunity, paying no penalty for their actions; this is often still true. This impunity comes from the fact that others with decision-making authority tended, and tend, to believe the police officer's version of the story. In contrast, when Black people target, harass, and kill police officers, they pay the penalty if captured.

Finally, police officers are virtually never blamed for being killed by Black people, while Black people are frequently blamed for being killed by police officers.[20]

Surfacing these distinctions between Black experiences and police experiences (while noting the experiences of Black police officers) clarifies that treating the Blue Lives Matter movement as equivalent to the Black Lives Matter movement ignores important distinctions that are themselves often grounded in the very racism being protested by the Black Lives Matter movement.

This brief introduction to moral alchemy and false equivalencies suggests the incredible range of forms that good-faith and bad-faith treatment can take. Moral alchemy is a straightforward example of the benefit of the doubt, in which valued people engaging in a particular behavior receive the benefit of the doubt while devalued people engaging in the same behavior have the benefit of the doubt withheld from them.

False equivalencies, which can be understood as the opposite of moral alchemy, also involve the benefit of the doubt; however, they engage it in a different way. By treating as equivalent situations that are decidedly not so, especially when their very real differences derive from a form of systemic inequality, false equivalencies mislead in one of two ways. They may characterize a situation as neutral with regard to inequality when in fact the situation serves to maintain or produce inequality (the "majestically equal" law that sounds class-neutral but punishes poor people). Alternately, they may proclaim two different groups as equal or equivalent (Blue Lives Matter and Black Lives Matter) when one group has more power or is more socially valued than the other group. In the second case, the experiences and perspectives of the less-powerful or less-valued group are likely to be unrecognized or ignored by anyone who treats the equivalency as legitimate.

---

19 This topic is covered more fully in Chapter 8.
20 This topic is covered more fully in Chapter 7.

Both outcomes serve to direct attention away from the inequality at hand, enabling those with power and privilege to avoid seeing how they benefit from the inequality while potentially reducing the credibility of members of devalued groups when they raise concerns about the inequality. Who, after all, could argue with the claim that "the way to stop discrimination on the basis of race is to stop discriminating on the basis of race," other than someone unreasonable—or biased?

Were a poor person to complain about the law forbidding sleeping under bridges, a rich person or one of their supporters could point out that the law is neutral and accuse the poor person of wanting "special treatment" or a "special right" to sleep under the bridge. Were a Black person to observe that calling a police support movement "Blue Lives Matter" trivializes the Black Lives Matter movement, many white people would object that all lives matter and disparage the Black person as irrationally prejudiced against police and, therefore, as unreasonable. In these hypothetical cases, false equivalencies allow those with power and privilege to avoid having to confront how inequality benefits them—and how it harms those who suffer from it. Writing off the poor person or the Black person in these scenarios is simply a way of withholding the benefit of the doubt from them, denying them the respect of being experts about their own lives and experiences.

Chapter 3 introduced a variety of assumptions that can inform good-faith and bad-faith treatment. Chapter 5 takes a closer look at some of those assumptions and expectations, as well as introduces the role of self-fulfilling prophecies in reproducing inequality over time and across space.

Discussion Questions

1. The chapter lists some examples of moral alchemy in gendered language. Can you think of any other ways in which the same behavior among men and women (or other valued and devalued groups) is described differently along these lines? How is the language used to approve or disapprove of behavior in moral alchemy situations?
2. How does the phrase "affirmative action for white people" make you feel? Have you heard it before? Do you agree that the historical laws and policies described in the chapter have served as affirmative action for white people? If so, why don't we call them by that name?
3. Can you think of any additional examples of false equivalencies that serve to support (or to hide the existence of) some form of systemic inequality?
4. The author argues that moral alchemy and false equivalencies both involve withholding the benefit of the doubt from members of devalued groups. Given that the two processes work in opposite ways, how can this be true? Try to explain the author's argument in your own words.

Chapter 5

ASSUMPTIONS, EXPECTATIONS, AND SELF-FULFILLING PROPHECIES

My wife broke her arm in 2023, and one of our many doctor visits involved an emergency room trip when an urgent care doctor suspected circulatory damage. I was in line to go through security behind a young Black woman. The (white) security guard stopped her before she entered the screening machine and asked whether she had any guns or knives. She said no. He stared at her and made her go through the screening machine very slowly.

Then, it was my turn. As I emptied my pockets, the guard glanced at me and waved me through the screening machine without saying anything. When I collected my things, I noticed that the guard had picked up a book and appeared to be absorbed in it. He had not even watched as I passed through the checkpoint.

While I will never know what that guard was thinking, either about the Black woman or about me, it's reasonable to think that the question the guard asked her—but not me—followed from an assumption. He thought there was a chance that she was armed, but not that I was. As with all those police officers who did not pull me over, I was understood to be innocent until proven guilty—a courtesy not extended to the woman in front of me.

In Chapter 3, I listed assumptions that can inform whether someone receives the benefit of the doubt or has it withheld from them. Many of those assumptions fall into one of three clusters: competence, morality, and dangerousness. This chapter discusses assumptions about competence, trustworthiness, and innocence.[1] It then addresses self-fulfilling prophecies, which are circumstances in which acting on an assumption changes reality such that the assumption becomes true even though it was not initially so.

---

1 Trustworthiness (and its opposite, suspicion) and innocence (and its opposite, guilt) represent the intersection of assumptions about morality and assumptions about dangerousness. This chapter does not address heterosexist and homophobic assumptions, but those tend to cluster around morality and dangerousness as well.

Competence

I'm white, so I'm expected to be smarter.[2]

Men are assumed to be competent until proven otherwise, whereas a woman is assumed to be incompetent until she proves otherwise.[3]

I was highly educated. I spoke in the way one might expect of someone with a lot of formal education. I had health insurance. I was married. All of my status characteristics screamed 'competent,' but nothing could shut down what my blackness screams when I walk into the room.[4]

In Chapter 4, I quoted a trans man who had been defined as aggressive when female but was now understood as "take-charge" as a man. The research study in which the man was quoted also found that interviewees who had been ignored, passed over for promotions, and assumed to be incompetent in their jobs when they were living as women were treated quite differently once they transitioned. As men, they "[found] themselves with more authority and with their ideas, abilities, and attributes evaluated more positively in the workforce."[5] In contrast, a trans woman observed, "Apparently, since I became a female, I have become stupid."[6]

Black professionals similarly report poor treatment based on assumptions about their role in a situation. A Black entrepreneur wearing a suit told a reporter about being handed a set of car keys by someone who thought he was a parking attendant. A Black lawyer reported being patted down by guards at a courthouse while his white colleagues entered the building without being searched; apparently, the guards thought he was more likely to be a defendant than a lawyer. Similarly, a Black politician reported being told that she did not "look like a legislator" by a guard who singled her out for a search when she entered the Statehouse. A Black doctor trying to help a sick passenger on a plane had her credentials questioned by flight attendants, while another Black doctor reported overhearing patients say they had not seen a doctor yet—right after she examined them. A third Black doctor told a reporter that patients hand her their meal tray when she enters the room, trying to order a meal from her.[7] Underlying these assumptions—that an

---

2 A white high school student, quoted in Lewis and Diamond 2015: 99.
3 Trans scientist Joan Roughgarden, quoted in Sieghart 2021: 42.
4 Cottom 2019: 89.
5 Schilt 2010, cited in Sieghart 2021: 43.
6 Sieghart 2021: 46.
7 Hauser 2018. Evans (2019) provides another example of a Black attorney being treated badly by a county deputy, who thought he was a client impersonating a lawyer.

entrepreneur is a parking attendant, a lawyer is a criminal, and a doctor is a nursing assistant—is the deeper assumption that Black people are not competent to be entrepreneurs, lawyers, or doctors.

Many forms of workplace discrimination involve variations on having one's competence questioned and not receiving the same opportunities as those whose competence is taken for granted.[8] Studies of business leaders, architects, lawyers, and researchers in science, technology, engineering, and mathematics (STEM) fields have found the following:

- Women in senior leadership positions are substantially more likely than men to report having their judgment questioned (with Black women, lesbian/bisexual women, and women with disabilities even more likely to report this experience).
- Women in senior leadership positions are substantially more likely than men to report that others received credit for their ideas (with lesbian/bisexual women and women with disabilities even more likely to report this experience).
- Women and BIPOC men are substantially more likely than white men to report experiencing "prove it again" bias in which they had to demonstrate their competence multiple times to be taken seriously, with BIPOC women having to prove themselves the most often.
- Women, BIPOC men, and LGBTQ people are substantially more likely than men, white people, and heterosexuals to report having to work harder to get the same recognition as their colleagues or to be perceived as a legitimate scholar.
- Women and BIPOC men are substantially more likely to report getting less respect than male and/or white colleagues for the same level and quality of work as their colleagues.
- Women and BIPOC men are substantially more likely than white men to report that colleagues were surprised when they did outstanding work.
- Women and BIPOC men are substantially more likely to report that others assumed they were less qualified, even when they had the same credentials as their white male peers.
- BIPOC women are substantially more likely to report being mistaken for administrative staff, court personnel (in the case of lawyers), or janitorial staff.[9]

---

8 Two anthologies describing the prejudice and discrimination experienced by BIPOC women in higher education are titled *Presumed Incompetent* (Gutiérrez y Muhs et al. 2012) and *Presumed Incompetent II* (Niemann et al. 2020); see also Settles et al. 2021.

9 Blair-Loy and Cech 2022; Ridgeway et al. 2022; Williams et al. 2018; "Women in the Workplace 2022."

Beyond accounts of real-life experiences, several audit studies show how assumptions of incompetence have the potential to impact opportunities. In one such study, researchers asked a sample of school counselors to evaluate student transcripts; the transcripts were identical except for the names, which were coded to indicate race and gender. School counselors were less likely to recommend Black female students for AP Calculus and more likely to rate them as being the least prepared among all the students. In contrast, male students garnered recommendations for advanced academic options even when the transcripts suggested that their academic achievement was "borderline."[10]

Similarly, physics professors from large public research universities were asked to read one of eight identical CVs depicting a hypothetical doctoral graduate applying for a postdoctoral position in their field and to rate the student for competence. The name on the CV was used to manipulate race and gender. The professors rated male candidates as more competent than identical female candidates, and white candidates as more competent than identical Black and Latinx candidates.[11]

Knowing that others assume us to be competent is empowering. This knowledge expands our self-confidence and gives us courage to work harder and try new things. Such assumptions are also empowering when they lead those with power over us to treat us well, to give us access to opportunities, experiences, and resources that will enrich our lives. Conversely, assumptions of incompetence are heartbreaking and infuriating, especially when the benefit of the doubt is denied us as a result. Bad-faith treatment based on bad-faith assumptions limits our opportunities and damages our lives. What others assume about our competence, and what we assume about the competence of others, can have profound real-world consequences.

Morality and Danger: Trustworthiness and Suspicion, Innocence and Guilt

[T]rust underlies the operation of social power and actually creates power. Those who hold trust hold power.[12]

Strangers with a dark skin are suspect until they can prove their trustworthiness.[13]

---

10 Francis et al. 2019. The opportunity granted to the men is a perfect example of the benefit of the doubt.
11 Eaton et al. 2020.
12 Lewis and Weigert 1985: 459.
13 Anderson 2022: 29.

Every time I shop in a supermarket or department store, I throw out my receipt as I leave the check-out line. There may be a security guard at the store entrance, but they never ask to see my receipt. About a decade ago, I noticed that BIPOC people not only held onto their receipts but often kept them out to show the security guard as they left a store. I then began watching how the guards interacted with the people leaving and it became clear why BIPOC shoppers kept their receipts visible: every single person I ever saw stopped by a guard and asked to show their receipt was Black or Latinx. Years have passed and the pattern has held: I have not seen many people asked for their receipts, but I have never seen a single white person asked to show theirs.

As I mentioned earlier, assumptions about trustworthiness and innocence can involve deeper expectations about morality and dangerousness, giving such assumptions tremendous potential weight in our lives. If assumptions of incompetence can lead to a loss of opportunities, assumptions of untrustworthiness can lead to a loss of freedom. We may be monitored, scrutinized, or even policed—whether by actual police or by others seeking to make sure we are harmless or trying to protect others from us.[14]

Sociologist Nicole Gonzalez Van Cleve worked with several student research assistants during her study of the Cook County courthouse in Chicago; some students were white and some were Black. Van Cleve describes how her assistants were treated differently depending on their race. When white students entered the courthouse, they received privileges such as the freedom to violate small security measures without penalty. In contrast, Black students were routinely assumed to be defendants. One such student was asked by a sheriff whether he needed help finding the courtroom where his case would be addressed.[15]

Assumptions of Black criminality extend far beyond courthouse treatment. "Ban the box" (BTB) policies restrict employers from asking about job applicants' criminal histories on their applications, and for this reason are sometimes thought to have the potential to reduce unemployment among Black men, who are more likely than white men to have criminal records.[16] Two research studies, however, suggest that BTB policies may have unanticipated negative outcomes.

---

14 Trustworthiness also intersects with credibility, as discussed in Chapter 2. Finding someone credible necessarily includes believing them to be trustworthy.

15 Van Cleve 2016: 25. I discuss the criminalization of Black people more fully in Chapter 8.

16 I discussed racism in the criminal justice system in Chapter 3.

In one audit study,[17] researchers sent approximately 15,000 fictitious job applications to employers in New Jersey and New York City both before and after the adoption of BTB policies, varying applicant names to imply race but otherwise keeping the applications identical. After BTB policies were instituted, the Black–white gap in callbacks grew dramatically at companies that removed the "criminal history" box, from a seven percent gap before removing the box to a 43 percent gap after removing it.

Another study[18] tested the effect of BTB policies on employment and found that BTB policies decreased the probability of employment by 5.1 percent for young, low-skilled Black men—exactly the group that employers would presume to have a criminal record.

On the face of it, these outcomes are the opposite of what we would expect. Shouldn't removing criminal history information reduce the racial gap in potential employer interest? Shouldn't it contribute to increasing the probability of employment for young, low-skilled Black men? Shouldn't BTB policies have leveled the playing field at least somewhat? They did not. Instead, they made it harder for Black men, suggesting that in the absence of actual information about criminal histories, employers were more likely to presume their Black applicants had such histories—and to treat them accordingly.

Another study, mentioned in Chapter 3, examined wrongful convictions in the United States.[19] The researchers found that Black people (who make up 14.2 percent of US Americans[20]) represented 47 percent of those wrongfully convicted of crimes and later exonerated. Why are Black people so likely to be wrongfully convicted? There may be many answers, but an assumption of untrustworthiness or guilt seems likely to be among them.

When bad-faith assumptions about untrustworthiness or guilt inform how people are treated, the outcome can range from mildly annoying (the inconvenience of having to keep a receipt out while juggling shopping bags) to life-changing (an unjust prison sentence). Moreover, those receiving bad-faith treatment learn that society deems them problematic and will expend time, energy, and resources to protect others from them, a devastating message when one has done nothing wrong except belong to a devalued group.[21]

---

17 Agan and Starr 2018.
18 Doleac and Hansen 2020.
19 Gross et al. 2017.
20 United States Census Bureau 2021.
21 I cover the issue of people as problems in Chapter 7.

Self-Fulfilling Prophecies

The self-fulfilling prophecy is, in the beginning, a *false* definition of the situation evoking a new behavior which makes the originally false conception come *true*.[22]

If [people] define situations as real, they are real in their consequences.[23]

Imagine a financially solvent, successful bank, one that is in no apparent danger of failing. What happens to this bank if many of the people who bank there come to believe, however inaccurately, that the bank is in financial trouble? If I thought my money was at risk at the credit union where I bank, I would withdraw the money and put it somewhere else. I would not do this to punish the bank; I would just want to protect my money. Most people would probably do the same thing.

If enough people believed that the bank was financially unstable and withdrew their money, what would happen to the bank? It would in fact become financially unstable, despite having been fine before the withdrawals. Once people withdrew their money, and once the bank became insolvent, the initially false assumption of the people who had banked there—that the bank was in trouble—would become true. The bank would now, in fact, be in trouble. The assumption of those withdrawing their money would be confirmed—but the assumption would only be confirmed because of the action they took (withdrawing their money) based on an initially incorrect assumption they had (that the bank was in trouble).

Had the people not come to believe that the bank was in trouble, and had they not therefore withdrawn their money, the bank would not have been in trouble. For that matter, had the people come to believe that the bank was in trouble but not acted on that belief, the bank would have remained solvent. Presumably, the people would then have realized that their assumption was incorrect, kept their accounts open, and kept the bank from failing.

Sociologist Robert Merton uses this example to describe the power of what he calls "self-fulfilling prophecies," situations in which incorrect assumptions or beliefs lead to actions that change reality, with the outcome that the initially incorrect assumptions or beliefs become true and thus are confirmed or reinforced.

Sociologist Michael Schwalbe provides us with a more recent example of this phenomenon. More than 500 candidates ran for president in the 2016

---

22 Merton 1948: 195; italics in the original.
23 Thomas and Thomas 1928: 72.

US presidential election. How did we wind up with so few serious contenders for the presidency? Schwalbe provides the following answer:

> [I]nformation about [alternative candidates] and their ideas is filtered out by the very organizations that are supposed to bring it to [us.] [...] One reason that alternative candidates are ignored is that media people see them as having no chance to win. Media people are right. Restrictive election rules and the high cost of television advertising make it hard for alternative candidates to compete. But what truly dooms them is a lack of coverage. In this way, a self-fulfilling prophecy is created. Alternative candidates are not covered because they are seen as having no chance to win, and they have no chance to win if they are not covered.[24]

While banking and presidential races make for good examples of self-fulfilling prophecies, good-faith and bad-faith assumptions and the actions that arise from them provide equally important examples and show how self-fulfilling prophecies can reproduce systemic inequality.[25]

Racism in the classroom

> We have so many kids that are very capable but, for whatever reason, have never been pushed to their limits. [...] It's really hard when you get them as juniors to try to do damage control there [...] because they've lost faith in themselves, they don't trust the system, and it's really hard to get them to realize what they're capable of doing in their lives.[26]

> [I started in the International Baccalaureate program in 9th grade but felt the teachers] didn't think I was going to be able to succeed and so it didn't seem like they were trying as hard or giving as much effort toward me learning the same things as the other people in my classes (a Black student who subsequently left the IB program).[27]

Though the teacher and the student quoted here were part of different studies, their comments point to the same phenomenon: low expectations of BIPOC students on the part of (generally white)[28] teachers that have an impact on the students over time, causing them to disengage or even to

---

24 Schwalbe 2018: 182.
25 I discuss self-fulfilling prophecies related to race and crime in Chapter 8.
26 A high school teacher, quoted in Lewis and Diamond 2015: 112.
27 Joseph et al. 2016: 16.
28 Gershenson et al. 2016.

leave an advanced course of study in frustration. Once students lose faith in themselves or the educational system, their need for dignity may lead them to focus their energies on more rewarding pursuits than school, which has become a place of disappointment and perhaps even shame. If they stop taking their schoolwork seriously, this may confirm to their teachers that they do not have much academic potential. Similarly, when the Black student left her advanced course of study because she did not receive as much attention or care as the white students, she may have confirmed to her IB teachers that she was not dedicated enough to stay in the program.

When white teachers at any level of education assume that white students are smarter and more dedicated to learning than BIPOC students, they teach more effectively to those white students. They provide the white students with more attention, care, encouragement, mentoring, patience, and energy. In doing so, they may set up a self-fulfilling prophecy in which the white students respond to the extra attention, care, encouragement, mentoring, patience, and energy with extra effort and strengthened self-confidence, enabling them to perform better in class.

At the same time, BIPOC students can receive the message that teachers are less convinced that they will succeed. Such students may disengage and learn less. Such situations can lead to self-fulfilling prophecies in which white students respond to the higher expectations of their teachers by rising to the challenge and performing well while BIPOC students confirm the lower expectations of their teachers, responding to low expectations by disengaging and performing less well.

Research by psychologists and education scholars confirms that such racialized self-fulfilling prophecies take place at different levels of education and in countries around the world. Specifically, researchers find the following:

- Positive teacher expectations are associated with student achievement level, high school graduation, college attendance, and college graduation.
- Teachers hold racially based stereotypes and biases about student academic abilities.
- Teacher expectations of achievement differ dramatically and systematically in ways that privilege white students and disadvantage Black students.
- Black students report that white teachers hold lower expectations of their academic abilities compared to their white peers, do not offer extra assistance in some cases when they request it, and generally treat them less well than white students.
- Teachers provide more rigorous and challenging assignments to students they believe are more capable, offering them more chances to grow academically.

- Teachers provide more support and attention to students for whom they have high expectations, exhibiting emotionally warmer behavior toward them.
- Teachers display greater rates of smiling, nodding, and eye contact in interactions with students for whom they have higher expectations.
- Teachers offer systematically different feedback to students for whom they have higher or lower expectations, with students in lower expectation groups receiving less positive and more negative feedback.
- Teachers tend to place young high-expectation students into more advanced reading groups.
- Students who perceive that their teachers have lower expectations of them develop lower perceptions of their own abilities over time, feel hopeless, and see little point in trying to learn in low-expectation classrooms.
- Teacher expectations have an indirect effect on student achievement in math by deepening low-expectation students' sense of academic futility.
- In high-bias classrooms, teacher expectancy effects can account for a difference of more than half a grade point in Black–white achievement gaps.
- Teachers' low expectations of BIPOC high school students can cause their test scores to drop far more than would be expected based on prior schoolwork.[29]

Stereotype threat

One kind of academic self-fulfilling prophecy involves stereotype threat, the fear that when you engage in an activity in which your group is thought to be less capable, you will underperform and confirm the stereotype. Psychologist Claude Steele began studying stereotype threat in an attempt to understand why academically strong women struggled in advanced college math courses and academically strong BIPOC students struggled in selective college settings.[30] Stereotype threat works by diminishing the cognitive resources (especially working memory)[31] available to those in stereotype threat circumstances.

---

29 Bergold and Steinmayr 2023; Carter Andrews and Gutwein 2017; Freidus and Noguera 2017; Johnston et al. 2019; McKown and Weinstein 2008; Murdock-Perriera and Sedlacek 2018; Wang et al. 2018.
30 Steele 2010.
31 Nasir et al. 2012: 296.

The following are the most important things we know about stereotype threat:

- It shows up most prominently in students with stronger academic confidence and skills. It is the very fact that these students have high expectations that makes them so susceptible to the pressure.
- Stereotype threat is caused by environmental cues that remind a person of their stereotyped identity and thereby of their risk of confirming a negative stereotype.
- The frustration experienced by people in stereotype threat circumstances indicates that those people fear confirming the stereotype of their lesser intellectual ability.
- These stereotypes can cause enough disruption to lead to documented underperformance, for example, on an academic test.
- Performing in a stereotype threat circumstance involves multitasking: trying to perform a task while trying to refute a stereotype. This experience is stressful and distracting, with the person's mind in a "racing and overloaded" situation. The person is preoccupied with worry about confirming the stereotype and the consequences of doing so as well as whether it is possible to perform well and dispel the stereotype. Such rumination takes up mental capacity that is no longer free for the intellectual task at hand.
- Cardiovascular stress (increased heart rate and blood pressure) and other physiological signs of anxiety also interfere with task performance.
- Underperformance in a stereotype threat situation does not have to do with either incompetence or not working hard. It is the combination of anxiety and the urge to multitask that makes people work less effectively.
- If the stereotype is removed, the threat is removed and underperformance dissipates. People in what would otherwise be a stereotype threat situation perform as well as others if there is no risk of confirming a negative stereotype.[32]

Career decisions among heterosexual dual-career couples

Another important self-fulfilling prophecy concerns dual-career heterosexual couples in professional workplaces. Egalitarian couples generally express commitments to valuing both people's professional lives equally and to trading off compromises so that both people in the couple can succeed in their careers. Over time, however, the man's career is often prioritized,

---

32 Steele 2010.

with the woman taking a lower-pay, lower-prestige position or dropping out of the workforce at least temporarily. Parenting plays some role in this situation, but there are important other factors at work.[33] What makes this situation a self-fulfilling prophecy is the way in which employers' lower expectations of women's commitment to the workplace sets a cycle in place that can, in many cases, eventually lower women's commitment to the workplace because of employer treatment.

Sociologist Jaclyn Wong[34] interviewed male–female couples in which both people aspired to and trained for professional careers. By interviewing the couples multiple times over six years, Wong identified different stages at which the individuals—and couples—reassessed their work situations.

The men in the couples generally experienced good-faith treatment and advanced in their careers, while many of the women faced doubts about their competence and slower career advancement. The men found their work environments hospitable while the women faced harassment and other kinds of poor treatment. The gendered pay gap[35] led couples to prioritize his career over hers when decisions needed to be made, which in turn led

---

33 If professional careers were not structured around male trajectories rather than female ones, pregnancy would not derail women's careers; instead, it would be common for women who have children to modify or pause their work lives temporarily and later return to the same level of work they left, picking up from there with no penalty. That most workplaces don't operate in this way is a reminder that most professional careers are still based on the assumption that someone other than the worker in question is taking care of the chores and the children. See Johnson 2014b: 7 on the sixty-hour-a-week career as based on men's experiences and priorities.

34 Wong 2023.

35 In 2022, US women earned an average of 82 percent of what men earned; the average in 2002 was 80 percent. For full-time, year-round workers, 2021 data showed that women made 84 cents for every male dollar in median earnings. If part-time and part-year workers are included, the gap grows to 77 cents for white women for every dollar paid for men, with a larger gap for Black, Latina, and Native women. When comparing women and men with the same job title, seniority level, and hours worked, there is still a gender gap of 11 percent. Women make less than men in 94 percent of occupations; in 2022, women earned less than men for full-time weekly work in 19 of the 20 largest occupations for women and in all 20 of the largest occupations for men. Female-dominated occupations have the lowest average earnings for both men and women. Moreover, a study of more than 50 years of data revealed that when women moved into a field in large numbers, wages declined even when controlling for experience, skills, education, and region; we can interpret this finding as suggesting that women's work is devalued because women do it. Aragão 2023; Bartnik et al. 2022; Gould and DeCourcy 2023; Haan and Reilly 2023; Institute for Women's Policy Research 2023; Kochhar 2023; Lepage and Tucker 2023; on the importance of gendered occupational segregation, see Glynn and Boesch 2022; Zhavoronkova et al. 2022.

to women doing more unpaid work at home even in relatively egalitarian couples. As the men's careers took off, the women faced career instability and difficulties that made it easier to "choose" traditionally gendered divisions of labor at home. Such decisions, while disappointing to the couples, made the most sense in light of how sexism played out in their workplaces.

Wong's couples may not realize that their gendered work decisions, however rational in context, confirm the assumptions of workplace decision-makers that men are more committed to their careers than women.[36] If those assumptions informed the good-faith treatment experienced by the men and the bad-faith treatment experienced by the women, the outcome among the couples became yet another self-fulfilling prophecy—one that damaged and sometimes ended the careers of people who trained diligently and showed tremendous promise, and one that sometimes ended the couples' relationships.

Bad-Faith and Good-Faith Cycles

In a sense, self-fulfilling prophecies are simply one example of how systemic inequality works; in another sense, they capture the cycle of reproduction at the heart of all forms of systemic inequality. For those on the devalued, bad-faith end of the interaction, the cycle looks something like Figure 4.[37]

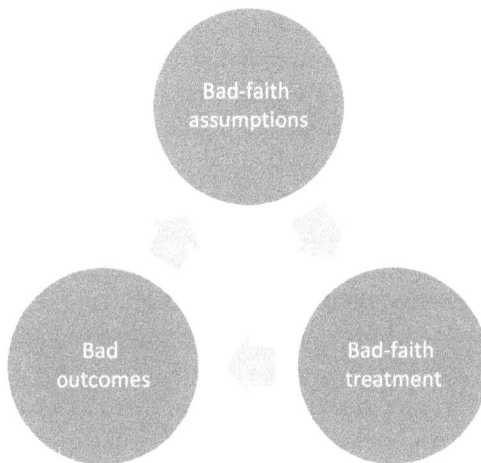

Figure 4. The bad-faith cycle.

---

36 Decision-makers' assumptions about men being more competent than women may also be confirmed if hostile workplace environments, slow advancement, and poorer pay make it harder for women to do their best work.

37 I am indebted to Dr. Helen Daly for proposing Figure 4.

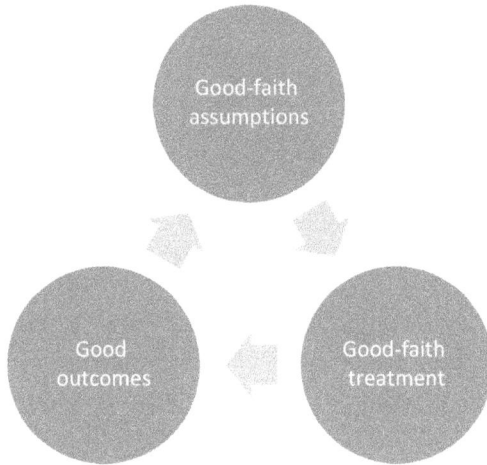

Figure 5. The good-faith cycle.

Bad-faith assumptions lead to bad-faith treatment in which members of devalued groups have the benefit of the doubt withheld from them. They are mistrusted and denied access to valuable opportunities; they may have their freedom restricted. Unsurprisingly, members of devalued groups struggle to be their best selves in the face of bad-faith treatment. They may be unable to succeed at school or work. Ultimately, they may lose trust in the systems that treat them badly and in the individuals who represent those systems. Those with cultural power can ensure that the failures and limitations of devalued groups receive more attention than their successes, which reinforces bad-faith assumptions about them. The cycle starts over.

As shown in Figure 5, the same kind of cycle takes place for members of valued groups, but with the opposite assumptions and the opposite outcomes.

Good-faith assumptions lead to good-faith treatment in which members of valued groups receive the benefit of the doubt. They are trusted and given access to life-enriching opportunities; their freedom is not restricted. Unsurprisingly, members of valued groups often respond to good-faith treatment with success and trust in the systems that support them. Those with cultural power can ensure that the successes of valued group members receive more attention than their failures, which reinforces good-faith assumptions about them. The cycle starts over.

The role of visibility, as suggested in both cycles, deserves more attention. Visibility (and invisibility) can be positive or negative, and the various forms of positive and negative "in/visibility" weave together at decision-making, cultural, and individual levels to contribute to sustaining inequality in all its forms. I consider how visibility and invisibility work in Chapter 6.

Discussion Questions

1. Why do assumptions about (in)competence play such an important role in our lives? Have you ever had your competence questioned? What was the experience like? Have you ever made assumptions about the competence of others based on their social groups?
2. Why do assumptions about (un)trustworthiness play such an important role in our lives? Have you ever had your trustworthiness or innocence questioned? What was that experience like? Have you ever made assumptions about the trustworthiness of others based on their social groups?
3. Explain what self-fulfilling prophecies are in your own words. Can you come up with any additional real-life examples?
4. Explain how the bad-faith and good-faith cycles work in your own words. Can you come up with any real-life examples beyond those mentioned in the book thus far?

Chapter 6

IN/VISIBILITIES, POSITIVE
AND NEGATIVE

[T]hose with status and power have the authority to render others visible, invisible, or hypervisible [because] power differentials [...] result in asymmetry around who controls their own visibility and that of others.[1]

What's visible is my race, what's invisible is my contribution.[2]

The bell rang and I wrapped up a lecture on sexism in my introductory sociology course. I was proud of myself for having mentioned the research on how professors give men more opportunities to talk in college classrooms; I wanted my material to be relevant to the students. Two of the women in the class stayed behind to speak with me. They looked uncomfortable.

One said, "So, about professors giving guys more airtime during class ..." and stopped.

The other one continued, "We decided to track the gender breakdown in who talked in class today. You know, there are two guys in the class, and twenty women. But you called on the guys almost half of the time. Did you do that on purpose to make your point?"

I suddenly felt a lot less proud of myself. I had not done it on purpose. I had not even been aware that I was doing it.

Every professor I've ever told this story to has their own version of it, including feminist-identified female professors. Men talking disproportionately is so normal that most of us don't notice it most of the time.

About a decade later, I ordered a Starbucks Frappuccino on a hot summer day. The barista squinted at me and said, "You do know this drink has like sixty carbs in it, right?"

I held my ground. "Do you tell everyone that, or just overweight women?"

---

1 Buchanan and Settles 2019: 2.
2 Kim et al. 2019.

She glared. "I'm just saying."

I ordered the drink anyway, but I didn't enjoy it.

Visibility plays a complicated role in systemic inequality, because being visible works to our advantage sometimes but being invisible can also work to our advantage. Similarly, visibility can be problematic, but so can invisibility, depending on the context. If you're in the socially valued group, both your visibility and your invisibility work in your favor: you receive positive attention without having to contend with unwanted attention. If you're in the socially devalued group, both your visibility and your invisibility work against you when you are "scrutinized but not recognized."[3]

Sociologist Allan Johnson observed the following about gendered invisibility:

In general, women are made invisible when they do things that might elevate their status, such as raising children into healthy adults or coming up with a brilliant idea in a business meeting. Men and manhood, however, are often made invisible when men's behavior is socially undesirable and might raise questions about the appropriateness of male privilege. Although most violent acts are perpetrated by men, for example, news accounts rarely call attention to the gender of those who rape, kill, beat, torture, and make war on others. [...] With numbing regularity, we hear reports of violent crimes perpetrated by men. [...] Yet rarely do we hear the simple statement that the perpetrators of such acts are almost always men.[4]

In this chapter, I consider ways in which visibility and invisibility are connected to good-faith and bad-faith treatment.

Positive Visibility, Negative Invisibility

When I started reading the *New York Times*, I noticed that there was a section devoted to "Business" but no section devoted to "Labor."[5] Theoretically, everyone in the workforce should be concerned about how "labor" is doing, as we are all "laborers"[6] but not all of us are "businesspeople." The *Times'* business section

---

3 Settles et al. 2019.

4 Johnson 2014b: 146–147.

5 This is still true of the online version of the *Times*.

6 This point could be expanded to include the extensive amount of unpaid and undocumented labor carried out by women the world over, upon which all formal economies depend.

identifies the reader with business interests almost exclusively from a corporate, managerial perspective—which is often not the perspective of workers lower down than the C-suite. The *Times'* editorial board thus uses its cultural power to lift up the importance and centrality of corporate management, generally rendering other workers and their needs and struggles invisible.

A different example comes from the film world, where women (more than 50 percent of the US population[7]) had just over a third of the speaking roles in top-grossing US films in 2022.[8] The same study found that women accounted for 38 percent of major characters, those who appear in more than one scene and who are instrumental to the story's action, while men accounted for 62 percent of major characters.[9] Go to a top-grossing US film from 2022 and you are sure to see—and hear—men on the screen.[10]

Still another example of positive visibility comes from US history curricula, where "[Black] history is still optional; it remains an elective"[11] even as attacks on "critical race theory" seek to limit teaching about BIPOC experiences and perspectives. Such approaches to history keep white experiences and perspectives squarely in view—as long as they are positive and not, say, about white racism.

Positive visibility is often a matter of being the center of attention; those deemed worthy of being the center of attention are understood to be important, powerful, and competent. Their opinions, perspectives, and decisions matter, so we are invited to pay attention to them.

A different kind of positive visibility results when a social group is defined as the default around which society is designed. Cars, climbing walls, and pianos are only some of the many items built with the male body in mind.[12] I've experienced the frustration of trying to play Romantic-era piano pieces with left-hand intervals that are simply too wide for me to reach, but that a man with an average hand size can manage.

---

7 World Bank 2022.

8 Lauzen 2023b.

9 The absence of nonbinary and genderqueer characters in these films represents another example of negative invisibility.

10 The "Bechdel test" is a measure of female representation in movies ("Bechdel test" n.d.). The test, identified by Liz Wallace and named after American lesbian cartoonist Alison Bechtel, sets the following threshold: a movie passes the Bechdel test if there are at least two female characters in the movie who have a conversation with each other about something other than a man. Readers may want to consider whether their favorite movies pass the Bechdel test or not.

11 Hannah-Jones 2021: xxxiii.

12 Criado Perez 2019b; Hamlett 2019.

The formula to determine the standard office temperature has also benefited men at the expense of women. This formula, developed in the 1960s, was based on the metabolic resting rate of the average 40-year-old, 154-pound man. A recent study, however, found that offices are, on average, five degrees too cold for women.[13]

Women involved in car crashes are 73 percent more likely to be seriously injured and 17 percent more likely to die than men because cars have been designed for men. The most commonly used crash test dummy is five feet nine inches tall; women on average are five feet four inches tall, and the differing heights (and other differences such as bone density and abdomen shape) mean that male and female bodies interact differently with seatbelts and steering wheels, leading to different outcomes in crashes.[14]

More broadly, as physician Alyson McGregor points out,

One of the biggest and most flawed assumptions in medicine is this: if it makes sense in a male body, it must make sense in a female one. *In every aspect, our current worldwide medical model is based on, tailored to, and evaluated according to male models and standards.* [...] All our methods for evaluating, diagnosing, and treating disease for both men and women are based on previous research performed on male cells, male animals, and male bodies. [...] However, recent research is revealing that female bodies are physiologically different from men's on every level—from our chromosomes to our hormones to our bodily systems and structures. Therefore, the medicine that works for men doesn't always work for, or even apply to, women.[15]

I mentioned how women's pain is not taken as seriously as men's pain in Chapter 1 (and I cover this topic more fully in Chapter 8); clearly, a medical model built on studying the bodies and believing the self-reports of men plays a role in women not receiving the pain medication they need.

This medical model also explains why women are up to three times more likely than men to die after a serious heart attack: as McGregor explains,

Women are far less likely than men to fit the textbook model of heart disease—but they are also more likely to die of a cardiac event [since]

13 Chang and Kajackaite 2019; Criado Perez 2019a.
14 Criado Perez 2019a; Holder 2019; Molinari and Brook 2021; Schmidt 2022. When female crash test dummies are used, they simulate women who are five feet tall and weigh 110 pounds; the average US woman is five feet four inches tall and weighs 171 pounds, so even the "female" dummies are not truly proportionate.
15 McGregor 2020: 7; italics in the original.

women are less likely to have 'traditional' heart attacks [...] that create the classic symptoms of acute chest and left arm pain.[16]

Medical professionals on the lookout for "traditional" heart attack symptoms may not recognize that a woman is having a heart attack because her symptoms don't match the ones we associate with heart attacks—a failure of recognition that results in lost lives and grief that would be avoidable if male heart attack symptoms were not the standard.

These examples of how society is built around men as the default gender point to a complex situation in which visibility and invisibility work together. As the default gender, men are invisible *as men*; they are simply the normal human beings around whom society's processes are organized. However, the products and resources created for men—the pianos, climbing walls, cars, office temperature settings, expectations about pain, and definitions of heart attack symptoms—are visible and normalized as though they were equally appropriate for everyone. We all encounter the same Subaru Outback, the same office temperature, and the same understanding of how a heart attack presents, and we rarely question its universality—until we realize, if we are female (or were assigned female at birth), that this aspect of society was not created with our bodies in mind and may not work for us.

Gendered language represents another kind of visibility in which maleness is universalized. Some months ago, while searching for new cooking competitions to watch, I found one on Hulu called "Man vs. Master: Chef Battle." More recently, I saw an ad for the game Royal Match in which one woman says to another, "Dude, I found the greatest game." Similarly, on almost a daily basis, I hear people use the term "guys" to refer to mixed-gender, or even all-female, groups. In all three examples, words that describe men in particular are also used to describe people in general. Both men and women were contestants on "Man vs. Master" but the network would never have put the same show forward with the title, "Woman vs. Master: Chef Battle." I have never heard people refer to a mixed-gender or all-male group as "women." Language for women refers to women only. Language for men includes everyone.[17]

Many people who care deeply about sexism believe that worrying about gendered language is a poor use of our energy, and that changing

---

16 McGregor 2020: 42, 43; see also Criado Perez 2019a on the negative outcomes of not including women in clinical drug trials.

17 Dichotomous gender language also, of course, excludes anyone who does not identify as a man or a woman.

such language is less important than addressing the gendered pay gap, rape, or the difficulty in electing female political leaders in the United States. But as sociologist Michael Schwalbe points out, these issues are related:

> [W]hat if our habitual ways of speaking and writing make certain groups of people invisible? What if [they] imply that certain groups of people (men) are standard and normal— representative of all humanity—while other groups (women) are different, deviant, or inferior? [...] Language is not merely a window to a sexist worldview; it is the main tool with which both the world and the view are continually rebuilt. [Women's] name-changing [upon marriage] and the use of male generics make women invisible. To refer to a group of first-year college students, half of whom are women, as fresh*men*, is to say, symbolically, that the presence of women doesn't matter. It is also to say, symbolically, that human = male. This linguistic practice thus reinforces a worldview in which women are not as important as men, not as fully human as men, not equal to men. [If] women are not seen as fully human, as the full equals of men, then it becomes easier to ignore them, abuse them, discriminate against them, restrict their freedom, and so on.[18]

In gendered language, maleness, by virtue of being neutral and thus universal, is visible everywhere. Femaleness, far from being universal, may not even be specified when women are involved—thus the female chefs on "Man vs. Master," a woman referring to another woman as "dude" in a video game ad, and the ubiquitous use of the term "guys."[19]

Men are not only more *visible*; they are more *audible*. In a recent study of 65,000 employees in more than 400 US companies, 36 percent of female senior leaders reported being interrupted or spoken over by men; only 15 percent of male senior leaders reported this experience.[20] A longitudinal

---

18 Schwalbe 2018: 48; italics in the original.
19 A similar point could be made about gendered language for God. The term "God" is usually gendered male or left ungendered. It is very rare to see "God—she" language except in intentionally progressive religious settings. "God" is thus both male and beyond gender. The term "Goddess," in contrast, is undeniably and only female.
20 "Women in the Workplace" 2021: 24.

study of a middle school found that teachers allowed sixth-grade boys to monopolize classroom conversations and challenge girls' opinions in ways that broke stated classroom rules—as long as the boys in question were white and affluent.[21] A separate study of gendered interaction in nine college classrooms found that men occupied what the researchers called "sonic space" 1.6 times as often as women and were more likely to speak out without raising their hands, to interrupt and to engage in prolonged conversations with one another.[22] The memory with which I began the chapter is part of a much larger pattern.

While I've been using gendered examples of positive visibility and negative invisibility, these patterns emerge in other forms of inequality as well, as with "missing white woman syndrome."

In September 2021, the disappearance of white 22-year-old Gabby Petito became a media sensation. Her remains were found in Wyoming, unlike the remains of hundreds of indigenous people who had been reported missing in Wyoming in the previous decade but never found. Petito became another example of what the late journalist Gwen Ifill described as "missing white woman syndrome," the media focus on missing white women to the exclusion of other missing persons.[23]

"Missing white woman syndrome" has been studied by criminologists and legal scholars. One analysis of news articles from 11 different newspapers over four years found that missing white women and children were overrepresented in the news and were more likely to receive repeated coverage, while missing BIPOC women were underrepresented.[24] Another study drew on FBI data and information from major news sources, finding race and gender disparities consistent with the idea of "missing white woman syndrome." The disparities involved both whether a missing person received any media attention at all and the level of coverage intensity among those who received coverage. The study noted that white overrepresentation and BIPOC underrepresentation could not be explained by differences in real-world victimization rates.[25] Even in their absence, white women were more visible than BIPOC women.

---

21 Musto 2019. Latino boys in lower-level sixth-grade classes were punished for engaging in the same behavior—another example of moral alchemy, as discussed in Chapter 4.
22 Lee and McCabe 2021.
23 Rosner 2021.
24 Slakoff and Fradella 2019.
25 Sommers 2017.

Negative Visibility, Positive Invisibility

> In sharp contrast to the marked, which is explicitly *accentuated*, the unmarked remains *unarticulated*. [...] Reflecting what we *assume by default*, it is thus effectively *taken for granted*.[26]

> It is normal for women to worry about being abnormal, because male behavior, male heroes, male psychology, and even male physiology continue to be the standard of normalcy against which women are measured and found wanting.[27]

> When it comes to political agenda-setting, white identity politics are the most successful identity politics in American history. The success of white identity politics rests upon an entrenched white normativity that refuses to see whiteness as a political identity and white interests as politics. In the mainstream media, white Americans are positioned as a default, universal, neutral category. Against this white baseline—considered just politics—the needs of people of color are considered 'special interests.'[28]

Our Bernese Mountain Dog had some early challenges that led us to work with a pair of orthopedic surgeons. The pair was a married couple, referred to by everyone in their practice as "Dr. Smith" and "Mrs. Dr. Smith."[29] When I asked a receptionist about why they were referred to in this way, she shrugged and said it was the easiest way to tell them apart.

More recently, a Facebook friend, knowing that I was working on this book, sent me a photo of her CPAP machine's configuration menu, which included the options "autoset" and "autoset for her."

Visibility and attention can be profoundly positive. They signal who's important, and who's worthy of interest. They let us know who has authority and credibility, and who we can expect to hear from most often. They tell us who matters—whose perspective matters and whose body, priorities, and experiences shape the world in which we live.

At the same time, as we've already seen, invisibility can be positive. To be unnamed and unmarked is powerful. It is to be the standard, the norm against which everyone else is measured and potentially found wanting.

---

26 Zerubavel 2018: 2; italics in the original.
27 Tavris 1992: 17.
28 Ray 2022: 117.
29 I have changed their last names.

Invisibility is also a way to avoid being held accountable for the harm you have done, because you cannot be defined as a problem or policed if your actions are not scrutinized. As antiviolence activist Jackson Katz has pointed out,

> We talk about how many women were raped last year, not how many men raped women. We talk about how many girls in a school district were harassed last year, not about how many boys harassed girls. We talk about how many teenage girls [...] got pregnant last year, rather than how many boys and men impregnated teenage girls. [...] Even the term 'violence against women' is problematic. [...] It's a bad thing that happens to women, but when you look at that term, 'violence against women,' nobody is doing it to them. It just happens to them. [...] Men aren't even a part of it.[30]

These aspects of sexism will remain a problem until men are named as the ones responsible for them and are held accountable for changing their behavior to end rape, other forms of violence against women, and unwanted pregnancies.

Invisibility often results from being the norm or the standard. Every February, I hear someone ask when we will have "white history month"; every March, I encounter a comment about "men's history month" and every June, I see calls for "straight pride month." The reality, however, is that we already have white history month, men's history month, and straight pride month; we simply have them all year long and they go unmentioned. The overwhelming majority of history taught in schools and celebrated on public holidays centers on the activities, experiences, perspectives, and power of men and white people. Every time an opposite-sex couple is affectionate in public, has photos of their spouses on their office desks without trouble, or gets married without someone trying to make their marriage illegal, it's straight pride month.

It's not that maleness, whiteness, and heterosexuality are unseen, it is that they are *taken for granted*, invisible in the sense of not inviting questions or concerns. In contrast, "Black history month," "women's history month," and "LGBTQ pride month" stick out, calling attention to themselves as something other than the norm, drawing our focus away from "regular," "plain old" history, and sexual politics. Similarly, we specify

---

30 Zarya 2017.

that some higher education institutions are "historically Black colleges and universities" but not that most of the others are "historically white colleges and universities."[31]

Positive invisibility, like positive visibility, shows up in the language we use. We don't have to state that the National Basketball Association involves men's basketball or that the Professional Golf Association focuses on men's golf. To talk about professional women's basketball or golf, however, we need to modify the norm to specify a focus on women, referencing the Women's National Basketball Association and the Ladies Professional Golf Association.[32]

The invisibility of normalcy can have profoundly negative effects on those outside the norm. As mentioned earlier, women are more likely than men to die after a serious heart attack because the symptoms we take as diagnostic of a heart attack are actually *male* heart attack symptoms in most cases. Calling these symptoms "textbook," "traditional," or "classic" universalizes them and implies that anyone without these symptoms is not having a heart attack.

Not only does such universalizing lead to doctors missing female heart attacks, it makes it harder to change the medical narrative about heart attack symptoms. Until multiple kinds of heart attack symptoms are covered in medical textbooks, the range of symptoms women experience when they have heart attacks will not be on the radar of medical professionals, and women will continue to die unnecessarily from undiagnosed heart attacks.

Individuality as positive visibility and positive invisibility

[T]he invisibility of the ideal worker norm being based on a White, male, middle-class, heterosexual worker hides the ways White, male, middle-class, heterosexual employees are advantaged by the design of workplace policies, procedures, standards, and expectations. Successes of privileged group members are therefore attributed solely to their personal efforts and characteristics (e.g., intelligence, hard work), and

---

31 Bonilla-Silva 2012. As sociologist Allan Johnson (2006: 104) points out, this aspect of in/visibility "[puts] subordinate groups in a double bind. If they don't call attention to themselves, the defaults built into systems of [inequality] make them invisible and devalued. If they do call attention to themselves, if they dare to put themselves at the center, they risk being accused of being pushy or seeking special treatment. This is why women and [BIPOC people], for example, are often labeled as 'special-interest groups' with biased agendas, whereas men and whites are not."

32 Friends of mine have suggested resisting this form of invisibility by creating and wearing t-shirts that read "male engineer" and "male pastor," among other categories.

because they are not subject to heightened surveillance, their failures and transgressions are often invisible.[33]

I mentioned in Chapter 3 that being treated as an individual is a kind of privilege. Most privilege lists include items such as the following:

- I am seen as an individual, not just as a member of my group.
- My failures and weaknesses reflect only on me, not on my group.
- I am not asked to represent all members of my group.

In an individualistic society, getting to be seen as an individual is a good thing. If I am seen as an individual, my bad habits, failings, and frailties are simply my own idiosyncrasies, while my strengths and successes are understood to be genuinely earned rather than "given" to me by someone else (for example, because "affirmative action" made them do it). We tend to grant individuals their full complexity, to acknowledge that they will have a mix of good and bad attributes, and to interact with them accordingly.

Individuality and visibility have a complicated relationship. Members of valued groups are visible *as individuals*, meaning that they are not treated only as members of their group. Their group status is unremarked-upon, socially invisible. Members of devalued groups, in contrast, are often reduced to their group memberships. They are forced to represent, stand in for, or speak for their group, and their group membership is seen as the most important thing about them. They are largely or entirely invisible as individuals.

I once saw a cartoon that demonstrated perfectly what individuality has to do with devalued group membership. The cartoon had two panels; each panel featured two people solving a math problem on a blackboard. In the first panel, both people were men and one of them said to the other, "Wow, you're terrible at math" (or something to that effect). In the second panel, the same man said to the other person, a woman, "Wow, girls are terrible at math." In this cartoon, the individual failing of a specific person is taken to demonstrate the stereotyped failing of a member of a social group—but only when the specific person is a member of a devalued group. Otherwise, it's just the one individual ("you") who is "terrible at math."[34]

Sociologist Howard Becker[35] came up with a term for reducing devalued group members to their devalued statuses. Becker referred to such a person

---

33 Buchanan and Settles 2019: 3.
34 Given that the two individuals in both panels are clearly adults, we might also consider how the term "girl," applied to an adult, contributes to sexist devaluation.
35 Becker 1973: 33.

as having a "master status," a devalued identity that "overrides all other statuses." As an example, Becker pointed out that a Black doctor will be "treated as [Black] first and [a physician] second"; we saw examples of how Black doctors face "master status" treatment in Chapter 5, where assumptions about Black (in)competence led people to mistake doctors for nursing assistants or to otherwise mistrust them.

All forms of discrimination come down to reducing people to their "master statuses"—whether in the reviewing of mortgage applications or in a police officer stopping a Black person without clear and reasonable cause. When heterosexual couples are more likely than equally qualified same-sex couples to be approved for a mortgage loan, the difference surely involves the sexuality of the same-sex couple. Similarly, the literature on racism in the criminal justice system, discussed in Chapter 3, suggests that when officers are asked why they stopped a Black person on the street or pulled them over, the officer will reply that the person "fit the profile." What profile did the person fit? The profile of a criminal, of course. On what basis did the person fit the profile? Too often, their race. Unique individuals are thus treated as members of a group rather than as individuals, and then punished because the group is devalued.

Negative visibility can take an especially upsetting and sometimes dangerous turn when someone's devalued identity inspires others to target them rather than leaving them alone. I consider two versions of this targeting briefly: public harassment and having one's body policed.

Negative visibility: public harassment

I got up to cheer when our team made a basket, and that's when it happened. When I started to sit down, I felt somebody [grab] my ass. I wanted to turn around but I couldn't—I heard him and his friends start laughing. One of his friends gave him a high five and said, '*Good one, Charles!*' I could feel myself turn red and tears came to my eyes. I told myself I'd ignore it but every time I thought of it, I started crying again. I couldn't help it. I don't remember the rest of the game. Don't remember who won.[36]

"Ooo-ee! Thank you for wearing a sundress!" "Hey you, hey sexy, you got a man?" "Bitch, get back here." "Don't worry, you're not THAT

---

36 Gardner 1995: 156; italics in the original.

cute!" "Bitch. You're lucky I don't rape you right here." "You should be scared of me!!" "I'm gonna rape [you]!"[37]

These examples of public harassment represent only a fraction of the range of forms such harassment takes. Women report harassers

- honking at them,
- leering or staring at them,
- whistling at them,
- making kissy noises,
- cat-calling them,
- calling them names,
- telling them to smile,
- giving them unsolicited advice,
- evaluating their bodies, whether approvingly or disapprovingly,
- referencing specific body parts,
- making sexually explicit comments or gestures,
- asking inappropriate sexual questions,
- gesturing for them to come over,
- offering them money for sex,
- threatening them,
- following them on foot or in a car,
- flashing them,
- touching or brushing up against them sexually, and
- sexually assaulting them.[38]

A 2019 nationally representative survey found that 81 percent of women reported experiencing some form of sexual harassment and/or assault, with 76 percent of women experiencing verbal sexual harassment and 49 percent of women reporting that they were sexually touched in an unwelcome way.[39] In a later study of 143 men, many respondents

---

37 Colorado Springs Independent 2019, capturing remarks women reported that men yelled at them while the women were minding their own business. Beyond the examples listed above, a group of 12-year-old girls reported a man yelling "Fucking whores!" at them.
38 DelGreco et al. 2021: 1412; Gardner 1995; University of California San Diego Center on Gender Equity and Health/Stop Street Harassment 2019: 9.
39 University of California San Diego Center on Gender Equity and Health/Stop Street Harassment 2019: 10.

reported engaging in street harassment behaviors toward women they did not know:

- 76 percent asked a woman for her name,
- 70 percent complimented a woman's appearance,
- 61 percent asked a woman for her phone number,
- 50 percent stared at a woman sexually while walking past her,
- 50 percent told a woman to smile, and
- 48 percent asked a woman if she had a boyfriend or was married.[40]

Public harassment happens to other groups as well, of course. I will never forget being followed and yelled at by 30 elementary school students while walking with a girlfriend in my college town in rural Ohio, or being stalked by a man while walking with another girlfriend in New York City years later. The first experience was humiliating, and the second frightening. The man in New York followed us closely and said, multiple times, "I love women who love women" with a leer and a threatening tone.

Public harassment is, above all, intrusive and disrespectful. It sends a clear message that the harassed person falls outside the harasser's moral community and is therefore fine to treat in ways that disempower them, leave them fearful, and ruin their day. Because of how infuriating, terrifying, and even traumatizing public harassment can be, it can lead to harassed people giving up some of their freedom to avoid further experiences of harassment. Ultimately, public harassment sends the message that public spaces belong to harassers and not to those they harass.

Negative visibility: surveilled bodies

I began this chapter with two stories, one of them about having my drink order questioned by a Starbucks barista in a way that likely never happens to men. As we navigate public places, we may do so freely without others interfering, or we may be surveilled, however, formally or informally. By *surveillance*, I mean someone's attempt to control, shape, or limit our activities.

My experience was as informal as such experiences can be, consisting only of a look and a comment; many women have their eating similarly surveilled.[41] On the other end of the spectrum, the criminalization of BIPOC people, discussed in Chapter 8, involves surveillance by police; such

---

40 DelGreco et al. 2021: 1412.
41 See Bates 2014 and Manjani 2019 for examples.

surveillance can control freedom in the most extreme of ways: by arresting or killing someone.

Whenever someone's body is seen as problematic—as out-of-control, as disgusting, as dangerous—with the result that someone else tries to limit what the person does, negative visibility is at play. The consequences may be minor or life-altering, or may fall somewhere in between. Regardless, and as with public harassment, surveillance signals moral exclusion. When someone is surveilled, they are treated as unworthy of the freedom to go about their day without interference—an uncomfortable and sometimes dangerous example of being denied the benefit of the doubt.

Surveilled bodies are, by definition, problematic bodies—or, at least, bodies that someone else finds problematic and tries to control. This point leads us to the last set of cultural processes that I discuss in this book: the various ways in which people and problems are connected. I address these issues in Chapter 7.

Discussion Questions

1. Consider the examples of positive visibility described in this chapter. How do they involve good-faith treatment or the granting of the benefit of the doubt? Can you think of additional examples?
2. Consider the examples of negative invisibility described in this chapter. How do they involve bad-faith treatment or the withholding of the benefit of the doubt? Can you think of additional examples?
3. Consider the examples of positive invisibility described in this chapter. How do they involve good-faith treatment or the granting of the benefit of the doubt? Can you think of additional examples?
4. Consider the examples of negative visibility described in this chapter. How do they involve bad-faith treatment or the withholding of the benefit of the doubt? Can you think of additional examples?
5. In your own words, explain how individuality is related to good-faith treatment and "master status" is related to bad-faith treatment.
6. In your own words, explain how public harassment and surveillance are examples of moral exclusion.

Chapter 7

PROBLEMS AND PEOPLE

Between me and the [white] world there is ever an unasked question: unasked by some through feelings of delicacy; by others through the difficulty of rightly framing it. All, nevertheless, flutter round it. They approach me in a half-hesitant sort of way, eye me curiously or compassionately, and then, instead of saying directly, How does it feel to be a problem? they say, I know an excellent colored man in my town; or, I fought at Mechanicsville; or, Do not these Southern outrages make your blood boil? At these I smile, or am interested, or reduce the boiling to a simmer, as the occasion may require. To the real question, How does it feel to be a problem? I answer seldom a word.[1]

Black girls and black women are problems. That is not the same thing as causing problems. We are social issues to be solved, economic problems to be balanced, and emotional baggage to be overcome.[2]

I own a book titled, *The Morality of Gay Rights*[3] and another titled, *What's Wrong with Homosexuality?*[4] As of this writing, amazon.com does not sell any books called either "The Morality of Heterosexual Rights" or "What's Wrong with Heterosexuality?"

Problems are part of the human condition and every individual has them, but our problems don't come down only to our individual experiences or our basic humanity. As suggested throughout this book, many of our problems stem from being denied the benefit of the doubt and grappling with bad-faith treatment. There is, however, more to say about the relationship between problems and systemic inequality. In this chapter, I consider three aspects of this relationship: the distinction between having a problem and being

---

1 Du Bois 1997: 37.
2 Cottom 2019: 10.
3 Ball 2003.
4 Corvino 2013.

a problem, the question of who is held responsible for dealing with particular problems, and the way in which victim-blaming emerges from and reinforces inequality.

Having a Problem vs. Being a Problem

Whether someone in a difficult situation is understood as *having* a problem or as *being* a problem is a particular kind of moral alchemy, one in which we tend to have compassion for the person who "has" the problem while judging the person who "is" the problem. When someone "has" a problem, we help them if possible; when someone "is" a problem, we control them if possible. Compassion and assistance are ways of granting the benefit of the doubt; judgment and restraint are ways of withholding it.

The most direct example of this process that I've found comes from educational ethnographer Alexandra Freidus.[5] She compared the treatment of a white girl and a Black boy at the same gentrifying elementary school. Both children misbehaved to similar degrees, yet the school defined the girl as a "child with a problem" and the boy as a "problem child." Teacher and administrator narratives about the two children continually framed the girl as innocent and the boy as culpable. She was eventually referred to a psychologist, while he was suspended.[6]

Other research has found a similar pattern of white medicalization and Black criminalization in school settings. One study found that schools and districts with larger BIPOC populations are more likely to implement criminalized disciplinary policies ranging from suspension and expulsion to police referrals and arrests, and less likely than whiter schools and districts to medicalize students by setting up behavioral plans for them.[7]

In a different arena, news media coverage of mass shootings—an undeniably criminal activity—medicalizes white shooters and criminalizes Black shooters, according to one sociological study. Researchers reviewed 433 news articles covering 219 mass shootings over three years. White shooters were about 19 times more likely than Black shooters to have their crime attributed to mental illness. White shooters with this attribution were framed as "victims of society," found to be of "good character" or "from a good environment" and had the shooting characterized as "unexpected" or "out of

---

5 Freidus 2020.
6 Chapter 8 covers the racialized school discipline gap in more detail.
7 Ramey 2015.

character." Black shooters were more likely to be described as public menaces or problems, to have their criminal history included in the coverage and to have their weapons described.[8]

The racial discrepancy in drug-related criminal justice practices, introduced in Chapter 3, similarly follows from how white and Black drug users are understood differently. Comparing the 1980s/1990s crack cocaine epidemic with the current opioid epidemic is instructive.[9] The federal government (including the criminal justice system), the media, and the health-care system all defined Black crack addicts as "crackheads" and "super-predators" who posed a danger to others and should be locked up, while white opioid users have mostly been understood as having an addiction problem and needing compassion.

Media coverage of white suburban and rural drug use often focused on how someone began using drugs—the conditions, situations, and events that explained their addiction. Coverage of urban Black users skipped the sympathetic background context and focused on arrests and criminal charges. White drug use, but not Black drug use, required an explanation.[10]

These perceptions have influenced federal funding decisions, with only about a quarter of the $1.7 billion Congress authorized to fight the crack epidemic in 1986 earmarked for treatment, rehabilitation, and prevention programs; the rest went to law enforcement (including incarceration). In contrast, in fiscal year 2018, three-quarters of the $7.4 billion Congress set aside to respond to the opioid epidemic was earmarked for treatment, recovery, and prevention programs, with another seven percent going to research; just under 20 percent went to law enforcement.

Ironically, during the worst years of the crack epidemic, most crack users were white,[11] yet whites were much less likely to be sent to prison or to be the subject of media coverage. In keeping with other racialized criminal justice system practices, when whites were sent to prison for crack use, their sentences were shorter than those of Black users.

---

8 Duxbury et al. 2018.

9 This section draws on Mullen et al. 2019 and Netherland and Hansen 2016.

10 This finding reminds us about presumptions of white innocence and Black guilt.

11 Fifty-two percent of people who admitted using crack between 1990 and 1991 were white and 38 percent were Black. In 2017, 4.5 percent of Blacks and 3.9 percent of whites reported having ever used crack in their lives; given that there are about four times as many whites as Blacks in the United States, the more recent data still indicate that more crack users were white.

Whose Problem Is It? The Matter of Responsibility

Sociologist Allan Johnson has observed that,

> Selective male invisibility shapes how we perceive and think about gender issues. The oppression of women, for example, is routinely discussed as a women's issue rather than as a men's issue, making male gender invisible as part of the problem. Whether it's job discrimination or harassment and violence, gender issues typically are seen as problems for women—the category of people who are victimized. Gender issues are rarely seen as problems for men, the category of people who actually do the victimizing. [...] Male invisibility [...] loads both responsibility and blame onto the victim by implying that oppression is an issue for those who suffer from it but not for those who benefit from or perpetrate it.[12]

The question of whose problem something is can be better understood as a question of whose responsibility it is. Who should have to address or correct the problem? In theory, the person or people who caused the problem should be held accountable for repairing the damage and making changes to end the problem. However, as Johnson points out, a key element of gender inequality is holding those who suffer from it responsible for fixing it rather than placing the accountability where it belongs.[13] In this section, I introduce two examples: women's responsibility for birth control and women's responsibility for sexual assault prevention.[14]

Women's responsibility for birth control

> I wish there was a male birth control, I really do. Instead of it always being our kind of responsibility, let it be theirs. [...] I think it should be their responsibility as well.[15]

In 2019, the US contraceptive market size was valued at around $8 billion. Of the dozens of contraceptive products, approximately 90 percent of them are created for women, purchased by women, and used by women.[16]

---

12 Johnson 2014b: 147.
13 This misallocation of responsibility is true of all forms of systematic inequality.
14 I cover victim-blaming later in the chapter.
15 Littlejohn 2021: 76, reporting a comment from one of her interviewees.
16 Blair 2022: 46.

It takes two people to create a pregnancy and both parties benefit from pregnancy prevention, yet women are normally understood as the ones responsible for preventing pregnancies. Women pay for their birth control, deal with the logistics of obtaining it, suffer the inconveniences and discomforts that go with using it, and are responsible for making sure that they use it consistently and correctly. It is women's time, attention, money, and energy that is taken up with pregnancy prevention for the most part. Sociologist Katrina Kimport estimates that the typical woman in the United States who has sex with men will spend about three decades of her life trying to avoid pregnancy—three decades of labor, expenses, and stress with which men are not burdened.[17]

The fact that men are not socially defined as equally responsible for birth control communicates that male pleasure matters more than female comfort. His dislike of condoms takes precedence over her dislike of the pill or other forms of birth control. Male and female dislike of birth control is not identical, however. As sociologist Krystale Littlejohn points out, the pill has a range of side effects that can include intense mood swings, acne, and nausea along with weight gain—a difficult issue for women whose body sizes and shapes are already routinely judged through private comments, public harassment, and both formal and informal surveillance.[18] Intrauterine devices, commonly called IUDs, often cause women pain.[19] Whatever else men may think about condoms, condoms do not bring the range of challenges that the pill does, so the casualness with which many men will suggest she "just go on the pill" shows how free men are not to think about the implications of birth control for women.

Men's lack of responsibility for birth control also sends a message that women's choices have consequences in ways that men's choices do not; as author Gabrielle Blair has put it, "There are zero consequences for men who ejaculate irresponsibly."[20] Men are free in relation to heterosexual sex in ways that women simply are not. The absence of consequences for men is another form of positive invisibility that will emerge again in our discussion of abortion in Chapter 8.

Ultimately, Kimport argues, women's responsibility for birth control is "both a product of and a contributor to gender inequality."[21] The relationship

---

17 Kimport 2018: 1096.
18 Littlejohn 2021: 59–65.
19 Bever 2022.
20 Blair 2022: 107.
21 Kimport 2018: 1096.

between male freedom and female obligations, and between male pleasure and female discomfort, indicate how men are valued and women are devalued. At the same time, women's birth control responsibilities take time, energy, attention, and resources away from (for example) professional careers in ways that are not true for men. While this particular obligation may be minor compared to parenting or housework obligations, it represents another way in which the path to success is made easier for men and harder for women.

Women's responsibility for sexual assault prevention

During his training, antiviolence educator Jackson Katz asks women what steps they take on a daily basis to prevent themselves from being sexually assaulted. Katz recounts some of their answers:

> Hold my keys as a potential weapon. Look in the back seat of the car before getting in. Carry a cell phone. Don't go jogging at night. Lock all the windows when I sleep, even on hot summer nights. Be careful not to drink too much. Don't put my drink down and come back to it; make sure I see it being poured. Own a big dog. Carry Mace or pepper spray. Have an unlisted phone number. Have a man's voice on my answering machine. Park in well-lit areas. Don't use parking garages. Don't get on elevators with only one man, or with a group of men. Vary my route home from work. Watch what I wear. Don't use highway rest areas. Use a home alarm system. Don't wear headphones when jogging. Avoid forests or wooded areas, even in the daytime. Don't take a first-floor apartment. Go out in groups. Own a firearm. Meet men on first dates in public places. Make sure to have a car or cab fare. Don't make eye contact with men on the street. Make assertive eye contact with men on the street.[22]

The extent to which women are held responsible for avoiding sexual assault is confirmed in a study by sociologists Nicole Bedera and Kristjane Nordmeyer. Bedera and Nordmeyer examined 494 rape prevention and risk reduction tips posted on the websites of 15 US colleges. They found that about four-fifths of the tips were directed at women. Less than one-sixth of prevention tips were directed at men and the only tip directed at men that appeared

---

22 Katz n.d.

on more than one college website was "no means no"—certainly useful, but probably not the only tip from which men might benefit. The tips for women conveyed four main messages: there are no safe places for women, women can't trust anyone, women should never be alone, and women are vulnerable. Reflecting on these findings, Bedera and Nordmeyer observe that, "Sexual assault prevention tips present a paradox for women in which they are always vulnerable to attack, yet expected to prevent their own sexual assaults."[23]

Missing or minimized in both examples is the extent to which men carry out the sexual assaults from which women are responsible for protecting themselves.[24] Once again men are invisible and therefore unaccountable, with the outcome that sexual assault is not stopped at its source. Moreover, defining women as responsible for preventing sexual assault can lead to blaming assault survivors for not doing enough to prevent the assaults they experienced, a phenomenon I discuss in detail in Chapter 8.

Blogger Gillan Lasic[25] offers a refreshing alternative to the common types of practices discussed above in her post, "10 Ways we can actually end rape." Nine of the ten items are variations on "don't rape"; the tenth instructs men to teach other men not to rape. All ten items are aimed at men. The rarity of lists such as Lasic's testifies to how much we take it for granted that preventing sexual assault is women's work and not men's.

Blaming the Victim

When something bad happens to a member of a socially valued group, we are likely to treat them with compassion, in part, because it would not occur to us that they are to blame for someone else's poor treatment of them. The compassion we afford them follows naturally from their being part of our moral community.

In contrast, when something bad happens to a member of a socially devalued group, we may be unsympathetic at a minimum and may even blame them for bringing harm to themselves. Blaming a victim for their victimization is connected both to negative visibility, as discussed in Chapter 6, and to *being* rather than *having* a problem, as discussed earlier in this chapter.

---

23 Bedera and Nordmeyer 2015: 540.
24 According to the United States Sentencing Commission (2022), 93.7 percent of sexual abuse offenders were men in fiscal year 2022.
25 Lasic 2018. The entire post is worth reading, as much for the commentary as for the list items.

One little-discussed example of victim-blaming is the "gay panic" or "trans panic" criminal defense strategy. "Gay/trans panic" is

> a legal strategy that asks a jury to find that a victim's sexual orientation or gender identity/expression is to blame for a defendant's violent reaction, including murder. [...] When a perpetrator uses an LGBTQ 'panic' defense, they are claiming that a victim's sexual orientation or gender identity not only explains—but excuses—a loss of self-control [on the part of the defendant] and the subsequent assault.[26]

This strategy, especially when used as part of a provocation or self-defense plea, moves the focus of the attack from the defendant to the victim and blames the victim for the attack. As civil rights attorney Omar Russo points out, the driving assumption behind the "gay panic" defense strategy is that "had the victim not been gay, he would not have been murdered."[27] Rarely is victim-blaming quite so straightforward.

We regularly encounter racialized victim-blaming as a bad-faith assumption in cases where a police officer or vigilante kills an unarmed Black person—not surprising given the ways in which suspicion and assumptions of guilt are racialized in the United States.[28] Among the studies that explore this kind of victim-blaming:

- Sociologist CalvinJohn Smiley and public health scholar David Fakunle showed that traditional mass media often portray Black male victims of police violence as "thugs" and criminals and blame them for their own deaths.[29]
- American Studies scholar Mia Moody-Ramirez and communications scholar Hazel Cole reviewed tweets following the deaths of Michael Brown and Eric Garner in 2014. The researchers found that Twitter users often used victim-blaming discourse to frame violence against Black men as punishment that they deserved. Common victim-blaming themes included criminal actions, physical features, and racial stereotypes, with the victims portrayed as drug lords, crack addicts, and criminals, and as innately savage and destructive.[30]

---

26 LGBTQ+ Bar n.d.
27 Russo 2019: 830.
28 I cover the criminalization of Black people in Chapter 8.
29 Smiley and Fakunle 2016.
30 Moody-Ramirez and Cole 2018.

- Criminologists Danielle Slakoff and Pauline Brennan studied front-page crime stories about female victims from four US newspapers, comparing how white victims and Latina/Black victims were described. They found that stories about white victims were more likely to contain sympathetic narratives while Latina/Black victims were more likely to be portrayed as "bad" women who lived in unsafe environments in which they should have expected violence.[31]

Victim-blaming is an effective way to draw attention away from systemic inequality while reproducing it at the same time. Blaming a gay man or Black person for their death distracts us from the homophobia and racism that likely played a role in that death while disparaging the deceased rather than mourning their passing.

Some journalists have compared media descriptions of Black victims and white killers, finding that white killers often receive more positive coverage than Black victims. Columnist David Harris-Gershon offered the example of Michael Brown, killed by a police officer in 2014:

> Michael Brown, 18, due to be buried on Monday, was no angel. [...] He lived in a community that had rough patches, and he dabbled in drugs and alcohol. He had taken to rapping in recent months, producing lyrics that were by turns contemplative and vulgar.[32]

Harris-Gershon invited his readers to compare this material with a description of white serial killer Ted Bundy:[33]

> His mother, Louise Bundy, said there was never a shred of evidence in her son's first 28 years, before he became a murder suspect for the first time, to hint at any aberrant behavior. People familiar with his early years say he was a Boy Scout, a B-plus college student; he loved children, read poetry and was a rising figure in Republican politics in Seattle. The year the murders began there he was the assistant director of the Seattle Crime Prevention Advisory Commission and wrote a pamphlet for women on rape prevention.[34]

---

31 Slakoff and Brennan 2019.
32 Harris-Gershon 2014, quoting *New York Times* reporter John Eligo.
33 Bundy kidnapped, raped, and murdered dozens of young women, eventually confessing to 30 murders committed during the 1970s and possibly responsible for many more ("Ted Bundy" n.d.).
34 Notice again the passive language: "the year the murders began there"—not "the year Ted Bundy began raping and murdering women."

Reporter Nick Wing[35] provided a number of similar examples. Here, first, are headlines about the deaths of some Black victims:

- "Montgomery's latest homicide victim had history of narcotics abuse, tangles with the law"
- "Trayvon Martin was suspended three times from school"
- "Police: Lakeland teen had been shot before; death possibly drug-related"
- "Ohio man was carrying variable pump air rifle—not a toy—when cops killed him: attorney general"
- "Deputy killed Marine out of fear for children's safety, officials say"[36]
- "Shooting victim had many run-ins with law"
- "Police: Warren shooting victim was gang member"

Here, in contrast, are headlines about some white killers (and one would-be killer) along with information about their actions:

- "Ala. suspect brilliant, but social misfit" (killed three people)
- "Son in Staten Island murders was brilliant, athletic—but his demons were the death of [his] parents" (killed his parents)
- "Oregon school shooting suspect fascinated with guns but was a devoted Mormon, his friends say" (killed a classmate and injured a teacher before turning the gun on himself)
- "Santa Barbara shooting: Suspect was 'soft-spoken, polite, a gentleman', ex-principal says" (Elliott Rodger, who shot and stabbed six people to death)
- "Ohio shooting suspect, T.J. Lane, described as 'fine person'" (killed three people)
- "Straight-A student plots to bomb high school"

Reading through these headlines quickly might lead you to think that the first group of people were the problems and the second group of people had problems, rather than the reverse. Such is the way bad-faith and good-faith treatment work. Even committing multiple murders doesn't suffice to deny white killers the benefit of the doubt; even being murdered doesn't merit granting Black victims that same benefit of the doubt.

We've now explored a number of cultural processes that contribute to the reproduction of systemic inequality. It's time to see how they work together

---

35 Wing 2017.
36 This unarmed father of two was killed by a police officer while entering a car in which his own children were sitting.

in examples ranging from women's pain to the criminalization of Black people. I address the intersection of these processes in Chapter 8.

Discussion Questions

1. How is being defined as "having a problem" an example of a good-faith assumption? How is defined as "being a problem" an example of a bad-faith assumption? Can you think of any circumstances beyond those described in the chapter in which some people are defined as "having a problem" and others are defined as "being a problem?"
2. How is the misalignment of responsibility for a situation (or a problem) an example of bad-faith treatment? Can you think of examples other than those in the chapter in which a group of people has to take sole responsibility when the responsibility should be shared? In which a group of people has to take responsibility for a situation that is someone else's doing?
3. How is victim-blaming an example of bad faith treatment? How does it contribute to inequality? Can you think of examples of victim-blaming beyond those described in the chapter?

Chapter 8

BRINGING THE PROCESSES TOGETHER

Thus far, we have explored connections between power and inequality; good-faith/bad-faith treatment and the benefit of the doubt; moral alchemy; assumptions related to competence, trustworthiness, and innocence; self-fulfilling prophecies; positive and negative in/visibility; and relationships between people and problems. While I've provided examples of how these processes work separately, they often combine to make situations of inequality even more troubling or dangerous. In this chapter, I discuss five situations of inequality in which multiple cultural processes work in tandem: women's pain, how we think about sexual assault, antiabortion discourse and laws, race and school discipline, and racial profiling outside of schools.

Women's Pain

Women's pain was mentioned in Chapter 1 as an example of whose comfort matters and whose does not. The discussion of heart attack symptoms in Chapter 6 also noted that women are more likely to die of heart attacks because the "textbook," "traditional," and "classic" heart attack symptoms (which involve pain) are universalized despite the fact that they describe male heart attacks rather than all heart attacks.[1] We know that women experience and report more pain than men, but receive less intensive and effective treatment for it.[2] Why?

---

1   Similarly, the *British Medical Journal* noted of coronary disease that "Women may have more atypical symptoms than men […] which makes the diagnosis more difficult" (Kohut 2019). In a non-sexist society, men's symptoms would not be seen as "typical" and women's as "atypical."
2   Lloyd et al. 2020.

Journalist Maya Dusenbery points to a knowledge gap and a trust gap as the factors underlying women's challenges in having their pain taken seriously:

> First, there is a knowledge gap: the average doctor does not know as much about women's bodies and the health problems that afflict them. It starts at the most basic level of biomedical research, where investigators overwhelmingly use male cells and animals in preclinical studies. And it continues through the clinical research process, where women remain underrepresented, analysis by gender is rare, and women's differing hormonal states and cycles are usually ignored entirely. Meanwhile, conditions that disproportionately affect women have often not been deemed worthy of research funding and time. [...] Second, there is a trust gap: women's accounts of their symptoms are too often not believed.[3]

As Dusenbery further observes,

> These two problems—the knowledge gap and the trust gap—are mutually reinforcing to such a degree that they've become stubbornly difficult to correct. Are women's complaints so often dismissed because doctors simply don't know enough about women's bodies, their symptoms, and the diseases that disproportionately affect them? Or are women's complaints so often dismissed because doctors hold an unconscious stereotype that women are unreliable reporters of their symptoms? Is it a lack of knowledge or a lack of trust? It seems to be both. The knowledge gap and the trust gap are so tightly interwoven at this point that they could be thought of as two sides of the same coin. Women's symptoms are not taken seriously because medicine doesn't know as much about their bodies and health problems. And medicine doesn't know as much about their bodies and health problems because it doesn't take their symptoms seriously.[4]

The knowledge gap and the trust gap described by Dusenbery involve a number of processes covered in this book:

• Decision-making/cultural power: those with the authority to decide whose pain is important in medical research have focused on men's pain.

---

3 Dusenbery 2019: 11.
4 Dusenbery 2019: 12.

- Individual power: men have more credibility than women when they report pain symptoms.[5]
- Moral alchemy: men in pain are regarded as "stoic" while women in pain are considered "emotional," "hysterical," "complaining," and "malingerers."[6]
- Assumptions: men are treated as competent, trustworthy reporters when it comes to pain.
- Positive visibility: male pain symptoms and experiences are universalized to all people. As reporter Lindsey Bever points out, when male pain sensitivity is the norm against which women are measured, women's response to pain is seen as an "overreaction" rather than a different but equally legitimate reaction.[7]
- Negative invisibility: medical conditions unique to women are not studied and go undiagnosed or misdiagnosed, sometimes for years.[8]
- People and problems: as a result of the intersection of the above processes, women reporting pain are often seen as being a problem rather than having a problem.

Psychologists Paige Lloyd, Gina Paganini, and Leanne ten Brinke discuss how gender stereotypes about emotionality can generate beliefs that women dramatize, overemphasize, or even make up their experiences of pain in ways not attributed to men. Multiple studies confirm this stereotype:

- Medical students and other research participants judged female patients more likely than male patients to fabricate or exaggerate their pain.
- Research participants identified expressions of pain on men's faces more quickly and accurately than they did on women's faces.
- Adult participants saw a video of a child apparently experiencing pain. All participants saw the same video, but the child was described as a boy in some cases and as a girl in others. Adults were asked to rate how much pain the child experienced and displayed. The "boy" was rated

---

5 Anushay Hossain refers to this phenomenon as a "credibility gap" (Bever 2022).
6 Bever 2022; Samulowitz et al. 2018: 5.
7 Bever 2022.
8 Endometriosis, a condition in which uterine tissue grows on bowels, kidneys, and other organs, is excruciatingly painful and frequently undiagnosed or diagnosed late. In one study, more than 60 percent of women and girls with the disease were initially told by health-care providers that nothing was wrong. Diagnostic delays often exceed ten years, with the mean reported delay in one study being more than eight years (Bever 2023; Bontempo and Mikesell 2020; Kohut 2019). An endometriosis expert told one author that, "Nobody in Congress really cares about the uterus when it doesn't have a baby in it" (Gross 2022: xii).

as experiencing more pain than the "girl" despite identical clinical circumstances and identical pain behavior across conditions.

- In another experiment, participants viewed facial video clips of male and female patients with chronic shoulder pain and estimated the pain intensity. Perceivers underestimated female patients' pain.[9]
- In one study, participants judged female patients as more likely to benefit from psychotherapy and male patients from pain medicine despite both groups reporting the same symptoms. Other research finds that women are more likely than men to receive a psychiatric diagnosis (especially an anxiety diagnosis) when they report pain symptoms identical to those reported by men across conditions ranging from irritable bowel syndrome to heart attacks.[10]

In short, men in pain receive the benefit of the doubt when they report pain symptoms, while women have it withheld from them. Men are treated in good faith, and women in bad faith. The sexism underlying this distinction is ultimately responsible for women experiencing pain that, in a good-faith society, would be treated more quickly and effectively, easing discomfort and, in some cases, saving lives.

Sexual Assault

Consider that a person who comes forward with an allegation of abuse makes a trio of claims: *This happened. It was wrong. It matters.* Each claim is crucial. If any one of them is rejected, whether by a loved one or by an official responder, the accuser will be dismissed. The listener may decide that the alleged conduct didn't happen. Or that it wasn't the fault of the accused, but the fault of the accuser. Or that it wasn't harmful enough to warrant concern. [...] Unless all parts of the allegation [...] are accepted, the allegation will be dismissed as untrue, unworthy of blame, or unimportant.[11]

[Brock Turner's act was] completely different from a woman getting kidnapped and raped as she is walking to her car in a parking lot. [...] That is a rapist, I know for a fact that Brock is not one of those people.[12]

---

9 Bever 2022; Earp et al. 2019; Hoffmann et al. 2022; Lloyd et al. 2020; Zhang et al. 2021.

10 Bever 2022; Hoffmann et al. 2022; McGregor 2020; Samulowitz et al. 2018; Zhang et al. 2021.

11 Tuerkheimer 2021: 10–11; italics in the original.

12 Manne 2020: 37, quoting one of Brock Turner's friends.

Chapter 1 introduced the idea that there is a "care gap" in which men accused of sexual assault receive more sympathy than their female accusers. Chapter 7 described how women are burdened with the prevention of sexual assault despite men overwhelmingly being the assailants.[13] This care gap and gendered burden are part of a larger set of sexist cultural processes surrounding rape:

- Decision-making power: Judges in circuit, district, and federal courts are overwhelmingly male.[14]
- Individual power: Men accused of sexual assault have more credibility than women who accuse them.
- Moral alchemy: The assumptions underlying how we understand rape treat male sexuality as positive and female sexuality as suspicious.
- Assumptions: Men are understood to be competent, trustworthy reporters when it comes to their sexual activities, while women are treated as incompetent and untrustworthy. As social psychologist Dana Weiser points out, "If women as a whole are viewed as untrustworthy, it is a natural progression, then, to not view women as trustworthy when they are reporting sexual violence."[15]
- Self-fulfilling prophecies: Common understandings of what counts as rape and what does not (rape myths) have led people to accept restrictive definitions of "real rape." These definitions exclude the majority of sexual assaults. Because only certain actions in certain contexts are defined as sexual assault, the common perception is that few women are sexually assaulted. However, rape myths lead many women who are assaulted to choose not to report it, often based on the fear that they will be blamed for what happened.[16] When between three-fifths and four-fifths of sexual assaults go unreported, rape myths remain unchallenged and the cycle continues.
- Positive invisibility/negative visibility: Women's behavior receives almost all of the focus when decision-makers determine whether a situation should be defined as sexual assault.[17]

---

13 Men also experience sexual assault, with male-on-male sexual assault representing five to ten percent of assaults in a given year (Thomas and Kopel 2023).
14 American Bar Association 2022; Center for American Progress 2020.
15 Weiser 2017: 47.
16 Klein 2022.
17 Trans activist Julia Serano (2020: 57–58) describes how this process often plays out: "'What were you wearing?' will be considered a legitimate question for her, but what he wore won't even matter. 'Had she been drinking?' will be considered germane, but whether he was drinking will seem far less important. 'Perhaps she's

- People and problems: Women are understood to be responsible for avoiding sexual assault and are often blamed for being sexually assaulted.

These processes come together most clearly in the rape myths that inform how most people think about sexual assault as well as how decision-makers respond to allegations of sexual assault. The remainder of this section focuses on the assumptions that make up rape myths and the impact they have on responses to rape allegations.

Common rape myths include the following:[18]

- Women "asked for it" by doing something or behaving in a certain way (dressing "provocatively," drinking alcohol, going home with a stranger, flirting, or not saying no strongly enough).[19]
- Women "really wanted it" because women secretly wish to be raped, enjoy force, and find rape arousing.
- Women lie about being raped and file false reports. They lead men on and "cry rape" afterward. They use made-up rape accusations to get back at men. They have sex willingly but change their minds afterward. They claim it was rape to protect their reputations if they get pregnant from consensual sex. False reports are common and make up the majority of rape allegations.[20]

---

misremembering things?' will seem like a valid question to ask of her, but few will suggest that his denial may be due to his misremembering or forgetting the incident. 'Perhaps she has an ulterior motive for coming forward?' will seem like a reasonable avenue of inquiry, while his very obvious potential motive for denying it (e.g., not wanting to [...] take responsibility for what he did) will rarely ever be mentioned. And delving into her past sexual history will seem pertinent, yet his past sexual history will likely be viewed as irrelevant."

18 Burt 1980; Edwards et al. 2011: 761; O'Neal 2019: 129; Shaw et al. 2017; Taylor 2020: 33–36; Tuerkheimer 2021: 38.
19 The essay "The Rape of Mr. Smith, 2012; With New and Improved Victim-Blaming" implicitly contrasts how police respond to sexual assault reports with how they respond to reports of robberies. In this fictional essay, police interview a man who reports being robbed on the street. The police blame Mr. Smith for not struggling with the robber (despite the robber being armed), for not crying out, for having given money away willingly in the past through philanthropic donations, for being out walking alone late at night, and for wearing an expensive suit that broadcasts his wealth.
20 In fact, reviews of research literature on false reporting of sexual assault suggest that only 4.5–5.9 percent of US sexual assault reports, and about three percent of UK sexual assault reports, are false (Ferguson and Malouff 2016; Weiser 2017).

- It wasn't really rape because:
  - He didn't use a weapon.
  - She had no physical injuries.
  - She did not fight back, scream, or go straight to the police.
  - She knew him already.
  - He was an upstanding citizen.
  - It did not take place in a dark alley.
  - She was not upset enough in the police station.
  - She didn't cry afterward.
  - She did not act "like a victim."[21]
  - He was drunk.
- He didn't mean to rape her. He just got carried away and didn't realize she was resisting.
- Rapists are just sexually frustrated.
- Men can be sexually provoked to a "point of no return," at which point the sex is not rape.
- Certain kinds of women cannot be raped, including sex workers, "promiscuous" women, and "ugly" women.
- A husband cannot rape his wife. If she has married him, she has consented to have sex whenever he wants sex.

Taken together, these understandings justify men's behavior and minimize the harm such behavior causes. They make sexual assault the responsibility and/or fault of women and denigrate women as conniving liars.

However inaccurate rape myths are, research shows that they influence the actions of those who have the discretion to hold or not hold assaulters accountable:

- Judgments that certain women are not credible reporters lead police officers not to test their sexual assault kits (thereby losing the chance to potentially identify offenders), to close cases, to designate reports as false, and to elect to take no action in pursuing an identified assailant. One officer told the researchers that kits that were not tested "were cases that we couldn't *or wouldn't* do anything about."[22]

---

21 Tuerkheimer (2021:41–47) describes the stereotype of a "perfect rape victim" and explains why so many women do not fit the profile. For example, many women may not fight back because they freeze up physically or emotionally in response to the trauma (see also Percy 2023), because there is more than one assaulter, because women are socialized to be nonviolent, or because they think fighting back might get them hurt more seriously or killed.

22 Campbell and Fehler-Cabral 2018: 87; italics in the original.

- Another study found that "real rape" myths motivate arrest decisions, including "whether (or not) an incident will garner a formal report, what resources are directed toward investigative efforts, what charges are listed on the report, whether (or not) the suspect is arrested, and whether (or not) the case is forwarded to prosecution."[23]
- A different study found that police officers differentiated between "false reports," "ambiguous cases," and "legitimate sexual assaults" based on rape myths that impacted credibility. One officer told the researcher, "The serious one is the stranger.... Okay, with a gun, with a knife, in the bushes. You know, people get raped like that."[24]
- Rape myths affect prosecutors' decisions to file charges in sexual assault cases.[25]
- A systematic review of nine research studies found that in eight of the nine studies, rape myths impacted whether jurors found a suspect guilty or not.[26]

Rape myths and their impact show clearly how good-faith assumptions made about men lead to good-faith treatment of men, and how bad-faith assumptions made about women lead to bad-faith treatment of women. When it comes to sexual assault, men receive the benefit of the doubt—not women.

Abortion

We've already considered abortion in the context of whose rights matter (Chapter 1), why it matters who's in power (Chapter 2), and moral alchemy (Chapter 4). The discussion of women's responsibility for birth control (Chapter 7) is also relevant here; when almost the entire burden of birth control falls on women, unwanted pregnancies become her problem—but not his problem.

There are two other important ways that the topic of abortion intersects with the cultural processes discussed in this book. First, the public discourse on abortion treats women and other people who can get pregnant who do not identify as women[27] as incompetent, untrustworthy, and often explicitly immoral. Second, antiabortion discourse and laws offer a complex lesson in positive and negative visibility and invisibility.

23 Acquaviva et al. 2022: 3866.
24 Venema 2016: 886. This comment implies that people do not get raped by people they know or in bedrooms or when weapons are not involved.
25 St. George and Spohn 2018.
26 Dinos et al. 2015.
27 I use the term "women" in this section, but want to be clear that other people who can get pregnant (such as trans men) face the same set of cultural processes, even if the specifics differ due to (for example) transphobia.

Bad-faith assumptions about women

Ethicist and pastor Rebecca Peters notes that,

> The criticism that women seek abortions out of convenience betrays both a profound lack of awareness or exposure to women who actually have abortions and a deep disregard for the serious moral agency and intellectual capacity of women to make informed and reasoned decisions about their bodies and their future.[28]

This observation comes from a book titled, *Trust Women: A Progressive Christian Argument for Reproductive Justice*, in which Peters points out multiple times how little our society trusts women to make the best decisions for themselves and their families.

Ethicist Katie Watson provides a more specific example:

> Those who defend waiting periods make a simple suggestion: Shouldn't a woman having an abortion think about it for at least a day? Sure. But why would you assume she hasn't? Waiting periods send women who've chosen abortion a degrading message: your state thinks you are so stupid that the first moment you would consider the consequences of ending your pregnancy is the moment you consented to a medical procedure that does exactly that. Instead of being treated as an adult who is wise enough to assess whether she is ready to act after that counseling conversation, the legislature thinks you need a toddler's time out to think about what you said.[29]

Women who choose to terminate a pregnancy do so for a variety of reasons other than fetal viability concerns:

- Having the child would put their health at risk.
- Having the child would interfere with their ability to care for their families (including children they already have).
- They are not financially prepared to have a(nother) child.
- Having the child would interfere with a career for which they have spent years preparing.
- Having the child would interfere with the education that will enable them to have the future they want.

---

28 Peters 2018: 180.
29 Watson 2018: 187.

- They are in an abusive or otherwise problematic relationship which would be worsened with a(nother) child.
- They are not mentally or emotionally prepared or mature enough to raise a(nother) child.
- They would not be able to provide the kind of life that the child would deserve.[30]

These are serious, thoughtful justifications in which women show that they are attentive to their own well-being and the well-being of those for whom they care. Why do so many people discount the legitimacy of these justifications? Why do so many people write off women's perspectives as moral callousness, selfishness, frivolity, or indifference to life? Put differently, why do so many people withhold the benefit of the doubt from women in these situations? The arguments in this book suggest that those people do not find women credible, competent, trustworthy, or moral when women explain why they want an abortion. This bad-faith response has the effect of harming women and those who love them.

Complexities of in/visibility

Public discussion of abortion has come to inexorably privilege fetal life over female life. The imaginary futures—the 'personhoods'—of the unborn have taken moral precedence over the adult women in whose bodies they grow.[31]

99 percent of abortions are the result of unwanted pregnancies, and men cause all unwanted pregnancies. Currently, conversations about abortion are entirely centered on women—on women's bodies, and whether women have a right to terminate an unwanted pregnancy. [...] An unwanted pregnancy doesn't happen because people have sex. An unwanted pregnancy only happens if a man ejaculates irresponsibly—if he deposits his sperm in a vagina when he and his partner are not trying to conceive. It's not asking a lot for men to avoid this.[32]

In antiabortion discourse and laws:

- Fetuses are positively visible even as women are negatively invisible.[33]
- Women are negatively visible even as men are positively invisible.

---

30 Foster 2020, Chapter 2.
31 Traister 2014.
32 Blair 2022: 1–2.
33 Arguably, children are also negatively invisible, in that when women want an abortion in order to prioritize the children they already have, this justification is uncompelling to those who oppose abortion.

Abortion opponents have been successful in directing society's attention toward the well-being of fetuses and away from the well-being of women. From images of fetuses that don't incorporate the woman in whose body the fetus is growing[34] to politicians who refer to pregnant women as "hosts" or "host bodies,"[35] antiabortion discourse in the United States has treated women and fetuses as virtually unrelated except in terms of the obligations that a pregnant woman has to the fetus inside her. An exclusive focus on the dignity, importance, and personhood of fetuses allows abortion opponents to ignore the dignity, importance, and personhood of women.

Two research studies, one on news media and one on legal opinions, suggest how fetal visibility is connected to the invisibility of women:

- One study analyzed 783 news and opinion articles from three major US newspapers that contained the term "abortion." The fetus was described as a person in a third of substantive stories, while women's personal experiences appeared in only 11 percent of substantive stories.[36]
- The other study involved a content analysis of over 220 legal opinions on abortion rights prior to the overturning of *Roe v. Wade*. Substantial attention was paid to describing the interests of the fetus in detail. In contrast, the woman's perspective and physical experiences of pain were mentioned vaguely if at all, and risks to women were presented in abstract and clinical terms.[37]

Even as women are *negatively invisible* in antiabortion discourse in the sense that their experiences and perspectives go ignored, they are *negatively visible* as those whose bodies and decisions must be regulated and surveilled. At the same time, men are *positively invisible* despite playing a central role in every pregnancy. Neither the federal government nor any state government has attempted to regulate men's sexuality as it pertains to pregnancy. Moreover, as author Kate Manning has noted,

> [N]one of the new laws forcing pregnant women to give birth have mandated consequences for the impregnator. When he causes an unwanted pregnancy and birth, these laws do not require him to share the medical expenses of childbearing or the lifelong cost of

---

34 Sanger 2017.
35 Clawson 2019; Smith 2017.
36 Woodruff 2019.
37 Laguardia 2022; see also Manning 2022.

child-rearing—emotional, physical, financial or practical. Economic hardships of government-forced childbirth include a woman's job or income loss, years of unpaid child care, and increased household expenses. Women most often bear the brunt of these costs when a child is unplanned and unwanted.[38]

Men's invisibility in this discourse and in these laws thus affords them sexual freedom with no consequences or accountability should that freedom lead to a pregnancy. When it comes to heterosexual sex, "life, liberty, and the pursuit of happiness" are male entitlements only.

Criminalizing Black People

[T]he problem is not simply that crime is racialized (when we think of crime, we have African Americans in mind); it is also that race is criminalized (when we think of African Americans, we have crime in mind).[39]

All kids do something wrong. Why do the blacks have to be the ones that always have to be disciplined and the white kids are supposed to be understood?[40]

We've already considered the criminalization of Black people at length in this book. Chapter 1 discussed police killings of Black people and the racialization of the death penalty. The discretion afforded to institutional decision-makers discussed in Chapter 2 included examples of racism in policing. Chapter 3 opened with the shooting of Tamir Rice and provided evidence of racial discrimination in the criminal justice system. In Chapter 4, I noted the framing of Black protests as dangerous and destructive. Chapter 5 provided evidence that Black people are seen as suspicious and guilty, in line with racist assumptions about their immorality and dangerousness. Chapter 6 mentioned how racial master status leads Black people to be treated as "fitting the profile" by police rather than being treated as individuals; the chapter also mentioned surveillance of Black people. Chapter 7 compared responses to the crack cocaine and opioid epidemics as an example of "being a problem" (Black people) versus "having a problem" (white people). The chapter also provided examples of how Black shooting victims are blamed for having been shot.

---

38 Manning 2022.
39 Carbado and Roithmayr 2014: 152.
40 A high school senior administrator, quoted in Diamond and Lewis 2019: 831.

Unfortunately, there is much more to be said about how cultural processes of inequality play out in the criminalizing of Black people. For example, our society talks a lot about Black-on-Black crime but not about white-on-white crime despite intra-racial crime rates being similar. Looking only at homicide, in 2019, 79 percent of white victims were killed by white offenders, while 89 percent of Black victims were killed by Black offenders.[41] If we took other kinds of crime into account, the intra-racial rates would be even more similar.[42] As it is, discussions of intra-racial crime that focus only on Black-on-Black crime gift white people with positive invisibility and burden Black people with negative visibility.

The remainder of the chapter covers racial discrimination in school discipline, racial profiling in white spaces, and being pulled over for "driving while Black." These topics demonstrate the role of bad-faith assumptions about guilt and dangerousness, along with visibility distinctions that allow white people to remain positively invisible even as Black people are made negatively visible. Police pullovers for "driving while Black" also involve decisions that can set up self-fulfilling prophecies.

School discipline

The following anecdote provides a powerful example of moral alchemy:

> When my son Nicky was in 2nd grade, a close friend, Jamal, kept getting 'lunch detention." Nicky wanted to sit with Jamal at lunchtime, so every time [Jamal] got a detention, Nicky would try to get one by doing exactly what Jamal had done, but he would only get a reprimand. At first, he was mystified by this phenomenon, so for 2 weeks he kept data on a scrap of paper in his desk: *Jamal throws a paper airplane, he gets a detention; I throw a paper airplane, I am told to pick it up and put it in the trash and go back to my seat. Jamal doesn't turn in his homework, he gets a detention; I don't turn in my homework, I am reminded to do it tonight and bring it in tomorrow.* After 2 weeks of this, Nicky told me he had finally figured out how you get a detention in school. Apparently, he said, "'You have to do one of the things on this list, and have brown skin. Mama, my skin's the wrong color,' he cried. 'I'll never get a detention!"[43]

---

41 United States Federal Bureau of Investigation n.d.
42 White-collar crime, for example, is largely a white-on-white phenomenon because of who is in positions of power that allow them to carry out such crime.
43 Broderick and Leonardo 2016: 60; italics in the original.

While school punishments may not always lead to encounters with the law, a substantial literature on racialization of the "school-to-prison pipeline"[44] suggests that racist school discipline can be seen as a kind of proto-criminalization that too frequently ends up in actual criminalization.

Several research studies show how bad-faith expectations lead to racialized differences in school discipline:

- A video experiment involving 1339 teachers in 295 US schools found that teachers watching a randomly assigned video of a white, Black, or Latino boy committing identical routine classroom misbehaviors were more likely to perceive Black and Latino boys as more "blameworthy" and refer them to the principal's office more often for identical misbehavior.[45]
- Decision-making discretion leads to teachers disciplining Black students more often than white students for the same behaviors as well as to Black students receiving more suspensions for discretionary reasons such as dress code violations or hair length violations.[46]
- The racial gap in school suspensions accounts for approximately one-fifth of Black–white reading and math achievement gaps in grades 6–10. As the authors point out, "the racial achievement gap for black students is reproduced in part through disproportionate exposure to exclusionary discipline in public schools."[47]

An in-depth ethnographic study of a racially mixed high school found that Black students were targeted for wrongdoing more often than similarly misbehaving white students:

> Black students' behavior was more closely scrutinized than the behavior of their White counterparts. As a result, when Black students did break the rules, their behavior was often interpreted differently. As one White student put it, 'Because when people look at me, they probably don't see me as any kind of threat' [...] or as another [white student] explained,

---

44 Keyes 2022.
45 Owens 2022.
46 Henderson and Bourgeois 2021; Morris and Perry 2017; Smolkowski et al. 2016. In the context of school discipline, a "discretionary" reason for discipline is one in which the teacher or administrator has the flexibility to decide whether the offense merits any discipline and, if so, what action to take. These findings are in keeping with the discussion of institutional decision-making discretion in Chapter 2.
47 Morris and Perry 2016: 81; italics in the original. See also Gopalan 2019; Pearman et al. 2019.

'I think, as a white student, I get away with a lot more. I'm not a target of racial profiling.' […] [D]iscipline was 'racialized' not only in terms of the often-discussed pattern of treating Black youth as inherently suspect, but also in terms of a pattern of treating White students as inherently innocent.[48]

The study describes racial differences in

- how students were treated when they came to class late,
- how students were treated when they swore in class,
- whether students were allowed to leave class to go to the bathroom,
- whether students had to show a hall pass to the security guards,
- whether groups of students making noise in the hall were told to "move along" or had security called on them,
- whether girls were sent home for dress code violations or not, and
- how students caught with marijuana were treated, with Black students receiving suspensions and white students receiving warnings.

As we will see throughout the rest of the chapter, white suspicion of Black people follows them from school into adulthood, especially when they move through "white space," places in which white people are in the majority.[49]

Racial profiling in "White Space"

[W]ould the police have been contacted had the actor been White? Alternatively, is the actor engaged in behavior for which the average White person would not be reported to the police?[50]

Black people are seen as threats by police officers, security guards, vigilantes, and other white people when they engage in legal and, indeed, perfect normal public behavior. Racial profiling in primarily white spaces is another example of moral alchemy: activities that are regular and even positive when white people engage in them are problematic when Black people engage in them.

The experience of "shopping while Black," for example, includes

- being followed by security guards or otherwise being treated with suspicion,
- being ignored while white customers receive attention,

---

48 Diamond and Lewis 2019: 838.
49 Anderson 2022; Cashin 2021.
50 McNamarah 2019: 351.

- being wrongly accused of or arrested for shoplifting, and
- being kicked out of a store along with all other Black shoppers because a different Black shopper was accused of stealing.[51]

Between 2018 and 2020, Black people had police or other security people called on them for

- accidentally touching the person seated next to them while flying in an airplane,
- asking for directions,
- attending a funeral,
- barbecuing in a public park,
- babysitting white children,
- birdwatching in Central Park,
- calling their mother in the lobby of the hotel where they were staying,
- campaigning for political election,
- canvassing for political re-election,
- cashing a paycheck,
- checking the alarm system of a store that they owned,
- complaining to an Uber driver who refused to take them to their requested location,
- crossing the street,
- delivering newspapers,
- delivering packages for Amazon,
- doing community service,
- eating at Applebee's,
- eating at Subway with their family,
- eating at Waffle House,
- eating breakfast in the university classroom in which they were a professor,
- eating ice cream in their own car,
- eating lunch in a dormitory dining hall at the college where they were a student,
- entering the condominium complex in which they lived,
- entering the law library at the university where they were a student,
- falling asleep in a common room in the college dormitory where they lived,
- getting into their own car,
- giving food to a homeless person,

51 Favro 2018; Gabbidon and Higgins 2020; Jacobs 2017; Pittman 2020; Siegel 2018; Singletary 2018; Wootson 2016.

- grilling in public,
- handing out flyers in public,
- knocking on the wrong door as a home-care nurse trying to find a new patient,
- leaving an Airbnb at which they had been staying,
- moving into a new apartment,
- mowing the lawn,
- not listening to a neighbor's complaints,
- picking up trash at their own house,
- playing golf "too slowly,"
- playing pickup basketball,
- quoting a rap song in earshot of a white neighbor,
- requesting a money order at a supermarket,
- selling food from a legally licensed food truck,
- selling water on the sidewalk in front of their home as an eight-year-old,
- sheltering from the rain while waiting for an Uber,
- shopping at Costco,
- shopping at Finish Line,
- shopping at Staples,
- shopping at T-Mobile,
- shopping at Walgreens,
- shopping for school prom outfits at Nordstrom's Rack,
- sitting in their own car,
- sitting in their college classroom with their feet on a chair,
- sitting near the pool at their apartment complex,
- smoking cigarettes in a parking lot,
- speaking Somali in their car at a Dunkin Donuts drive-through,
- standing in a parking lot in an apartment complex in which they lived,
- standing near a white person,
- standing outside their car in front of their house having a conversation,
- stopping at a gas station convenience store to buy drinks,
- supervising a custody visit in a frozen-yogurt shop,
- swimming in a public pool,
- trying to enter their own gated community,
- trying to establish a community garden,
- trying to file a claim for luggage damage following a flight,
- trying to get a refund on movie tickets,
- trying to get change from their own car for a parking meter,
- trying to return a Hobby Lobby purchase,
- trying to return a Victoria's Secret purchase,
- trying to use coupons while shopping,

- trying to visit a library children's story period as part of a school assignment,
- waiting for a friend in Starbucks,
- walking across a college campus,
- walking in a park with their infant son,
- walking their own dogs on their own block,
- watching their son play soccer,
- wearing a bandanna to school,
- wearing a costume,
- wearing a protective mask in Walmart during COVID-19,
- working as a firefighter,
- working as a real estate investor, and
- working out at a gym where they were a member.[52]

I have personally experienced 52 of the 79 situations described above—more than once in many cases—and have never had police called on me for engaging in these activities. I suspect most white people in the United States could say the same thing, at least in the context of their whiteness.[53]

To be unable to carry out the routine activities of one's life without suspicion and surveillance on the part of strangers is surely one of the most exhausting and infuriating ways of being denied the benefit of the doubt. Moreover, many of the articles describing the events listed above indicated that this was not the first time the person had experienced this kind of policing. Some of them described the mistrust and surveillance as routine. Bad-faith treatment emerges readily when enough bad-faith assumptions are in place.

Driving while Black

Joe was pulled over by an officer hunting for an arrest. Another officer wanted to see where Deanna was going. Lisa was followed home from work every night for two weeks. Darrell was stopped while driving through a white neighborhood and then held on the sidewalk in handcuffs for an hour, only to be let go. Billy was stopped and searched yet again while driving to visit a critically ill uncle.[54]

---

52 "Central Park Bird Watching Incident" n.d.; Henderson and Jefferson-Jones 2020; Jan 2020; McNamarah 2019; Niedringhaus 2019. Some of the situations listed happened to multiple people in different places, such as sitting in one's own car or swimming in a public pool.

53 Earlier in my life, I had problems carrying out some of these activities while visibly queer, but those problems involved routine harassment, not calls to the police.

54 Epp et al. 2014: 134.

While racial profiling can happen in a wide range of contexts, as discussed above, racially motivated police pullovers are common and well-documented. Black drivers are 20 percent more likely to get pulled over than white drivers, according to a study of nearly 100 million traffic stops from around the United States.

The authors of the study that found this discrepancy carried out a second kind of analysis of the data to try to make sure that their findings reflected racism rather than some other phenomenon:

> [They used] what they called the 'veil of darkness' test. Essentially, they looked at the racial breakdown of only the traffic stops made after dark, when the race of a motorist is harder to discern. Even when applied to different subsets of data, the results '[showed] a marked drop in the proportion of drivers stopped after dusk who are black, suggestive of discrimination in stop decisions'.[55]

Multiple studies have reviewed data related to police searches of stopped cars, finding that police are more likely to search Blacks than whites during a traffic stop and to do so on the basis of less evidence than would be required to search white drivers. These searches rarely yield much contraband (drugs, unlicensed guns, or suspicious cash). If Black drivers were more likely than white drivers to possess contraband, searching them should be disproportionately successful. In fact, searching Black drivers produces less contraband than searching white drivers, indicating that the greater rates of Black driver searches are attributable to racism.[56]

Sociologist Jenny Stuber explains how racialized police searches set a cycle in motion:

> Because law enforcement officers do sometimes find drugs when they search minorities, racial profiling becomes a self-fulfilling prophecy: Inevitably, it appears justified because you find what you seek. If you stop and search lots of Black and Hispanic drivers, you're likely to turn up some illegal activity. Yet when looking at data from drivers who were searched, researchers find that white drivers are actually more likely to have contraband—illegal drugs or weapons—in their cars. [...] Given the disproportionate focus on minority drivers, the ACLU alleges that 'white drivers receive far less police attention, many of the drug dealers and possessors among them go un-apprehended, and the perception that whites commit fewer drug offenses than minorities

---

55 Willingham 2019; see also Kovera 2019; Pierson et al. 2020.
56 Balko 2020; Kovera 2019; Pierson et al. 2020; Willingham 2019.

is perpetuated'. [...] In fact, Black and white Americans use and sell drugs at similar rates, but Black Americans are 2.7 times more likely to be arrested for a drug-related offense.[57]

In Chapter 3, I discussed my experiences of speeding past police cars without being stopped and pointed out how those experiences were based on police assumptions of white innocence while also reinforcing those same assumptions, since the police had no opportunity to find out whether I was innocent or not unless they stopped me. The phenomenon of "driving while Black" is the flip side of my experience. I received the benefit of the doubt for "driving while white" every time I was not pulled over. Black drivers are denied the benefit of the doubt every time they are pulled over for "driving while Black."

In the past few chapters, we have seen how cultural processes of inequality play out over a wide range of situations, but we have not yet addressed one of the more uncomfortable realities of systemic inequality: the fact that members of devalued groups collude in their own devaluation and mistreatment. While such collusion is never the whole story, and while members of devalued groups often struggle powerfully against their devaluation, they also sometimes play a role in the making of forms of inequality from which they suffer. Chapter 9 discusses collusion.

Discussion Questions

1. Consider any of the examples provided in this chapter. How, in your own words, do you see two or more cultural processes of inequality at work in the example?
2. Can you think of any other examples of inequality (of any sort) where two or more cultural processes contribute to creating or reproducing the inequality?
3. Based on the examples in this chapter, how are cultural processes of racism and sexism similar and different? What extra challenges might Black women and other BIPOC women face as they navigate both forms of bad faith and bad treatment?
4. In Chapter 3, the author claimed that the idea of "the benefit of the doubt" can help us better understand how systemic inequality works. Now that you have read most of the book, how would you describe (in your own words) the role of the benefit of the doubt in continuing inequality over time and across space?

---

57 Stuber 2022: 346. Self-fulfilling prophecies also occur when police patrol majority-Black neighborhoods looking for crime while ignoring white neighborhoods; see Boddie 2022: 483 for an example.

Chapter 9

COLLUSION

I have learned that I have a quiet shame that lurks in the corners of my psyche. It colors and influences the way I interact with the world, form relationships, and understand myself. It operates by causing me to second guess myself when I know I am right. It makes me select a male name from the phonebook when I am looking for a doctor and feel immediately embarrassed when I realize what I am doing. It makes me resent other LBGT individuals who 'talk about gay stuff all the time,' which is something I recently found myself saying to my girlfriend. [This shame] is a catch-22 because no matter how hard I try, I cannot be without shame. I am ashamed of my shame. I hate that there is a part of me that hates a part of me.[1]

The more you're treated as if you don't know what you're talking about, the more you begin to question whether or not you do in fact know what you're talking about.[2]

As we've seen throughout this book, cultural processes of inequality are extensive enough and harmful enough when practiced by members of valued groups. Unfortunately, members of devalued groups can also withhold the benefit of the doubt from their own groups. Women defend accused sexual offenders.[3] Supreme Court Justice Clarence Thomas opposes antiracist social policies while Justice Amy Coney Barrett opposes feminist social policies. The five police officers who beat Tyre Nichols to death on January 7, 2023, were all Black.[4] Until we know something about the cultural processes behind collusion, we will not have a complete understanding of how systemic inequality relies on both valued and devalued people to keep it going.

---

1 David and Derthick 2014: 21–22, quoting a lesbian.
2 Sieghart 2021: 46, quoting a trans woman.
3 Blackburn Center 2017; Wright 2017.
4 Lenthang et al. 2023.

The topic of collusion is complicated and fraught. Pointing out that some people participate in devaluing their own social groups can look like—or turn into—blaming the victim. Moreover, focusing on such collusion can draw attention away from how those who benefit from the inequality in question are responsible for reproducing it. Describing the role of cultural processes in collusion, as this chapter does, may defuse the victim-blaming somewhat; colluders are as influenced as members of valued groups by cultural messages about who matters and who does not (as the two quotes that begin the chapter suggest). We all act in response to how we are taught to see the world; when we are taught that some people matter and others don't, it is difficult not to absorb that message to at least some extent.

At the same time, it would be simplistic to claim that members of devalued groups are completely unable to resist the messages of devaluation they receive. Some members of devalued groups resist inequality strenuously and consistently while others struggle deeply with internalized oppression. Many members of devalued groups fall in between the two extremes. When I reflect on my own experiences of sexism and heterosexism, I find that I have had a range of responses. I've felt rage, humiliation, terror, and a sense of inadequacy or wrongness at times. At other times, I've felt a deep sense of strength, a passion to educate others or engage in activism, and a sureness that the problem is inequality—not me. I doubt my experience in this is unusual.

So, we must be able to honor the complexity of how inequality works on devalued people. This complexity includes the many times devalued people struggle against inequality along with their co-conspirators from valued groups; it also includes those times when devalued people collude in their own devaluation.

Socialization and Subjectivity

A key insight of sociologists is that we become who we are through *socialization*. We learn who and how to be in the world, and how to be a member of society. We learn what is true, what is desirable, what is normal, and what is possible. We learn what experiences we should try to have or seek to avoid. We learn how to behave in different social settings. We learn virtually everything that enables us to survive and thrive in society, which includes knowing who matters and who doesn't.

We learn these lessons from our families, friends, teachers, religious leaders, and others we love and trust. We learn them from social media, movies, books, TV, and other places where stories are told and morals are stated or implied. We learn these lessons at stores, at the doctor's office, and on the basketball court. These lessons permeate song lyrics, legal briefs, textbooks, and newspaper articles.

Our self-understandings and interpretations of the world are thus socially shaped. Our desires, beliefs, values, and certainties come to us courtesy of society. Even our biological needs are socially shaped; for example, we need to eat, but what we want to eat has a lot to do with what we learn about what foods are tasty, what foods are good for us, what foods are disgusting, and so on. Moreover, since the way we interpret the world impacts how we act in the world, our actions are also socially shaped.

Socialization matters for inequality because we are introduced to the cultural processes discussed in this book as we grow up and we encounter them throughout our lives. We experience moral alchemy or false equivalencies at work. We hear our parents talk about different kinds of people in good-faith or bad-faith ways, treating them as trustworthy or not, competent or not. Examples of positive and negative visibility and invisibility make their way into our lives even if we do not identify them as such. This is as true for members of devalued groups as it is for members of valued groups. Everyone in a society shaped by inequality is at least touched by that inequality; most of us are formed by it to some degree.

Ultimately, socialization shapes our sense of self, our very subjectivity. Our individual identities are bound up in our group identities. Because of the way privilege works as the systematic granting of the benefit of the doubt, we may not be aware of how privilege shapes our subjectivities, and how we come to take access and ease and trust for granted. If we are members of devalued groups, however, we receive strong messages about how badly we should be treated and why. We take those messages in, whether we accept them, struggle with them or some of both. If we learn that our well-being does not matter, we may feel shame. If we learn that society thinks we are incompetent, we may come to believe this ourselves at some level. If we face discrimination, mistrust, and surveillance regularly enough, we will become self-conscious and fearful. Such shame, insecurity, self-consciousness, and fear become a part of who we are. These are not self-understandings that we can just wish away, and they can impact how we think of others like us as well as how we treat them.

Cultural Power and Ideology

[I]deological domination [works] through institutional control over education, religion, media, culture, and economic systems, [enabling valued] groups in society [to spread] ideas which serve to justify inequalities of status and power.[5]

---

5 Jost 1995: 398.

Because of how socialization works, we grow up encountering ideas and values without necessarily understanding the power structures behind them. When we are young, we may learn that certain people are important and other people are problematic but unless we are part of a devalued community, we may not learn the role inequality plays in who matters more and who matters less.

In fact, those with cultural power—the power to shape how we see the world, as discussed in Chapter 2—are often members of valued groups. They can influence our understanding of reality in ways that benefit them but not the rest of us. At the same time, they can use their cultural power to convince the rest of us that values, laws, or norms that benefit only them are actually good for everyone. Alternately, they may try to convince the rest of us that those values, laws, and norms are just the way things are and cannot be changed.

In Chapter 7, I pointed out that women are held responsible for preventing both sexual assault and pregnancy, despite the central role of men in both activities. Historically and still today, men are in most positions of cultural power, and it is in men's interests to make sure women are the ones defined as responsible for preventing sexual assault and pregnancy.[6] I say it is in men's interests because when most people in society believe this, men are not held accountable for sexual assaults, nor do they have to spend their time, energy, and money on birth control that they do not enjoy using. It is not surprising, therefore, that men are invested in having women believe that it is women's responsibility to keep from getting assaulted or pregnant. Men have much more cultural power than women, with the result that both women and men largely hold this belief about responsibility even when women resent it and complain about it. When women believe that women are responsible for preventing sexual assault, it is not surprising that they will defend assaulters and blame the assaulted—even when the people assaulted are other women.

When ideas reflect the interests of the group in power but are represented as reflecting everyone's interests, we call them "ideologies." Sociologist Karen Pyke describes how ideologies work, including how they flow through society and impact members of devalued groups:

> The [valued] group controls the construction of reality through the production of ideologies or 'knowledge' [...] that circulate throughout society where they inform social norms, organizational practices, bureaucratic procedures, and commonsense knowledge. In this way the

---

6 Those interests include maintaining power, remaining unaccountable for the harm they cause, getting to have their way when there is a conflict, and continuing to be understood as mattering more than other people.

interests of the [valued group] are presented as reflecting everyone's best interests, thereby getting [devalued] groups to accept the [valued] group's interests as their own. [Devalued people] inculcate, seemingly by cultural osmosis, negative stereotypes and ideologies disseminated as taken-for-granted knowledge.[7]

This last point is particularly important. Bad-faith assumptions about members of devalued groups are simply "how it is" and "what everyone knows." They represent understandings that most people take for granted and do not question. Otherwise, women could not be held accountable for actions taken by men—and otherwise, Black people could not be racially profiled for partaking in legal, normal everyday activities that white people do routinely with no difficulty.

Internalized Oppression

Internalizing your inferiority is violent.[8]

Given the impact of socialization in the context of cultural power and the ideologies it enables, it is not surprising that the taken-for-granted knowledge that fuels inequality has a negative impact on members of devalued groups. This negative impact is often referred to as "internalized oppression." Social psychologist Gail Pheterson provides a useful definition and description of internalized oppression:

Internalized oppression is the incorporation and acceptance by individuals within an oppressed group of the prejudices against them within the dominant society. Internalized oppression is likely to consist of self-hatred, self-concealment, fear of violence and feelings of inferiority, resignation, isolation, powerlessness, and gratefulness for being allowed to survive. Internalized oppression is the mechanism within an oppressive system for perpetuating domination not only by external control but also by building subservience into the minds of the oppressed groups.[9]

---

7 Pyke 2010: 556.

8 Cottom 2019: 58.

9 Pheterson 1986: 148. Similarly, internalized racism has been defined as "the situation that occurs in a racist system when a racial group oppressed by racism supports the supremacy and dominance of the dominant group by maintaining or participating in the set of attitudes, behaviors, social structures, and ideologies that undergird the dominating group's power and privilege and limits the oppressed group's own advantages" (Bivens n.d.: 45–46).

Again, we need to be careful to note that such "subservience" coexists with resentment, resistance, and attempts to change the cultural narrative, some of which are successful over time. For example, same-sex marriage would not be legal in the United States today if cultural narratives were unchangeable. At the same time, internalized oppression helps maintain inequality by inculcating shame and doubt in the minds and spirits of devalued people, as the quotations opening the chapter suggest.

An example: internalized sexism

> [The] cumulative effects of sexism are pervasive, impacting how women shape their personalities and identities, negotiate their relationships, feel about themselves, make meaning out of their experiences, and make choices about their lives over the short and long term. Internalized sexism refers to women's incorporation of sexist practices, and to the circulation of those practices among women, even in the absence of men.[10]

Growing up, I learned that boys were better at math than girls. I don't know when exactly I internalized that belief but I must have done so, since I have been afraid of math for most of my life. Basic math is easy for me, and I carry out bivariate statistical analysis for my job, but I continue to feel like a fraud when I run more complex statistical tests or work with advanced mathematical concepts. I've struggled with these feelings for more than half a century, but thus far they run too deep to root out—a perfect example of internalized sexism.

Internalized sexism also helps explain why women sometimes defend abusive men. Blackburn Center, an organization that supports sexual violence survivors, refers to such defenses as an example of "internalized misogyny":

> This is a phenomenon where girls hear stereotypes and myths about women from a young age, often from trusted adults such as parents and teachers. As a result, they often internalize these messages, believing false stereotypes such as 'women often make up allegations of rape' or that women who were sexually abused, were 'asking for it.' *It's important to note that this is not a voluntary process, but an involuntary one where women absorb messages over time.* The messages call into question the worth and value of any woman.[11]

---

10 Bearman et al. 2009: 11. One common example of a sexist practice is invalidation, in which "women discount their own feelings and thoughts, specifically when they don't match male standards" (Bearman and Amrhein 2014: 199).

11 Blackburn Center 2017.

I've emphasized that internalized misogyny is an involuntary process because of how important this point is—for any kind of internalized oppression. We are better able to address collusion and avoid participating in it ourselves, if we understand that it comes from socialization that is unavoidable and often unwanted. I did not choose to believe that women were bad at math and that I was therefore bad at math. This belief was essentially forced on me. Knowing that has allowed me to struggle against it and learn enough math to use some of it professionally. Similarly, as women come to understand and accept fully that women are not responsible for being sexually assaulted, women will stop defending assailants.

More broadly, members of all devalued groups have the opportunity to wrestle with the ideologies that they learned as "just how things are," ideologies that harm them while benefiting members of valued groups. Perhaps, over time, this wrestling will diminish the amount of collusion that props up inequality in all its forms.

Of course, members of valued groups also have a great deal of work to do if they (we) want to bring about a good-faith society, one in which everyone receives the benefit of the doubt. In Chapter 10, I discuss what some of that work might look like.

Discussion Questions

1. Why, according to the author, is it important to acknowledge the role that members of devalued groups can play in colluding with their own devaluation? In your own words, what are the challenges of acknowledging collusion?
2. What role does socialization play in collusion? Can you think of any examples beyond those given in the chapter?
3. What role does ideology play in collusion? Can you think of any examples beyond those given in the chapter?
4. Define internalized oppression in your own words. Have you experienced any form of internalized oppression yourself? If so, what effect do you think it has had on you?

Chapter 10

TOWARD A GOOD-FAITH SOCIETY

[D]ignity affects quality of life just as much as material resources do. When we think about how to improve society, then, we cannot ignore worth any more than we can poverty or inequality. We need to focus on the extent to which different groups are 'seen' by others, whether they have a seat at the table, and whether they feel welcomed, valued, and listened to. We know it is possible to do all this because worth is socially determined. That is to say, it is not handed down from above based on neutral criteria. Rather, *we* decide who matters—all of us, every day, by creating, supporting, and spreading new narratives about the worth of all groups. This is why worth should be factored in explicitly—in every social interaction on the street, as well as every legal and policy decision that our elected officials make. This is not to say that money and power do not matter. But whether groups are recognized and afforded dignity is *just as* important to their flourishing as human beings, just as vital to their drive to be all they can be.[1]

We know boundaries are changeable because *we make them*—they are created through a process that we all participate in.[2]

I used to live in a city with many universities. The women's basketball team at one of the universities was terrific, powered by a point guard who could hit any player on the team with a mid-court toss unless she felt like sinking a three-pointer from way outside instead. I attended the team's games regularly. The men's team at the same university wasn't very good. Unsurprisingly, the men played in a large arena with a fancy jumbotron and an impressive sound system. The women played in a small gym with an intermittently failing sound system. Maybe the court was full-size, maybe not.

---

1 Lamont 2023: 4; italics in the original.
2 Lamont 2023: 58; italics in the original.

As of 2023, both teams at this university play in the same large arena. Change is possible.

Years ago, my mother had a hard time finding an anniversary card for my wife and me that was specific to a female couple. She eventually found one in a gay neighborhood in New York City.

As of 2023, the local supermarket in my conservative city has a Mother's Day card section that includes cards for two moms, for a female couple, and for "LGBTQIA+" people. Change is possible.

Throughout this book, we've explored cultural processes of inequality in detail. As I see it, the main reason to study these processes is to learn how we can change them. In this chapter, I address change in two ways: first, by revisiting the cultural processes we've considered, and second, by suggesting concrete steps those of us in valued groups can take to work against inequality from which we benefit.

No matter how we approach our work against systemic inequality, it's important to keep our goal in mind at all times. This goal is to *create societies where everyone matters*—where the comfort, education, rights, health, and life of every single person are valued. In such a society, everyone would receive good-faith treatment. Everyone would have reasonable access to important resources, experiences, and opportunities. No one would be surveilled or policed based on stereotype-driven suspicions. Everyone would be understood to be part of the moral community within which it is ethically required to treat people fairly and justly. Cultural processes of inequality prevent us from building that kind of society, which is why we must dismantle them.

Treating everyone in good faith involves leveling up, not leveling down.[3] The point is not for police officers to treat white people as badly as they currently treat Black people, but for police officers to treat Black people as well as they currently treat white people. Teachers should start with the assumption that all students are able to learn and want to learn. Women should be believed when they report a sexual assault. LGBTQ people should have access to the same education, rights, and medical care as heterosexual, cisgender people. The point is not to get rid of the benefit of the doubt; the point is to *universalize* it.

Of course, some people will demonstrate that they cannot be trusted with good-faith treatment and they may need to be treated differently from others. However, this will happen because those people act in harmful ways, not because of any social identity they may have. Granting the benefit of the doubt does not deny that some people are in fact non-credible, incompetent,

---

3 Thanks to Dr. Helen Daly for suggesting this language.

untrustworthy, and so on. It means treating them as credible, competent, and trustworthy until we have clear evidence that they are not. This evidence cannot come down to the biases we received as part of our socialization; it must be based on what someone has said or done that shows them to require cautious treatment.

Universalizing the benefit of the doubt means uncoupling group statuses from either good-faith or bad-faith assumptions and treatment. In fact, universalizing the benefit of the doubt arguably means uncoupling bad-faith assumptions from bad-faith treatment entirely. How we treat people will be based, not on our stereotypes and biases, but on the evidence that they have shown us of who they are. In this sense, universalizing the benefit of the doubt means treating everyone as innocent until proven guilty, competent until proven incompetent, and so on.

Right now, some people benefit from the good-faith cycle described in Chapter 5, in which good-faith assumptions lead to good-faith treatment, with good outcomes for all involved. Others suffer from the bad-faith cycle, in which bad-faith assumptions lead to bad-faith treatment, with bad outcomes for those so judged. In a society without systemic inequality, every person would begin on the good-faith cycle and would only fall away from that cycle if they acted in such a way as to demonstrate that they did not deserve good-faith treatment.

A society in which everyone matters is an aspirational goal. It may not be possible to create such a society. However, I'm sure about three things. First, it's a worthy goal to pursue: a society in which everyone has a real chance of flourishing. Second, our only chance of making this aspiration a reality is to believe in the aspiration enough to work hard at bringing it to life. Third, we need to understand cultural processes of inequality in order to push against them, challenge them, and perhaps diminish their power.

Addressing Cultural Processes of Inequality

Consider moral alchemy, the process by which behavior that is defined as good for a valued group is defined as problematic for a devalued group. Once we understand how moral alchemy works, we can challenge it by defining the same actions as uniformly positive (or uniformly negative) no matter who engages in them. If marriage is good for heterosexual couples, it's good for same-sex couples. If "Black-on-Black" crime is understood to be a problem, "white-on-white crime" must be understood to be a problem as well. If we value male leaders who are "take-charge," we need to value female leaders who are "take-charge." Overturning moral alchemy will involve changing the language we use, changing the laws we enforce, and changing the social rewards we offer and the social punishments we inflict.

Because false equivalencies represent the opposite of moral alchemy, we need to respond to them by clarifying how exactly they are false and why the laws, policies, or movements (for example) they describe are not in fact equivalent. I provided an example of how to do this in comparing the Black Lives Matter and Blue Lives Matter movements. Because historical and current inequality so often provides the context within which the equivalency is false, we need to understand the role played by inequality in these situations.

It's not hard to grasp what's wrong with the "majestically equal" law mentioned by Anatole France that punishes all people for behaviors in which only the poor are forced to engage. We know that wealthy people do not need to beg and that poor people do. It is harder to argue with Justice John Roberts when he writes that, "The way to stop discrimination on the basis of race is to stop discriminating on the basis of race." This point sounds eminently reasonable. It only becomes unreasonable when we have enough context to understand that:

- Our society's history is built on discrimination against BIPOC people.
- Our society currently discriminates against BIPOC people.
- Roberts's objection is only to laws that "discriminate" in favor of BIPOC people in order to help them overcome historic and current discrimination against them.
- Roberts is not objecting to racial discrimination when it benefits white people, only when it benefits BIPOC people.
- Roberts is not, therefore, objecting to "discrimination on the basis of race" at all; quite the contrary, he is supporting it.

Consider good-faith and bad-faith assumptions and the good-faith and bad-faith actions they drive. We can monitor our own assumptions and actions to see how these patterns play out in our own lives, whether we are acting as individuals or in contexts of decision-making or cultural power. Who do we expect to be credible and why? Competent? Trustworthy? Innocent? As we get to know our assumptions, we may be horrified to see how readily we fall into bad-faith patterns of denying people the benefit of the doubt for dubious reasons. If we can live with the discomfort and deepen our understanding of our expectations and behaviors, we may be able to change them—again, both in our individual lives and in contexts where we make institutional decisions that impact other people.

Consider self-fulfilling prophecies. We can interrupt these cycles of inequality before they reach completion by recognizing our assumptions *and not acting on them*. If we realize that we believe white students to be smarter, we can pour more effort and focus into teaching BIPOC students. If we recognize that pulling over Black drivers or policing in majority-Black neighborhoods reproduces the criminalization of Blackness, we can pull over white drivers and patrol white neighborhoods.[4] If we grasp how careers are male-identified, we can begin, however modestly, to change the expectations of those careers so that they are not gendered. These changes would include paying women what men make for the same work, giving female workers the benefit of the doubt about their competence, and rethinking how careers are structured so that they can incorporate pregnancies rather than forcing pregnancies to compete with them.

Consider positive and negative visibility and invisibility. Raising questions about, and challenges to, the naturalness and normalcy of current in/visibility practices will make it possible for more people to change these taken-for-granted patterns. We can ask who is missing in a situation, who is receiving less attention, and whose interests or well-being are not represented. We can ask who is normal and what assumptions hang on their normalcy. We can resist the idea that anyone should have a "master status" and strive to treat all people as individuals—especially people who are usually reduced to their devalued group memberships now.

We can work against the harms of public harassment, surveillance, and other forms of negative visibility. My response to the barista who body-shamed me for ordering a Frappuccino was not particularly effective, but what if everyone who was body-shamed responded by inviting the shamer to deeper compassion? What if everyone who witnessed an occurrence of body-shaming did the same, in solidarity with the person being shamed? What if every man who saw another man harass a woman on the street held the harasser accountable? These are not easy actions to take, but we can practice taking them and ask others to join us.

Consider the relationship between people and problems. We can reject the idea that people "are" ever problems. We can expand our understanding of how people have problems and the effect those problems have on them. This rethinking helps us to universalize the benefit of the doubt. If drug addictions associated with white people merit a focus on treatment and prevention, for example, so too should drug addictions associated with BIPOC people.[5]

---

4 I hope that in a few years, some police officer who read this book (perhaps as a sociology student) pulls me over for speeding. I don't want it to happen but I hope it does. It would only be fair, after all.

5 Here, it's worth remembering that more white people used and use crack cocaine than Black people. We need to be honest about who is impacted by a particular problem in order to provide the help they need.

We can redefine whose problem something is so that everyone involved with the situation has a role to play in addressing the problem. Burdens such as birth control should be the responsibility of everyone who benefits from them, not just one group. Since both men and women benefit when unwanted pregnancies are avoided, the burden should be shared equally. This principle can be applied to a wide range of situations.

We can hold people who cause harm accountable for what they do, making their role visible and ceasing to blame victims for their victimization. We can replace the phrase "violence against women" with the phrase "male violence against women" if that's the phenomenon we are considering. As a specific but powerful example, we can commit the time, money, and energy needed to test all rape kits; imagine the message it would send about women's lives and well-being mattering if every police department made testing all rape kits a priority. Many other such interventions are possible.

Similarly, we can work to change media coverage of the killing of Black people so that headlines do not treat white mass murderers as more humane—even more human—than Black victims. We can push the media to hold the killers accountable. Imagine the difference it might have made if the standard headline about Tamir Rice's killing, found on news media across the country, had been: "Emotionally unstable, unfit police officer kills boy within two seconds of arrival on scene." Perhaps such a headline would eventually have saved a Black life—or many Black lives.

Consider the cultural processes underpinning collusion. We can recognize the power of socialization in enabling us to take inequality for granted even when we suffer from it; this may allow us to imagine new ways to socialize ourselves, each other, and the next generation.[6] We can learn about how ideology works and develop ways to resist it more effectively. If we are members of valued groups, we can learn how to support members of devalued groups in struggling against their own internalized oppression—not because we are somehow "saving" them but because we recognize that our well-being is bound up with theirs.

Consider moral exclusion more broadly. Once we have written off a person or a group as unworthy of moral treatment, it is hard to "write them back in," but we can use our capacity for compassion and empathy to do so. If, for example, we are white and are tempted to criminalize Black people, we might look hard at our own histories. Have we really never broken the law? If the criminal justice system were actually race-neutral, might we

---

6 I like to think that books such as this one can help with resocializing us toward greater humanity, compassion, and equality.

not have criminal records of our own? Can recognizing our own (capacity for) criminality help us jettison some of our racism?

Ultimately, we will need to change our language, our minds, our hearts, our meaning systems, and our institutions in order to push back against cultural processes of inequality. We will need to stop taking things for granted, start raising questions, and risk angering people who may have more power than us. If we are in valued groups, it is very easy to go along silently and take advantage of our valued status. If we want to be part of the solution, we will need to make some noise and take some chances, both with and on behalf of devalued groups.

Suggestions for Members of Valued Groups

There are many concrete actions that members of valued groups can take as part of working and living in solidarity with devalued groups toward the goal of ending social, political, and economic devaluation. I use "we" language here because this part of the chapter is inspired by antiracism work that I do with white people as a white person.

We can develop a fierce commitment to the well-being of members of the devalued group, to treating them with good faith, and to giving them the benefit of the doubt. This includes trusting devalued group members as experts on their own lives, even when they have things to say that we would rather not hear.

We can get comfortable with the inevitable discomfort of addressing our roles in inequality as people who benefit from it. It's natural to be uncomfortable when we address inequality head-on, whether we benefit from it or suffer from it. Individualism is an ideology that benefits the valued, well-off, and successful by distracting us from how systemic inequality works and who it benefits and harms. Any time we resist taken-for-granted narratives about how things are, we will be uncomfortable. We can learn to reject fragility, defensiveness, and emotional withdrawal. We can learn to tolerate and even welcome vulnerability along with the grief and rage that inequality should evoke in us. Such emotions can fuel our work to change society for the better.

There's more to say about the kind of discomfort members of valued groups may experience when taking seriously forms of inequality from which we benefit. We are used to receiving the benefit of the doubt, to being treated in good faith, to having privilege. Whether consciously or not, we know at some level that we receive these benefits and this trust precisely because other people do not receive them. This feels natural and normal to us.

Attempts to universalize the benefit of the doubt and to treat everyone in good faith may well feel unfair or unjust to us. For example, being pulled over as a white person, or being expected to pull one's weight with birth control as a man, will disrupt the taken-for-granted expectations with which we have lived for so long. When our lives have consisted of getting our way and having our perspective valued over the perspectives of others, it will feel strange to get our way less often, to have alternative perspectives receive as much respect as our own. We may even feel oppressed, as though we are now valued less than others. When those formerly denied the benefit of the doubt are granted the benefit of the doubt, we may feel as though we are suddenly receiving bad-faith treatment. This is not the case, of course, but because we no longer receive special entitlements, it can feel that way. We must be alert to these feelings, recognize them for what they are, and let them go. They are natural and understandable but they do not serve equality, justice, or the well-being of all people.

We can educate ourselves about the history and present reality of the relevant form of inequality as well as the social, economic, political, psychological, and other impacts that it has on members of the devalued group. There are extensive resources available for learning about any kind of inequality: books, blogs, podcasts, movies, TV shows, magazines, journals, trainings, and other courses. Some of these resources focus on, or include material about, solutions as well as background about the nature of the problems.[7]

Once we have educated ourselves enough, we can take responsibility for educating other members of our valued group. Because of the way credibility works under systemic inequality, our friends may take what we have to say about the inequality more seriously than they would take something said by a member of the devalued group. We can use this unfortunate fact to our advantage by educating and advocating for equality and justice.

---

7 Rothstein and Rothstein 2023 have many suggestions for challenging racial segregation. Sieghart 2021 (chapter 15) has pages of suggestions for how we can challenge our assumptions about women's competence in our roles as individuals, romantic partners, parents, colleagues, employers, teachers/educators, media workers, and government workers. Lamont 2023 (chapter 8) discusses ways in which societies can enhance recognition of devalued groups of people as a way of contributing to re-valuing them; more broadly, her book discusses what she calls "recognition chains," defined as "a network of change agents and organizations that scales up and disseminates messages of recognition. In these chains, change agents join forces with foundations and other organizations to benefit from their infrastructure, and ultimately to see their recognition work reverberate far beyond their own individual or institutional reach" (Lamont 2023: 77).

We can use our institutionally legitimated decision-making authority to support devalued individuals and communities. This work involves pushing against historical and institutional paths of least resistance in which decision-making authority has overwhelmingly been used to support valued people and communities at the expense of devalued people and communities. We must not underestimate how difficult this kind of change may be to make or how uncomfortable it will make us and others.

We can use our resources (including money), talents, time, energy, gifts, and passion to support devalued individuals and communities. For example, we can do the following:

- Donate money to advocacy and justice organizations.
- Buy from businesses owned by members of devalued communities.
- Bank with a financial institution that does not have an egregious history of supporting inequality.
- Volunteer with advocacy and justice organizations and support justice initiatives offered by broader organizations (such as driving people to the polls or doing other get-out-the-vote activities).
- Research the various communities, organizations, and commercial venues with which we interact, deciding whether we need to move some of our time, money, and energy elsewhere.

The last point I want to make is that *we can and should use our unique gifts and talents in the service of our dream of a good-faith society.* We don't all have to be "social justice warriors," though some of us certainly should be. Some of us can be social justice artists, using our creativity to work against inequality. Some of us can be social justice comedians, using humor to point out the absurdity of inequality to people who are not ready to hear about it in other ways. Or we can be social justice accountants, social justice project managers, social justice professors, or social justice athletes. The list of ways we can bring our gifts, vocations, and work lives to this struggle is practically endless.

When we use our gifts and talents in these ways, we know we are bringing our best selves to our work for a better world—the skills that we have spent years developing, the talents that bring us and others such joy when we put them to work (and play). Inequality is a huge, complex, messy, sprawling, monstrous phenomenon. Bringing only our rough edges, frailties, and sorrows to working against it is not sustainable. We need to bring our strengths, our power, our cleverness, our silliness, our joy, and our training. All forms of inequality are both harmful enough and unnecessary enough that it behooves us to bring our whole selves to the work against them. Our world and all the people in it deserve our A-game.

There is no guarantee that our work will lead to great changes, or that we will somehow eradicate the cultural processes that fuel inequality. Each of us, however, has the chance to make at least a small difference. All of us are invited to do so. I hope you will take up the invitation.

Discussion Questions

1. The author discusses universalizing the benefit of the doubt. In your own words, describe what this might look like and how it would work. How might your own life be different if everyone received good-faith treatment by default?
2. The author suggests ways to challenge cultural processes of inequality. How might you do this in your own life?
3. The author suggests actions that members of valued groups can take to work against forms of inequality that benefit them. Consider a valued group to which you belong. Which item on the author's list would be a good place for you to start working against this form of inequality?
4. The author believes that we can and should all use our unique gifts and talents in the struggle against inequality. What are some of your particular gifts and talents? How might you use them to help create a world of moral inclusion and good-faith treatment?

APPENDIX: THINKING LIKE A SOCIOLOGIST

Perhaps this book or the course in which you are reading it is your first introduction to sociology. If so, this appendix is for you. It introduces sociology as a discipline, along with some of the most important insights sociologists have about how society works. Some language in the appendix assumes that you've already read the book.

What Is Sociology?

Sociology is the academic study of social patterns (and exceptions to them) at all levels and in all contexts through the use of empirical research. Sociology is also a perspective or way of seeing the world, about which I say more later.
   Sociology studies the following:

- Ways in which we are free and ways in which we are not
- How structure and culture enable and constrain us
- How belonging to a social group shapes our beliefs
- How our interactions with people change based on the context
- How our actions differ depending on the setting
- How social inequality works
- How different organizations and institutions interact with one another
- How our self-understanding is socially shaped
- How social patterns continue over time and how they change
- How individuals make sense of their lives
- How people interact with each other
- What people learn from culture
- What people believe, value, and assume, and how those beliefs, values, and assumptions impact our actions
- How organizations and large-scale institutions work separately and collectively

- How these facets of life come together to make societies that keep going over time while changing constantly

Since everything we do in our lives involves our relationships with others and with society more broadly, nothing human is off limits to sociology and virtually everything human is of interest to at least a few sociologists.

Some sociologists focus on the smallest levels of human social life: perceptions, values, ideas, identity development, meaning-making, individual behavior, and interpersonal interactions. Some sociologists are more interested in how organizations work, how cultural norms and ideals are disseminated across a society, or how social change movements come into existence, have an effect (or don't), and fall away again. Some sociologists study the largest-scale institutions of a given society, how nations interact with each other, or globalization and other patterns that span multiple countries.

Some sociologists are most interested in how different institutions interact with each other, such as the family and the workplace. Others wonder what happens when different social levels interact, what (for example) individual-level experiences and relationships look like in the context of organizations or federal laws or changes in the global economy. In real life, all of these aspects of society are completely interwoven and most of them are invisible to people on a day-to-day basis. We tend to focus on our immediate obligations and opportunities without normally thinking about, say, institutional social patterns or globalization or how culture gets disseminated. Sociologists want to understand how all the aspects of our social world intersect but it is not possible to study everything at one time, so we pick an area to highlight, extricate it from the other facets of society in which it is embedded, and focus on its specifics, trying not to lose sight of the larger context.

What Are Social Patterns?

My favorite definition of social patterns comes from sociologist Michael Schwalbe, who defines them as "people doing things together in orderly ways on a regular basis."[1] Social patterns include the following:

- How we see ourselves and the world and make sense of our lives; our meaning systems (ideas, values, attitudes, beliefs, perceptions, assumptions, worldviews, inclinations, dispositions, priorities, etc.) and how these are

---

1 Schwalbe 2018: xv.

shaped by the groups and communities to which we belong
- How we behave differently depending on the situation and context
- How we present ourselves to the world
- How we interact with others and how those interactions are shaped by larger contexts
- How we partake of cultural products and norms, how we make culture, how it shapes us, and what we learn from it
- How our experiences, perceptions, memories, knowledge, skills, and consciousness solidify and change our identities and commitments over time
- How we reproduce and change society both individually and collectively
- The organizations in which we participate and groups to which we belong (a particular family, a particular college, a particular workplace, a particular sporting team, a particular church/synagogue/mosque, etc.), and their policies, practices, and interpersonal relationships
- The large-scale institutions (education, the family, the state/government, religion, the economy/marketplace, industry/the workplace, the arts, science, the media, sports, health care/medicine, criminal justice/legal system, the military, etc.) that enable our society to survive over time
- How social inequality is produced and reproduced through assumptions, actions, culture, and institutional practices
- How these different aspects of human life intersect with and influence each other; how they continue and change over time

Put differently, social patterns focus on the following:

- People, perspectives, and practices, and the relationships between them
- "Ideologies, institutions, interests, identities, and interactions"[2] and the intersections between them

Social patterns are different from individual experiences or anecdotes. Just because something happened to you doesn't mean it happens regularly, and just because something has not happened to you does not mean it doesn't happen to all or most people in a particular social group or social setting. Social patterns can have exceptions; they don't have to be universal. But if something is a social pattern, it happens with regularity in a particular context, and it is connected to other social patterns.

Sociology's passion and genius is in teasing apart the strands of our lives to better understand what social patterns have to do with each other, how they make us who we are, how we make them what they are, and how we might

2 Hughey 2015.

change them in order to build a society where everyone has a real chance to flourish.

The Sociological Imagination

> The sociological imagination enables us to grasp history and biography and the relations between the two within society. That is its task and its promise.[3]

Sociology may be even more important as a mindset or as an analytic framework than it is as an academic discipline. C. Wright Mills spoke of the "sociological imagination," the capacity to see the way that society forms individuals even as individuals create society. People with a sociological imagination understand the complexity of human freedom and its limits, which I discuss below. The sociological imagination is helpful in inviting us to "zoom out" and study society from a broader perspective rather than focusing only on individuals, individual actions, and individual successes and failures. Once we have "zoomed out," the sociological imagination invites us to zoom back in and see how the larger social patterns impact individual lives. The rest of the appendix expands on some insights offered by the sociological imagination.

The Social Construction of Reality

Michael Schwalbe is particularly skilled at describing the sociological imagination for those new to sociology. He writes:

> If there is a first step in being sociologically mindful, it is learning to see the social world as humanly made. Because we are all born into pre-existing groups—families, communities, societies, nations—with established cultures and ways of doing things, it can seem like the social world is just there. [...] But this is not really so. All parts of the social world—all the groups, organizations, institutions, political and economic systems; all our beliefs, values, symbols, and practices—were created, once upon a time, by people. [...] Yet we often experience [the social world] as apart from us, or over and above us. This experience is reflected in how we talk about the social world. We say that the *market* did this or that, or that the *economy* did this or that, or

---

3 Mills 2000: 6. Schwalbe (2018: 3–5) uses the term "sociological mindfulness" and Jacobs (2021) uses the term "sociological curiosity" to refer to the same capacity.

that *technology* drives change, or that *globalization* is transforming society, and so on. [...] [W]e think about and talk about the social world [...] as if it were made of things and forces that are independent of human action. [We] often talk about organizations—universities, banks, armies, hospitals, corporations—and institutions—higher education, government, the family, the market—as *things*, but these 'things' are really just people interacting in patterned ways on a regular basis. One kind of pattern we call a university, another kind we call a bank, another kind we call a corporation, another kind we call a sports team, and so on.[4]

Consider a particular college or university. Perhaps you are, or were, a student there. The school existed before you got there and will exist after you leave. You probably encounter it as something apart from you and larger than you. It is a complex place with many offices, departments, people, and things. Your ability to have an impact on it is limited, particularly as an individual. It seems to be, as Schwalbe puts it, "just there."

And yet this school is a human creation, the product of ideas and labor, plans and building materials, organizational charts, and lesson plans, all of which are also human creations. People brought this school into being. People keep it in existence through their daily actions: going to work, going to class, teaching, eating in a dining hall, and meeting with a student group. People modify the policies or practices of the institution, changing the curriculum or transforming the demographics of the student body. People decide to make such changes, and they act to put them into practice. This school, and every organization, and indeed every aspect of society, is a collective human enterprise.

Put differently, human action underlies every aspect of society— specifically joint human action, "people doing things together in orderly ways on a regular basis" as Schwalbe puts it. We make reality what it is as we interact with one another in the various venues of our lives.

At the same time, reality makes us who we are; we are part of the "reality" that is socially constructed. I discussed socialization in Chapter 9, the process by which we learn how to be ourselves from the people in our lives and the information we encounter. Over the course of our lives, we continue to learn and grow, to better understand society and our place in it, and the impact we want to have on it. We, like the school mentioned above, are thus "socially constructed."

Eventually, we teach the next generation how to become themselves through the same socialization processes—as parents, siblings, teachers,

---

4 Schwalbe 2020: 4–5, 12.

employers, or in other ways. They, too, encounter society as separate from them and greater than them, and they, too, are tempted to think that society is "just there." If they study sociology, they too will learn how both they themselves and the world they encounter are socially constructed.

The Relationship between Individuals and Society

Individual lives must always be understood in terms of larger social contexts, while larger social contexts are always made up of the values, beliefs, assumptions, priorities, and actions of individuals. Two sociologists have come up with useful analogies to explain the relationship between individuals and society. Allan Johnson writes about the trees, the forest, and the relationship between them.[5] Johnson and Jenny Stuber both write about the players, the game, and the relationship between them.[6]

Most of us know that there is a relationship between a forest and the trees in it. Many individual trees make up a forest, but the forest is more than just the individual trees. The forest has its own ecosystem, which includes plants and animals. Even the trees may not be as individual as they look on the surface; tree roots intertwine underground to make up a larger, interconnected system. To understand the forest, we need to understand the individual trees, but to understand each individual tree, we also need to understand something about the forest of which it is a part. Human society is similar. We cannot understand individual people without knowing something about the larger contexts in which they live, dream, worry, and act. And we can't make sense of a society without knowing the kinds of individuals who populate it. Sociology at its best helps us to recognize the forest, the trees, and the relationship between them when it comes to people and society.

The analogy with games is also helpful. As I mentioned in Chapter 1, a game is only a set of rules or a box of materials (conceived of and produced by people) unless someone is actually playing it, yet the game has an impact on its players. I am almost never competitive; one of the few times in which I am is when I am playing a game. You might say that playing the game "makes" me competitive. In this sense, the game "makes" the players even as the players "make" the game.

It's easy to forget that people created the game in the first place and could choose to change it if they wanted to. As a small example, when I play cards or dominoes games, I usually do not keep score across rounds or hands; thus,

---

5 Johnson 2014a.
6 Johnson 2014a; Stuber 2022: 8.

there is not an overall winner in those games. This change makes the games less competitive and more fun for me, but it is definitely not the way the games were conceived. Most of the time, though, most of us do not change the rules of the game—whether it's a board game, the "game" of "college," the "game" of "career," or the "game" of "racism." We encounter these experiences, obligations, and situations as external to us. They are "just there." The path of least resistance[7] is for us to "play" all of these "games" as we have learned them, whether that is from the instructions or from the ways in which our families "play" them. We do not always take the path of least resistance but many of us do so much of the time. And thus, we make the games and the games make us and the cycle continues.

Human Interdependence

Individuals and the social patterns we live out are interconnected. Our lives are woven together through our interactions. Our lives are also knit together through the ways in which we rely on one other for the resources we need to live, for the ideas that give our lives meaning, and for the very existence of all the socially constructed reality around us.

Everything you know, believe, do, and possess is "yours" because of other people. Every thought in your mind, every action you take, and everything you own came to you from someone else. Other people taught you what you know and enabled you to believe what you believe. Other people modeled how to act and socialized you to find some actions preferable to others. Other people made the items you own or taught you how to make them yourself. Other people gave you your possessions or enabled you to buy them (by giving you an allowance or hiring you for pay).

Someone else built the street that you walk or drive on. Someone else manages the health-care system that you use. Someone else prepared the food that you buy at a supermarket or fast-food store. These examples could be multiplied endlessly across your entire life.

You, in turn, keep society going through your words, actions, and individual contributions as a family member, friend, student, and worker and through your other activities and connections. You do this along with every other member of society.

We co-create society together, interdependently.[8] This does not mean that we are never independent; we are independent in certain ways, just as we are dependent

---

7 Johnson 2006: 79.

8 We can also destroy society interdependently through actions that cause systematic harm to people, other living beings, and the planet.

on others in certain ways. But the core truth about humanity that sociology lifts up is our interdependence in making the world in which we live.

The Importance of the Taken-for-Granted

Socialization, discussed in Chapter 9, is important for many reasons. Part of its importance is that it leads to our having taken-for-granted assumptions that shape our lives. We learn what's true, right, desirable, and appropriate. We learn what counts as success and how to succeed. As this book has demonstrated, we learn who matters and who doesn't. Much of the time, this knowledge lives in us without our needing to pay much attention to it. The social patterns we take for granted become invisible, normal, and just how things are. When we take them for granted, we tend to act in ways that reproduce them rather than changing them. This reproduction might occur through self-fulfilling prophecies, as discussed in Chapter 5, or it might occur because we do not question our assumptions and therefore do not challenge them; we merely keep acting on them.

In Chapter 8, I discussed our tendency to blame women for being sexually assaulted, a common example of victim-blaming in sexist societies and one that we generally take for granted. If we stopped taking such blame for granted and really thought about it, we might find that it does not fit with our normal understanding of responsibility. For example, while we encourage people to protect themselves against robbery and scams, we don't usually blame them for being robbed or scammed; we blame the robber or scammer.

Sociologists are interested not just in what we take for granted but in the effect that the taking-for-granted has on us. Taking for granted that it is women's responsibility to prevent sexual assault has the effect of protecting sexual assaulters from being held accountable for their actions. It also contributes to broader processes that enable misbehaving men to remain invisible, making it harder to change cultural narratives about men being more credible and trustworthy than women.

Ultimately, sociologists seek to unearth taken-for-granted assumptions and expose them to the light of day. We want to know where they come from, what purpose they serve, who they benefit, and who they harm. If they are assumptions about how reality works, we want to test them to find out whether they are accurate or not. If they are values, we want to know what impact they have and whether most people would be better off without them.

Freedom and Its Limits

How free are we, really? Philosophers have debated this question for millennia, joined more recently by natural scientists. Sociologists make the following observations about freedom:

- In individualistic societies, we are likely to overestimate how much freedom someone has because *we can observe the choices that they make but not the choices that are not available to them.* We do not know about options that are either genuinely not available to them (due to lack of access to resources, for example) or that might be available but about which they have no information (due to lack of access to social networks, for example).
- Socialization limits our freedom by training us to see certain options as positive and others as negative; we are theoretically free to choose negative options but our understanding that we should not do so will act as a deterrent for many of us.
- We all know that laws limit our freedom, but informal social control does so as well. We face negative consequences when we question certain things or act in ways that are "out of line." A rude comment can be a form of social control, as can a vigilante killing a member of a BIPOC community, and there are many forms of social control that fall between these two extremes. Am I really free to act in a certain way if I expect people to judge me for doing so and if I really care what they think? Similarly, is a Black person really free to go into a certain neighborhood if doing so means taking their life in their hands? Technically, I may be free in the first case and the Black person may be free in the second case, but both freedoms may be close to meaningless.
- Our freedom is also limited by decisions made by those with institutional decision-making power. When a state government restricts what schools can teach about racism, teachers lose the freedom to teach about racism in the ways they find most appropriate (unless they are willing to lose their jobs or risk other punishment). When the Supreme Court overturns the federal right to abortion access, women in states with antiabortion political leadership lose the ability to control their reproductive lives (unless they have the resources to travel elsewhere for abortions or to move). This type of limit on freedom is often tied to cultural processes of inequality, such that some groups of people have systematically less freedom than others. As this book demonstrates, white people have more freedom than Black people in the United States, men have more freedom than women, and heterosexual cisgender people have more freedom than LGBTQ people.

- Finally, sometimes the very social realities that enable and empower us also constrain us and limit our freedom. Consider language. Having words and a grammatical structure to describe our experiences enables us to speak, to build relationships, to obtain things we want, and to survive in society. We could not think without language and we could not communicate without words and grammar. At the same time, language limits what we can say and even what we can think. If there is no word for a particular idea in one's language, that idea is literally "inconceivable."

Sociology Can Be a Force for Equality

Sociology is not inherently ethical or unethical, liberatory or repressive, and humane or inhumane. It can be used for good or evil. Understanding how inequality works helps both those against and those in favor of inequality; understanding how social control works can help us fight it or enforce it. Both fictional and real-world authoritarian societies tend to be sociologically savvy and to use sociological insights to deepen and expand their authoritarian reach.

That said, a sociological understanding of how systemic inequality works can help us struggle against it more effectively. No form of inequality is inherently natural or immutable; all forms of inequality come down to historic and present-day human choices. *Different choices can always be made.*

When we stop taking the cultural processes that fuel inequality for granted, we recognize that they are socially constructed (though no less harmful for that) and that, therefore, they can potentially be deconstructed. Sociology can open up options that we may not have known were there previously, from how we use language to how we engage in politics. In this sense, sociology is anti-fatalistic. It offers us no guarantees but it has the potential to expand the horizons of the possible.

Sociology reminds us that the most rigid and apparently unyielding social structures are actually made and remade with every human action and interaction. This reality means that those social structures can be (and sometimes are) unmade by actions that reject the taken-for-granted assumptions upon which the structures depend. Women having the legal right to vote was inconceivable—until it wasn't. The legalization of same-sex marriage was inconceivable—until it wasn't. A Black President of the United States was inconceivable—until it wasn't.

At the same time, most human actions reproduce inequality rather than changing it, especially when those with power have stakes in maintaining the inequality. For example, the United States has not yet found it "conceivable" to provide free housing for all as a human right, to elect a female President, or to treat addiction to illegal drugs as a health-care problem rather than a criminal matter.[9] A thoughtful sociological approach to inequality acknowledges both the possibilities for which so many of us yearn and the harsh realities keeping those possibilities from coming to be. At the same time, thoughtful sociology offers insights and tools to struggle against those harsh realities.

It remains to be seen whether enough of us have the insight, energy, resources, and passion to succeed against social forces perpetuating inequality. Those forces reside behind closed doors in government buildings and other places where institutional and cultural decision-making occurs. The same anti-equality forces reside in our own hearts, embedded there during our socialization. We will need to struggle against these forces in both kinds of locations and many others as well. Sociology can help with that struggle. I hope that this book can, in its small way, contribute to the creation of a more humane, ethical, and equal world—one where everyone matters and where moral exclusion is a thing of the past.

---

9 Or, perhaps better put, it has not yet found it conceivable to do so for all people.

AFTERWORD

The 2024 U.S. elections clarify vividly the power of cultural processes of inequality. Electing a president may be one of the most important ways in which we grant or withhold the benefit of the doubt, and it has stark consequences for U.S. society and the world. A plurality of voters withheld the benefit of the doubt from a competent, smart, ethical, compassionate mixed-race woman with a concrete plan for improving the lives of working Americans. These same voters gave the benefit of the doubt to a white man who is a multiply convicted felon, adjudicated sex offender, serial adulterer, inveterate liar, and longtime racist, misogynist, homophobe, and xenophobe—someone who delights in cruelty and in inciting violence, someone whose fascist and authoritarian tendencies were public knowledge. In voting for Trump, these citizens treated in good faith someone who, by any normal understanding, had forfeited their right to be so treated based on his well-publicized acts of corruption, thievery, and an attempted overthrow of the government in order to retain power illegally.

We see the consequences of this particular granting of the benefit of the doubt in the new administration's moral exclusion of huge swaths of the country. Executive orders, cabinet appointments, public speeches, and other actions make it clear that women and other people who can get pregnant, members of Black, Indigenous, and People of Color (BIPOC) communities, immigrants, Muslims (and everyone else who is not an evangelical Christian), Lesbian, Gay, Bisexual, Transgender, Queer Plus (LGBTQ+) people, poor people, workers, and people with disabilities are being defined as outside the moral community of those whose rights and well-being matter. Indeed, the current administration's moral community really only includes wealthy white men and evangelical Christians. Ironically, some of the people who strongly supported the administration are beginning to learn that their rights and well-being do not matter to those they elected. The administration's authoritarian attack on democracy, and its resulting consolidation of power, will simply make it easier for them to punish members of devalued groups while rewarding the wealthiest and most right-wing individuals.

Several cultural processes of inequality discussed in the book are clearly on display in the actions of this administration. Rights, freedom, and liberties are defined as essential for white heterosexual conservative Christian men but are to be stripped away from BIPOC people, women, LGBTQ+ people, and members of other religious traditions—a clear case of moral alchemy. Religious freedom and freedom of speech are only important values until a religious leader such as Episcopal Bishop Mariann Edgar Budde pleads with the new administration to be merciful toward those who are now afraid, at which point religious freedom and freedom of speech are treated as problematic. Such values are fine—but only for certain people with certain messages about what religion is and what it demands.

Similarly, the president's executive order affirming the "biological reality of sex" over and against "gender ideology" is itself a fine example of gender ideology since the definition of sex provided in the executive order is not based on a scientific understanding of sex or gender. The order's declaration that "sex" is determined "at conception" has no scientific basis or merit. In this example of moral alchemy, an unscientific definition of "biological reality" that erases the lived experience of trans, intersex, and non-binary people is used to justify changing laws and practices across the land, while a more scientifically rigorous definition of "biological reality" that affirms and celebrates trans, intersex, and non-binary people is rejected as "ideology."

In Chapter 10, I discussed a particular false equivalency, Justice John Roberts' assertion that, "The way to stop discrimination on the basis of race is to stop discriminating on the basis of race." Given the extensive evidence of historic and current discrimination on the basis of race in the United States (some of which is documented in this book), I concluded that, far from opposing discrimination on the basis of race, Roberts actually supports it as long as the discrimination favors white people. For Roberts, "discrimination" is only really discrimination (and therefore problematic) if it helps BIPOC people succeed against the onslaught of racism that they face.

In ending "DEI" (diversity, equity, and inclusion) initiatives in education, workplaces, and elsewhere, the current administration has expanded on Roberts' earlier language and logic, putting policies and practices into place that benefit white people at the expense of BIPOC people. Through executive orders, departmental "dear colleague" letters and in other ways, the administration has stripped away opportunities for the United States to wrestle with, accept, and work against its historic and current racism while harming members of BIPOC communities in the process. This attack on DEI initiatives once again establishes a false equivalency between the racism undergirding U.S. history and current society on the one hand, and attempts to end that racism and make life fairer for all people in the country on the other.

Consider the language the administration uses to characterize DEI initiatives:

- "Discrimination on the basis of race, color, or national origin"
- "Illegal preferences and discrimination"
- "Racial preferences"
- "A violation of civil rights"
- The overturning of "merit-based order"
- "Illegal and morally reprehensible"
- "Repugnant race-based preferences"

On the face of it, such "discrimination" and "preferences" sound problematic, perhaps even "repugnant" and "morally reprehensible," potentially "illegal," and certainly a challenge to "civil rights" and "merit-based order." Before we accept the administration's interpretation of DEI, however, we need to put this interpretation in context:

- DEI initiatives were developed to make it possible for qualified BIPOC people to have a fair chance to compete against equally (or less) qualified white men for job opportunities and access to other resources, and would not have been necessary in a society without the degree of racism the United States has today and has always had.
- The current administration overturned the 1965 Equal Employment Opportunity Act executive order that requires equal opportunity in hiring and promotion (among other areas) regardless of race, color, religion, sex, or national origin. In overturning this executive order, the administration signaled that equal opportunity is no longer important—which means that the administration actually supports the very "preferences and discrimination" it claims to oppose as long as those preferences are for white men and as long as that discrimination benefits white men.
- Treating preferences that benefit white men as acceptable while treating preferences that benefit anyone else as unacceptable (a form of moral alchemy) signals that, from the perspective of the administration, white men are entitled to these jobs, such opportunities should be for white men and not for anyone else, and any laws that grant other people access to the opportunities meant only for white men are illegitimate.
- Overturning the equal opportunity executive order means supporting affirmative action for white men. Jettisoning equal opportunity overturns the very "merit-based order" to which the administration claims to be returning. A true merit-based order is not possible without equal

opportunity; otherwise, equally qualified BIPOC people will not be able to compete fairly against white men.

- The administration's selection of underqualified and unqualified white men (and a few white women) for cabinet positions based solely on the race and gender of those individuals (and their loyalty to the new administration) makes a mockery of any claim that the administration is prioritizing merit over other considerations.
- Finally, these actions are based on the assumption that white men are always and inevitably more qualified than BIPOC people, a clear example of giving white men the benefit of the doubt while withholding it from other people.

One last cultural process of inequality is worth mentioning in this context: the many ways in which trans, intersex, and non-binary people (and, to a lesser extent, lesbian, gay, and bisexual people) are being forced back into the kind of invisibility that I refer to as "negative invisibility" in Chapter 6. We see this most clearly in an early executive order stating that the federal government no longer recognizes the existence of trans people due to its definition of sex. This order means (among other things) that passports, social security records, and other government-issued identification documents must reflect every person's sex as assigned at birth; the documents are restricted to the designations "male" and "female." To the extent that the federal government and its documentation represents or speaks for the country, this executive order literally erases the legal existence of anyone whose gender identity falls outside the male/female binary as well as anyone whose gender identity is not identical to the identity they were assigned at birth.

Additional attacks on the visibility and well-being of trans people have included

- instructions from the Department of Education to end all trans-inclusive policies, programs, contracts, regulations, practices, and public media information;
- an order that schools receiving federal funding may not allow students to use bathrooms or lockers that best fit their gender identity or to play on the athletic teams best aligned with their identity;
- plans on the part of the Pentagon to remove all trans service members who are not willing or able to serve while identified with the sex they were assigned at birth;
- the National Parks Service's (NPS) removal of the letters "TQ+" and all mention of trans people from the Stonewall National Monument as well as the NPS website about the monument; and
- attempts to restrict gender-affirming healthcare for trans people.

More broadly, federal offices and departments that have purged all LGBTQ+ content from their websites under the new administration include the White House, the Department of State, the Department of Education, the Department of Justice, the Department of Defense, the Department of Health and Human Services, and the Department of Labor. The removed websites included extensive information of use to LGBTQ+ people and those who love them as well as providing educational information to the rest of the country about the experiences, struggles, and perspectives of these communities. Erasing the information sends a strong message that these communities, their contributions, and their well-being do not matter to the federal government.

Fortunately, many people are working to protect members of targeted communities and to challenge the above actions legally where possible. However, the extent to which the administration has chosen to use its time, energy, and resources to exclude and harm its own people (rather than using that time and energy and those resources to make life better for everyone in the country) is profoundly disturbing. Clearly, the cultural processes of inequality discussed in the book remain central to life in the United States of America and are in fact being taken up by those with the power to cause tremendous damage. Those of us who want to live in a country that gives everyone the benefit of the doubt and refuses to morally exclude people based on their identities have a lot of work ahead of us. I remain hopeful that the ideas presented in this book will equip us to work more effectively against systemic inequality now and in the days ahead.

BIBLIOGRAPHY

Abrams, Stacey, Carol Anderson, Kevin M. Kruse, Heather Cox Richardson, and Heather Ann Thompson. *Voter Suppression in U.S. Elections*. Athens, GA: University of Georgia Press, 2020.

Acker, Joan. "Hierarchies, Jobs, Bodies: A Theory of Gendered Organizations." *Gender & Society* 4 (1990): 139–158.

Acker, Joan. "Inequality Regimes: Gender, Class, and Race in Organizations." *Gender & Society* 20 (2006): 441–464.

Acquaviva, Britany L., Katherine A. Meeker, and Eryn N. O'Neal. "Blameworthy Suspects and 'Real Rape': Assessing the Effects of Rape Culture-Specific Suspect Capability Factors on the Police Decision to Arrest." *Violence against Women* 28 (2022): 3865–3885.

Adelman, Larry. "A Long History of Racial Preferences—For Whites." *PBS*, 2003. https://www.pbs.org/race/000_About/002_04-background-03-02.htm.

Agan, Amanda, and Sonja Starr. "Ban the Box, Criminal Records, and Racial Discrimination: A Field Experiment." *The Quarterly Journal of Economics* 133 (2018): 191–235.

Ahmad, Aamra, and Jeremiah Mosteler. "After 35 Years, Congress Should Finally End the Sentencing Disparity between Crack and Powder Cocaine." *The Hill*, October 27, 2021. https://thehill.com/blogs/congress-blog/politics/578693-after-35-years-congress-should-finally-end-the-sentencing/.

American Association of University Women. "Fast Facts: Women Working in Academia." *AAUW*; accessed October 24, 2023. https://www.aauw.org/resources/article/fast-facts-academia/.

American Bar Association. "New Report on Profession Focuses on Judicial Demographics." *American Bar Association*, August 1, 2022. https://www.americanbar.org/news/abanews/aba-news-archives/2022/08/new-report-on-profession/.

American Civil Liberties Union. "A Tale of Two Countries: Racially Targeted Arrests in the Era of Marijuana Reform." *ACLU*, July 1, 2020. https://www.aclu.org/sites/default/files/field_document/tale_of_two_countries_racially_targeted_arrests_in_the_era_of_marijuana_reform_revised_7.1.20._0.pdf.

Anderson, Carol. *One Person, No Vote: How Voter Suppression Is Destroying Our Democracy*. New York: Bloomsbury, 2018a.

Anderson, Carol. "Voting While Black: The Racial Injustice that Harms Our Democracy." *The Guardian*, June 7, 2018b. https://www.theguardian.com/commentisfree/2018/jun/07/black-voter-suppression-rights-america-trump.

Anderson, Elijah. *Black in White Space: The Enduring Impact of Color in Everyday Life*. Chicago: University of Chicago Press, 2022.

Anderson, Elizabeth. *The Imperative of Integration*. Princeton, NJ: Princeton University Press, 2010.

Anderson, Kathryn F. "Racial Residential Segregation and the Distribution of Health-Related Organizations in Urban Neighborhoods." *Social Problems* 64 (2017): 256–276.

Aragão, Carolina. "Gender Pay Gap in U.S. Hasn't Changed Much in Two Decades." *Pew Research Center*, March 1, 2023. https://www.pewresearch.org/short-reads/2023/03/01/gender-pay-gap-facts/.

Arnold, David, Will Dobbie, and Crystal S. Yang. "Racial Bias in Bail Decisions." *The Quarterly Journal of Economics* 133 (2018): 1885–1932.

Asch, David A., and Rachel M. Werner. "Segregated Hospitals Are Killing Black People. Data from the Pandemic Proves It." *Washington Post*, June 18, 2021. https://www.washingtonpost.com/opinions/2021/06/18/segregated-hospitals-are-killing-black-people-data-pandemic-proves-it/.

Avery, Dan. "Nearly Half of LGBTQ Adults Are Religious, U.S. Study Finds." *NBC News*, November 29, 2020. https://www.nbcnews.com/feature/nbc-out/nearly-half-lgbtq-adults-are-religious-u-s-study-finds-n1249273.

Bailey, Zinzi D., Justin M. Feldman, and Mary T. Bassett. "How Structural Racism Works—Racist Policies as a Root Cause of U.S. Racial Health Inequities." *New England Journal of Medicine* 384 (2021): 768–773.

Bailey, Zinzi D., Nancy Krieger, Madina Agénor, Jasmine Graves, Natalia Linos, and Mary T. Bassett. "Structural Racism and Health Inequities in the USA: Evidence and Interventions." *The Lancet* 389 (2017): 1453–1463.

Balko, Radley. "There's Overwhelming Evidence that the Criminal Justice System Is Racist. Here's the Proof." *Washington Post*, June 10, 2020. https://www.washingtonpost.com/graphics/2020/opinions/systemic-racism-police-evidence-criminal-justice-system/.

Balko, Radley. "What Black Cops Know about Racism in Policing." *Washington Post*, April 13, 2022. https://www.washingtonpost.com/opinions/2022/04/13/black-police-know-racism-law-enforcement/.

Ball, Carlos A. *The Morality of Gay Rights: An Exploration in Political Philosophy*. New York: Routledge, 2003.

Banco, Darcy, Jerway Chang, Nina Talmore, Priya Wadhera, Amrita Mukhopadhyay, Xinlin Yu, Siyuan Dong, Yukun Lu, Rebecca A. Betensky, Saul Becker, Basmath Safdar, and Harmony R. Reynolds. "Sex and Race Differences in the Evaluation and Treatment of Young Adults Presenting to the Emergency Department with Chest Pain." *Journal of the American Heart Association* 11 (2022): 1–10.

Barnes, Robert. "Supreme Court Rejects Race-Based Affirmative Action in College Admissions." *Washington Post*, June 29, 2023. https://www.washingtonpost.com/politics/2023/06/29/affirmative-action-supreme-court-ruling/.

Bartnik, Dominica, Paul Edward Gabriel, and Susanne Schmitz. "The Impact of Occupational Feminization on the Gender Wage Gap and Estimates of Wage Discrimination." *Applied Economic Letters* 29 (2022): 1605–1609.

Bates, Laura. "'Are You Really Going to Eat That?' Yes, and It's Nobody Else's Business." *The Guardian*, July 24, 2014. https://www.theguardian.com/lifeandstyle/womens-blog/2014/jul/24/women-meal-choices-control-female-bodies-food-policing.

BBC Editorial Staff. "Tamir Rice: US Police Kill Boy, 12, Carrying Replica Gun." *BBC*, November 24, 2014. https://www.bbc.com/news/world-us-canada-30172433.

Beacon Press. "Book Banning in the U.S.: What's Happening, Why It's Important, and What You Can Do to Fight Back." Accessed June 24, 2023. http://www.beacon.org/assets/PDFs/freethebook.pdf.

Bearman, Steve, and Marielle Amrhein. "Girls, Women, and Internalized Sexism." In *Internalized Oppression: The Psychology of Marginalized Groups*, edited by E.J.R. David, 191–225. New York: Springer Publishing Company, 2014.

Bearman, Steve, Neill Korobov, and Avril Thorne. "The Fabric of Internalized Sexism." *Journal of Integrated Social Sciences* 1 (2009): 10–47.

"Bechdel Test." Accessed February 11, 2024. https://en.wikipedia.org/wiki/Bechdel_test.

Becker, Howard S. "Whose Side Are We On?" *Social Problems* 14 (1967): 239–247.

Becker, Howard S. *Outsiders: Studies in the Sociology of Deviance*. New York: Free Press, 1973.

Bedera, Nicole, and Kristjane Nordmeyer. "'Never Go Out Alone': An Analysis of College Rape Prevention Tips." *Sexuality & Culture* 19 (2015): 533–542.

Berdejó, Carlos. "Criminalizing Race: Racial Disparities in Plea-Bargaining." *Boston College Law Review* 59 (2018): 1188–1249.

Bergold, Sebastian, and Ricarda Steinmayr. "Teacher Judgments Predict Developments in Adolescents' School Performance, Motivation, and Life Satisfaction." *Journal of Educational Psychology* 115 (2023): 642–664.

Berman, Ari. "Rigged: How Voter Suppression Threw Wisconsin to Trump." *Mother Jones*, November/December 2017. https://www.motherjones.com/politics/2017/10/voter-suppression-wisconsin-election-2016/.

Bever, Lindsey. "From Heart Disease to IUDs: How Doctors Dismiss Women's Pain." *Washington Post*, December 13, 2022. https://www.washingtonpost.com/wellness/interactive/2022/women-pain-gender-bias-doctors/.

Bever, Lindsey. "Severe Period Pain Is Often Dismissed in Teens. Many Have Endometriosis." *Washington Post*, June 26, 2023. https://www.washingtonpost.com/wellness/2023/06/26/endometriosis-period-pain-teens/.

Bivens, Donna. "What Is Internalized Racism?" Accessed March 24, 2020. https://philanthropynewyork.org/sites/default/files/files/events/What_is_Internalized_Racism.pdf.

Blackburn Center. "Why Some Women Defend Abusive Men." Blackburn Center, December 6, 2017. https://www.blackburncenter.org/post/2017/12/06/why-some-women-defend-abusive-men.

Blair, Gabrielle. *Ejaculate Responsibly: A Whole New Way to Think about Abortion*. New York: Workmen Publishing, 2022.

Blair-Loy, Mary, and Erin A. Cech. *Misconceiving Merit: Paradoxes of Excellence and Devotion in Academic Science and Engineering*. Chicago: University of Chicago Press, 2022.

Blakemore, Erin. "How the GI Bill's Promise Was Denied to a Million Black WWII Veterans." The History Channel, June 21, 2023. https://www.history.com/news/gi-bill-black-wwii-veterans-benefits.

Bland, Meredith. "Politician Opens Mouth and Reminds Us Why Men Should STFU about Abortion." ScaryMommy, December 9, 2016. https://www.scarymommy.com/politician-opens-mouth-and-reminds-us-why-men-should-stfu-about-abortion.

Blow, Charles M. "The Other Children in the DeSantis Culture War." *New York Times*, March 8, 2023. https://www.nytimes.com/2023/03/08/opinion/education-ron-desantis-crt.html.

Blumenfeld, Warren. "He's 'Assertive,' She's 'Bossy': The Double-Standard Language of Gender." *The Good Men Project*, October 14, 2017. https://goodmenproject.com/social-justice-2/hes-assertive-shes-bossy-the-double-standard-language-of-gender-wcz/.

Boddie, Elise C. "Racially Territorial Policing in Black Neighborhoods." *University of Chicago Law Review* 89 (2022): 477–498.

Bonilla-Silva, Eduardo. "The Invisible Weight of Whiteness: The Racial Grammar of Everyday Life in America." *Michigan Sociological Review* 26 (2012): 1–15.

Bonilla-Silva, Eduardo. "Rethinking Racism: Toward a Structural Interpretation." *American Sociological Review* 62 (1996): 465–480.

Bontempo, Allyson, and Lisa Mikesell. "Patient Perceptions of Misdiagnosis of Endometriosis: Results from an Online National Survey." *Diagnosis* 7 (2020): 97–106.

Brainstetter, Gillian. "How the ACLU Tracks Anti-LGBTQ Bills, and How We're Fighting Back." American Civil Liberties Union, January 23, 2023. https://www.aclu.org/news/lgbtq-rights/how-the-aclu-tracks-anti-lgbtq-bills.

Branch, Enobong Hannah, and Christina Jackson. *Black in America*. Medford, MA: Polity Press, 2020.

Brennan Center for Justice. "The Impact of Voter Suppression on Communities of Color." Brennan Center for Justice, January 10, 2022a. https://www.brennancenter.org/our-work/research-reports/impact-voter-suppression-communities-color.

Brennan Center for Justice. "Voting Laws Roundup: May 2022." Brennan Center for Justice, May 26, 2022b. https://www.brennancenter.org/our-work/research-reports/voting-laws-roundup-may-2022.

Brennan Center for Justice. "Voting Laws Roundup: February 2023." Brennan Center for Justice, February 27, 2023. https://www.brennancenter.org/our-work/research-reports/voting-laws-roundup-february-2023.

Breslin, Maureen. "Federal Judge in Texas Rules in Favor of Religious Businesses over LGBTQ Discrimination Claims." *The Hill*, November 3, 2021. https://thehill.com/legal/579816-federal-judge-in-texas-rules-in-favor-of-religious-businesses-over-lgbtq-discrimination/.

Broderick, Alicia A., and Zeus Leonardo. "What a Good Boy: The Deployment and Distribution of 'Goodness' as Ideological Property in Schools." In *DisCrit: Disability Studies and Critical Race Theory in Education*, edited by David J. Connor, Beth A. Ferri, and Subini A. Annamma, 55–67. New York: Teachers College Press, 2016.

Broome, Brian. "This Supreme Court Pits Us against Them." *Washington Post*, June 30, 2023. https://www.washingtonpost.com/opinions/2023/06/30/supreme-court-deepens-divisions/.

Buchanan, NiCole T., and Isis H. Settles. "Managing (In)visibility and Hypervisibility in the Workplace." *Journal of Vocational Behavior* 113 (2019): 1–5.

Burt, Martha R. "Cultural Myths and Supports for Rape." *Journal of Personality and Social Psychology* 38 (1980): 217–230.

Campbell, Rebecca, and Giannina Fehler-Cabral. "Why Police 'Couldn't or Wouldn't' Submit Sexual Assault Kits for Forensic DNA Testing: A Focus Concerns Theory Analysis of Untested Rape Kits." *Law & Society Review* 51 (2018): 73–105.

Campbell, Walter, Elizabeth Griffiths, and Joshua Hinkle. "The Behavior of Police: Class, Race, and Discretion in Drug Enforcement." *Police Practice and Research* 23 (2022): 337–354.

Carbado, Devon W., and Daria Roithmayr. "Critical Race Theory Meets Social Science." *Annual Review of Law and Social Science* 10 (2014): 149–167.

CarolinaForward. "NC Republican Congressman Greg Murphy: Abortion Isn't Needed Because Rape Doesn't Exist." June 29, 2022. https://www.dailykos.com/stories/2022/6/29/2107129/-NC-Republican-Congressman-Greg-Murphy-Abortion-isn-t-needed-because-rape-doesn-t-exist.

Carter Andrews, Dorinda J., and Melissa Gutwein. "'Maybe That Concept Is Still with Us:' Adolescents' Racialized and Classed Perceptions of Teachers' Expectations." *Multicultural Perspectives* 19 (2017): 5–15.

Case, Kim A., ed. *Deconstructing Privilege: Teaching and Learning as Allies in the Classroom.* New York: Routledge, 2013.

Cashin, Sheryll. *White Space, Black Hood: Opportunity Hoarding and Segregation in the Age of Inequality.* Boston: Beacon Press, 2021.

Center for American Progress. "Examining the Demographic Compositions of U.S. Circuit and District Courts." Center for American Progress, February 13, 2020. https://www.americanprogress.org/article/examining-demographic-compositions-u-s-circuit-district-courts/.

Center for American Progress. "State Attacks against LGBTQI+ Rights." Center for American Progress, April 13, 2022. https://www.americanprogress.org/article/state-attacks-against-lgbtqi-rights/.

"Central Park Bird Watching Incident." Wikipedia, accessed June 15, 2023. https://en.wikipedia.org/wiki/Central_Park_birdwatching_incident.

Century Foundation, The. "Closing America's Education Funding Gaps." The Century Foundation, July 22, 2020. https://tcf.org/content/report/closing-americas-education-funding/.

Chang, Tom Y., and Agne Kajackaite. "Battle for the Thermostat: Gender and the Effect of Temperature on Cognitive Performance." *PLoS ONE* 14 (2019): e0216362. https://doi.org/10.1371/journal.pone.0216362.

Chen, M. Keith, Kareen Haggag, Devin G. Pope, and Ryne Rohla. "Racial Disparities in Voting Wait Times: Evidence from Smartphone Data." National Bureau of Economic Research, working paper 26487, November 14, 2019. https://www.nber.org/papers/w26487#:~:text=Relative%20to%20entirely%2Dwhite%20neighborhoods,minutes%20at%20their%20polling%20place.

Chung, Christine. "Cleveland Officer Who Killed Tamir Rice Swiftly Exits New Police Job." *New York Times,* July 7, 2022. https://www.nytimes.com/2022/07/07/us/tamir-rice-timothy-loehmann-pennsylvania.html.

Clarke, Janet. "Parents Should Not Control Curriculum." *LancasterOnline*, March 28, 2023. https://lancasteronline.com/opinion/letters_to_editor/parents-should-not-control-curriculum-letter/article_b1a22eca-ccc4-11ed-b905-2fe8ed6594bb.html.

Clawson, Laura. "Incoming Florida State Speaker of the House Calls Pregnant Women 'Host Bodies'." *Alternet.org*, March 1, 2019. https://www.alternet.org/2019/03/incoming-florida-state-speaker-of-the-house-calls-pregnant-women-host-bodies/.

Colorado Springs Independent. "On the Streets of Colorado Springs…" *Colorado Springs Independent*, June 26–July 2, 2019: 12.

Congressional Research Service. "Cocaine: Crack and Powder Sentencing Disparities," November 9, 2021. https://sgp.fas.org/crs/misc/IF11965.pdf.

Corvino, John. *What's Wrong with Homosexuality?* New York: Oxford University Press, 2013.

Cottom, Tressie McMillan. *Thick and Other Essays.* New York: The New Press, 2019.

Criado Perez, Caroline. "In a World Designed for Men, the Effects for Women Range from Inconvenient to Fatal." *Washington Post*, March 11, 2019a. https://www.

washingtonpost.com/entertainment/books/in-a-world-designed-for-men-the-effects-for-women-range-from-inconvenient-to-fatal/2019/03/11/2d3b671e-41e0-11e9-a0d3-1210e58a94cf_story.html.

Criado Perez, Caroline. *Invisible Women: Data Bias in a World Designed for Men*. New York: Abrams Press, 2019b.

Dallas, Mary E. "'Religious Refusal Laws' May Take Mental Health Toll on LGBT Americans." *US News & World Report*, May 23, 2018. https://health.usnews.com/health-care/articles/2018-05-23/religious-refusal-laws-may-take-mental-health-toll-on-lgbt-americans.

Daniels, Gilda R. *Uncounted: The Crisis of Voter Suppression in America*. New York: New York University Press, 2020.

Darrah-Okike, Jennifer, Nathalie Rita, and John R. Logan. "The Suppressive Impacts of Voter Identification Requirements." *Sociological Perspectives* 64 (2021): 536–562.

David, E. J. Ramos, and Annie O. Derthick. "What Is Internalized Oppression, and So What?" In *Internalized Oppression: The Psychology of Marginalized Groups*, edited by E. J. R. David, 1–30. New York: Springer Publishing Company, 2014.

Dearden, Lizzie. "Tamir Rice: 12-Year-Old Boy Playing with Fake Gun Dies after Being Shot by Ohio Police." *UK Independent*, November 24, 2014. https://www.independent.co.uk/news/world/americas/cleveland-police-shooting-boy-with-fake-gun-dies-after-being-shot-by-ohio-officer-9878700.html.

Death Penalty Information Center. 2023. "Facts about the Death Penalty." https://dpic-cdn.org/production/documents/pdf/FactSheet.pdf.

DelGreco, Maria, Amy S. Ebesu Hubbard, and Amanda Denes. "Communicating by Catcalling: Power Dynamics and Communicative Motivations in Street Harassment." *Violence against Women* 27 (2021): 1402–1426.

Desmond, Matthew. *Poverty, by America*. New York: Crown, 2023.

Diamond, John B., and Amanda E. Lewis. "Race and Discipline at a Racially Mixed High School: Status, Capital, and the Practice of Organizational Routines." *Urban Education* 54 (2019): 831–859.

Dillbary, J. Shahar, and Griffin Edwards. "An Empirical Analysis of Sexual Orientation Discrimination." *The University of Chicago Law Review* 86 (2019): 1–76.

Dinos, Sokratis, Nina Burrowes, Karen Hammond, and Christina Cunliffe. "A Systematic Review of Juries' Assessment of Rape Victims: Do Rape Myths Impact on Juror Decision-Making?" *International Journal of Law, Crime, and Justice* 43 (2015): 36–49.

Doleac, Jennifer L., and Benjamin Hansen. "The Unintended Consequences of 'Ban the Box': Statistical Discrimination and Employment Outcomes When Criminal Histories Are Hidden." *Journal of Labor Economics* 38 (2020): 321–374.

Du Bois, William Edward Burghardt *The Souls of Black Folk*. Boston, MA: Bedford/St. Martin's Press, 1997.

Dusenbery, Maya. *Doing Harm: The Truth about How Bad Medicine and Lazy Science Leave Women Dismissed, Misdiagnosed, and Sick*. New York: HarperOne, 2019.

Duxbury, Scott W., Laura C. Frizzell, and Sadé L. Lindsay. "Mental Illness, the Media, and the Moral Politics of Mass Violence: The Role of Race in Mass Shootings Coverage." *Journal of Research in Crime and Delinquency* 55 (2018): 766–797.

Earp, Brian D., Joshua T. Monrad, Marianne LaFrance, John A. Bargh, Lindsey L. Cohen, and Jennifer A. Richeson. "Gender Bias in Pediatric Pain Assessment." *Journal of Pediatric Psychology* 44 (2019): 403–414.

Eaton, Asia A., Jessica F. Saunders, Ryan K. Jacobson, and Keon West. "How Gender and Race Stereotypes Impact the Advancement of Scholars in STEM: Professors' Biased Evaluations of Physics and Biology Post-Doctoral Candidates." *Sex Roles* 82 (2020): 127–141.

Edgell, Penny, Evan Stewart, Sarah Catherine Billups, and Ryan Larson. "The Stakes of Symbolic Boundaries." *The Sociological Quarterly* 61 (2020): 309–333.

Edwards, Frank, Hedwig Lee, and Michael Esposito. "Risk of Being Killed by Police Use of Force in the United States by Age, Race-Ethnicity, and Sex." *Proceedings of the National Academy of Sciences* 116 (2019): 16793–16798.

Edwards, Katie M., Jessica A. Turchik, Christina M. Dardis, Nicole Reynolds, and Christine A. Gidycz. "Rape Myths: History, Individual and Institutional-Level Presence, and Implications for Change." *Sex Roles* 65 (2011): 761–773.

Edwards, Torrie K., and Catherine Marshall. "Undressing Policy: A Critical Analysis of North Carolina (USA) Public School Dress Codes." *Gender and Education* 12 (2020): 732–750.

Ellis, Nicquel T. "Homes in White Neighborhoods Are being Appraised at Higher Values than in Communities of Color, New Report Finds." *CNN*, November 3, 2022. https://www.cnn.com/2022/11/03/us/home-appraisal-inequity-study-reaj/index.html.

English, Devin, Sharon F. Lambert, Brendesha M. Tynes, Lisa Bowleg, Maria Cecelia Zea, and Lionel C. Howard. "Daily Multidimensional Racial Discrimination among Black U.S. American Adolescents." *Journal of Applied Developmental Psychology* 66 (2020). https://doi.org/10.1016/j.appdev.2019.101068.

Epp, Charles R., Steven Maynard-Moody, and Donald Haider-Markel. *Pulled Over: How Police Stops Define Race and Citizenship*. Chicago: University of Chicago Press, 2014.

Equal Justice Initiative. "Report Documents Racial Bias in Coverage of Crime by Media." Equal Justice Initiative, December 16, 2021. https://eji.org/news/report-documents-racial-bias-in-coverage-of-crime-by-media/.

Evans, Erin E. "Black Attorney Says Deputy Thought He Was a Suspect and Detained Him at Court." *NBC News*, March 27, 2019. https://www.nbcnews.com/news/nbcblk/black-attorney-says-deputy-detained-him-court-because-he-thought-n988111.

Faber, Jacob W. "Segregation and the Geography of Creditworthiness: Racial Inequality in a Recovered Mortgage Market." *Housing Policy Debate* 28 (2018): 215–247.

Faber, Jacob W., and Terri Friedline. "The Racialized Costs of 'Traditional' Banking in Segregated America: Evidence from Entry-Level Checking Accounts." *Race and Social Problems* 12 (2020): 344–361.

Farmer, Paul. "Paul Farmer Quotes." Goodreads, accessed October 7, 2018. https://www.goodreads.com/author/quotes/6684.Paul_Farmer.

Favro, Marianne. "San Jose Woman Accuses Macy's of Racial Profiling in Stop-and-Search Incident." *NBC Bay Area*, May 15, 2018. https://www.nbcbayarea.com/news/local/San-Jose-Woman-Accuses-Macys-of-Racial-Profiling-in-Stop-and-Search-Incident-482738761.html.

Fernandez, Anita F., and Lovoria B. Williams. "A View of Health Disparities among African Americans through a COVID-19 Lens." *Journal of Health Care for the Poor and Underserved* 33 (2022): 437–450.

Ferguson, Claire E., and John M. Malouff. "Assessing Police Classification of Sexual Assault Reports: A Meta-Analysis of False Reporting Rates." *Archives of Sexual Behavior* 45 (2016): 1185–1193.

Ferrell, Nikki. "Cleveland Police Name Timothy Loehmann, Officer Who Shot Tamir Rice, 12, on West Side." News 5 Cleveland, November 26, 2014. https://www.news5cleveland.com/news/local-news/cleveland-metro/cleveland-police-name-timothy-loehmann-officer-who-shot-tamir-rice-12-on-west-side.

Fitzsimmons, Emma G. "12-Year-Old Boy Dies after Police in Cleveland Shoot Him." *New York Times*, November 23, 2014. https://www.nytimes.com/2014/11/24/us/boy-12-dies-after-being-shot-by-cleveland-police-officer.html.

Fleischmann, Lesley, and Marcus Franklin. "Fumes across the Fence-Line: The Health Impacts of Air Pollution from Oil & Gas Facilities on African American Communities." *NAACP*, November 2017. catf.us/resources/publications/files/FumesAcrossTheFenceLine.pdf.

Flores, Andrew R., Mark L. Hatzenbuehler, and Gary J. Gates. "Identifying Psychological Responses of Stigmatized Groups to Referendums." *Proceedings of the National Academy of Sciences* 115 (2018): 3816–2821.

Foden-Vencil, Kristian. "Emergency Medical Responders Confront Racial Bias." Kaiser Health News, January 11, 2019. https://khn.org/news/emergency-medical-responders-confrnt-racial-bias/.

Foster, Diana G. *The Turnaway Study: Ten Years, a Thousand Women, and the Consequences of Having—or Being Denied—an Abortion.* New York: Scribner, 2020.

France, Anatole. *The Red Lily.* Volume 1. New York: J. Lane, 1910.

Francis, Dania V., Angela C. M. de Oliveira, and Carey Dimmitt. "Do School Counselors Exhibit Bias in Recommending Students for Advanced Coursework?" *The B.E. Journal of Economic Analysis & Policy* 19 (2019): 1–17.

Freidus, Alexandra. "'Problem Children' and 'Children with Problems': Discipline and Innocence in a Gentrifying Elementary School." *Harvard Educational Review* 90 (2020): 550–572.

Freidus, Alexandra, and Pedro A. Noguera. "Making Difference Matter: Teaching and Learning in Desegregated Classrooms." *The Teacher Educator* 52 (2017): 99–113.

Fricker, Miranda. *Epistemic Injustice: Power and the Ethics of Knowing.* New York: Oxford University Press, 2007.

Gabbidon, Shaun L., and George E. Higgins. *Shopping while Black: Consumer Racial Profiling in America.* New York: Routledge, 2020.

Gaddis, S. Michael. "Discrimination in the Credential Society: An Audit Study of Race and College Selectivity in the Labor Market." *Social Forces* 93 (2015): 1451–1479.

Garcia, Emma. "Schools Are Still Segregated, and Black Children Are Paying a Price." Economic Policy Institute, February 12, 2020. epi.org/files/pdf/185814.pdf.

Gardner, Carol Brooks. *Passing By: Gender and Public Harassment.* Berkeley, CA: University of California Press, 1995.

Gershenson, Seth, Stephen B. Holt, and Nicholas W. Papageorge. "Who Believes in Me? The Effect of Student-Teacher Demographic Match on Teacher Expectations." *Economics of Education Review* 52 (2016): 209–224.

Glantz, Aaron, and Emmanuel Martinez. "For People of Color, Banks Are Shutting the Door to Homeownership." *Reveal News*, February 15, 2018. https://revealnews.org/article/for-people-of-color-banks-are-shutting-the-door-to-homeownership/.

Glaser, Jack, Karin D. Martin, and Kimberly B. Kahn. "Possibility of Death Sentence Has Divergent Effect on Verdicts for Black and White Defendants." *Law and Human Behavior* 39 (2015): 539–546.

GLSEN. "The 2021 National School Climate Survey: Executive Summary." *GLSEN*; accessed October 18, 2022. https://www.glsen.org/sites/default/files/2022-10/ NSCS-21-Executive_Summary-EN.pdf.

Glynn, Sarah Jane, and Diana Boesch. "Connecting the Dots: 'Women's Work' and the Wage Gap." U.S. Department of Labor Blog, March 14, 2022. https://blog.dol. gov/2022/03/15/connecting-the-dots-womens-work-and-the-wage-gap.

Golash-Boza, Tanya. "A Critical and Comprehensive Sociological Theory of Race and Racism." *Sociology of Race and Ethnicity* 2 (2016): 129–141.

Goldstone, Lawrence. *On Account of Race: The Supreme Court, White Supremacy, and the Ravaging of African American Voting Rights*. Berkeley, CA: Counterpoint, 2020.

Goosby, Bridget J., Jacob E. Cheadle, and Colter Mitchell. "Stress-Related Biosocial Mechanisms of Discrimination and African American Health Inequities." *Annual Review of Sociology* 44 (2018): 319–340.

Gopalan, Maithreyi. "Understanding the Linkages between Racial/Ethnic Discipline Gaps and the Racial/Ethnic Achievement Gaps in the United States." *Education Policy Analysis Archives* 27 (2019): 1–33.

Gould, Elise, and Katherine DeCourcy. "Gender Wage Gap Widens Even as Low-Wage Workers See Strong Gains." Working Economics Blog, March 29, 2023. https:// www.epi.org/blog/gender-wage-gap-widens-even-as-low-wage-workers-see-strong-gains-women-are-paid-roughly-22-less-than-men-on-average/.

Goyal, Monika K., Nathan Kuppermann, Sean D. Cleary, Stephen Teach, and James M. Chamberlain. "Racial Disparities in Pain Management of Children with Appendicitis in Emergency Departments." *JAMA Pediatrics* 169 (2015): 996–1002.

Graves, Joseph L. Jr., and Alan H. Goodman. *Racism Not Race: Answers to Frequently Asked Questions*. New York: Columbia University Press, 2022.

Green, Amy E., Myeshia Price-Feeney, Samuel H. Dorison, and Casey J. Pick. "Self-Reported Conversion Efforts and Suicidality among US LGBTQ Youths and Young Adults, 2018." *American Journal of Public Health* 110 (2020): 1221–1227.

Greenbaum, Susan D. *Blaming the Poor: The Long Shadow of the Moynihan Report on Cruel Images about Poverty*. New Brunswick, NJ: Rutgers University Press, 2015.

Griffith, Nicola. "Men Are Afraid that Women Will Laugh at Them." November 8, 2014. https://nicolagriffith.com/2014/11/08/men-are-afraid-that-women-will-laugh-at-them/.

Grissom, Jason A., and Christopher Redding. "Discretion and Disproportionality: Explaining the Underrepresentation of High-Achieving Students of Color in Gifted Programs." *AERA Open* 2 (2016): 1–25.

Gross, Daniel A. "How Elite US Schools Give Preference to Wealthy and White 'Legacy' Applicants." *The Guardian*, January 23, 2019. https://www.theguardian.com/us-news/ 2019/jan/23/elite-schools-ivy-league-legacy-admissions-harvard-wealthier-whiter.

Gross, Rachel E. *Vagina Obscura: An Anatomical Voyage*. New York: W.W. Norton & Company, 2022.

Gross, Samuel R., Maurice Possley, and Klara Stephens. "Race and Wrongful Convictions in the United States." National Registry of Exonerations, March 7, 2017. https://www.law.umich.edu/special/exoneration/Documents/Race_and_Wrongful_ Convictions.pdf.

Gutiérrez y Muhs, Gabriella, Yolanda Flores Niemann, Carmen G. Gonzalez, and Angela P. Harris, eds. *Presumed Incompetent: The Intersections of Race and Class for Women in Academia*. Logan: Utah State University Press, 2012.

Haan, Kathy, and Kelly Reilly. "Gender Pay Gap Statistics in 2023." *Forbes*, February 27, 2023. https://www.forbes.com/advisor/business/gender-pay-gap-statistics/.

Hajnal, Zoltan, Nazita Lajevardi, and Lindsay Nielson. "Voter Identification Laws and the Suppression of Minority Votes." *The Journal of Politics* 79 (2017): 363–379.

Hamilton, Colleen. "How Drag Artists Became the Far Right's Ultimate Villains." *Them*, December 23, 2022. https://www.them.us/story/drag-gop-right-wing-attacks-explained.

Hamilton, Rebecca. "The Sure-Fire Way to Win an Election Is..." Patheos.com, October 28, 2018. https://www.patheos.org/blogs/publiccatholic/2018/10/voter-suppression-in-10-the-sure-fire-way-to-win-an-election-is/.

Hamlett, Melanie. "Men Rigged a World Built for Them and Called It 'Neutral'—Women Call Bullshit." *Glamour*, May 7, 2019. https://www.yahoo.com/lifestyle/men-rigged-world-built-them-181714108.html.

Hannah-Jones, Nikole. *The 1619 Project: A New Origin Story*. New York: OneWorld, 2021.

Hanson, Andrew, Zackary Hawley, Hal Martin, and Bo Liu. "Discrimination in Mortgage Lending: Evidence from a Correspondence Experiment." *Journal of Urban Economics* 92 (2016): 48–65.

Harnois, Catherine E., and João L. Bastos. "Discrimination, Harassment, and Gendered Health Inequities: Do Perceptions of Workplace Mistreatment Contribute to the Gender Gap in Self-Reported Health?" *Journal of Health and Social Behavior* 59 (2018): 283–299.

Harriot, Michael. "An Incomplete List of Things Black People Should Avoid Doing So They Won't Be Killed by Police." *The Root*, March 23, 2018. https://www.theroot.com/an-incomplete-list-of-things-black-people-should-avoid-1824032408.

Harris, Fred, and Alan Curtis, eds. *Healing Our Divided Society: Investing in America Fifty Years after the Kerner Report*. Philadelphia, PA: Temple University Press, 2018.

Harris-Gershon, David. "Comparing How the New York Times Described Mike Brown & Ted Bundy." *Tikkun Daily*, August 29, 2014. https://www.tikkun.org/tikkundaily/2014/08/29/comparing-how-the-new-york-times-described-mike-brown-ted-bundy/.

Harvey, David. *A Brief History of Neoliberalism*. New York: Oxford University Press, 2005.

Haupt, Angela. "The Rise in Book Bans, Explained." *Washington Post*, June 9, 2022. https://www.washingtonpost.com/books/2022/06/09/rise-book-bans-explained/.

Hauser, Christine. "How Professionals of Color Say They Counter Bias at Work." *New York Times*, December 12, 2018. https://www.nytimes.com/2018/12/12/us/racial-bias-work.html.

Henderson, Howard, and Jennifer Wyatt Bourgeois. "Penalizing Black Hair in the Name of Academic Success Is Undeniably Racist, Unfounded, and against the Law." The Brookings Institution, February 23, 2021. https://www.brookings.edu/blog/how-we-rise/2021/02/23/penalizing-black-hair-in-the-name-of-academic-success-is-undeniably-racist-unfounded-and-against-the-law/.

Henderson, Taja-Nia Y., and Jamila Jefferson-Jones. "#LivingWhileBlack: Blackness as Nuisance." *American University Law Review* 69 (2020): 863–914.

Hesse, Monica. "The Right-Wing Drag Panic Is Not about Men Wearing Women's Clothing." *Washington Post*, March 16, 2023. https://www.washingtonpost.com/lifestyle/2023/03/16/right-wing-drag-panic-is-not-about-men-wearing-womens-clothing/.

Hewes, Hilary A., Mengtao Dai, N. Clay Mann, Tanya Baca, and Peter Taillac. "Prehospital Pain Management: Disparity by Age and Race." *Prehospital Emergency Care* 22 (2018): 189–197.

Hoffman, Jeremy S., Vivek Shandas, and Nicholas Pendleton. "The Effects of Historical Housing Policies on Resident Exposure to Intra-Urban Heat: A Study of 108 US Urban Areas." *Climate* 8 (2020). https://doi.org/10.3390/cli8010012.

Hoffman, Kelly, Sophie Trawalter, Jordan R. Axt, and M. Norman Oliver. "Racial Bias in Pain Assessment and Treatment Recommendations, and False Beliefs about Biological Differences between Blacks and Whites." *Proceedings of the National Academy of the Sciences* 113 (2016): 4296–4301.

Hoffmann, Diane E., Roger B. Fillingim, and Christin Veasley. "The Woman Who Cried Pain: Do Sex-Based Disparities Still Exist in the Experience and Treatment of Pain?" *The Journal of Law, Medicine & Ethics* 50 (2022): 519–541.

Holder, Eric, with Sam Koppelman. *Our Unfinished March: The Violent Past and Imperiled Future of the Vote: A History, A Crisis, A Plan.* New York: OneWorld, 2022.

Holder, Sarah. "A Clue to the Reason for Women's Pervasive Car-Safety Problem." CityLab, July 18, 2019. https://www.citylab.com/transportation/2019/07/car-accident-injury-safety-women-dummy-seatbelt/594049/.

Howell, Junia, and Elizabeth Korver-Glenn. "Neighborhoods, Race, and the Twenty-first-century Housing Appraisal Industry." *Sociology of Race and Ethnicity* 4 (2018): 473–590.

Hughey, Matthew W. "The Five I's of Five-O: Racial Ideologies, Institutions, Interests, Identities, and Interactions of Police Violence." *Critical Sociology* 41 (2015): 857–871.

Human Rights Campaign. "Anti-LGBTQ+ Bills in 2022." HRC, 2022. https://www.hrc.org/campaigns/the-state-legislative-attack-on-lgbtq-people#state-legislative-tracker-map.

Human Rights Campaign. "LGBTQ+ Americans under Attack: A Report and Reflection on the 2023 State Legislative Session." Human Rights Campaign, June 8, 2023. https://hrc-prod-requests.s3-us-west-2.amazonaws.com/Anti-LGBTQ-Legislation-Impact-Report.pdf.

Human Rights Campaign Foundation. "An Epidemic of Violence." November 2023. https://reports.hrc.org/an-epidemic-of-violence-2023.

Igler, Eva C., Ellen K. Defenderfer, Amy C. Lang, Kathleen Bauer, Julia Uihlein, and W. Hobart Davies. "Gender Differences in the Experience of Pain Dismissal in Adolescence." *Journal of Child Health Care* 21 (2017): 381–391.

Institute for Policy Studies. "The Souls of Poor Folk: Auditing America 50 Years after the Poor People's Campaign Challenged Racism, Poverty, the War Economy/Militarism and Our National Morality." IPS, April 2018. https://ips-dc.org/wp-content/uploads/2018/04/PPC-Audit-Full-410835a.pdf.

Institute for Women's Policy Research. "Women Earn Less than Men whether They Work in the Same or in Different Occupations." Institute for Women's Policy Research, March 2023. https://iwpr.org/women-earn-less-than-men-whether-they-work-in-the-same-or-in-different-occupations/.

Isenberg, Nancy. *White Trash: The 400-Year Untold History of Class in America.* New York: Penguin Books, 2016.

Izadi, Elahe, and Peter Holley. "Video Shows Cleveland Officer Shooting 12-Year-Old Tamir Rice within Seconds." *Washington Post*, November 26, 2014. https://www.washingtonpost.com/news/post-nation/wp/2014/11/26/officials-release-video-names-in-fatal-police-shooting-of-12-year-old-cleveland-boy/?utm_term=.8e8c283772f7.

Jackson, Katharine. "US Equal Rights Amendment Blocked Again, a Century after Introduction." Reuters, April 27, 2023. https://www.reuters.com/legal/government/us-equal-rights-amendment-blocked-again-century-after-introduction-2023-04-27/.

Jacobs, Jerry A. "Sociological Curiosity: Updating C. Wright Mills." *Contexts* 20 (2021): 34–39.

Jacobs, Tom. "More Evidence that Black Shoppers Are Subject to Racism." *Pacific Standard Magazine*, November 10, 2017. https://psmag.com/economics/more-evidence-that-black-shoppers-are-subject-to-racism.

Jan, Tracy. "Two Black Men Say They Were Kicked Out of Walmart for Wearing Protective Masks. Others Worry It Will Happen to Them." *Washington Post*, April 9, 2020. https://www.washingtonpost.com/business/2020/04/09/masks-racial-profiling-walmart-coronavirus/.

Jbaily, Abdulreahman, Xiaodan Zhou, Jie Liu, Ting-Hwan Lee, Leila Kamareddine, Stéphane Verguet, and Francesca Dominici. "Air Pollution Exposure Disparities across US Population and Income Groups." *Nature* 601 (2022): 228–233.

Johnson, Allan G. *The Forest and the Trees: Sociology as Life, Practice, and Promise.* Third Edition. Philadelphia, PA: Temple University Press, 2014a.

Johnson, Allan G. *The Gender Knot: Unraveling Our Patriarchal Legacy.* Third Edition. Philadelphia, PA: Temple University Press, 2014b.

Johnson, Allan G. *Privilege, Power, and Difference.* Second Edition. Boston, MA: McGraw-Hill, 2006.

Johnston, Olivia, Helen Wildy, and Jennifer Shand. "A Decade of Teacher Expectations Research 2008–2018: Historical Foundations, New Developments, and Future Pathways." *Australian Journal of Education* 63 (2019): 44–73.

Joseph, Nicole M., Kara Mitchell Viesca, and Margarita Bianco. "Black Female Adolescents and Racism in Schools: Experiences in a Colorblind Society." *The High School Journal* 100 (2016): 4–25.

Jost, John T. "Negative Illusions: Conceptual Clarification and Psychological Evidence Concerning False Consciousness." *Political Psychology* 16 (1995): 397–424.

Kamin, Debra. "Home Appraised with a Black Owner: $472,000. With a White Owner: $750,000." *New York Times*, August 18, 2022a. https://www.nytimes.com/2022/08/18/realestate/housing-discrimination-maryland.html.

Kamin, Debra. "Widespread Racial Bias Found in Home Appraisals." *New York Times*, November 2, 2022b. https://www.nytimes.com/2022/11/02/realestate/racial-bias-home-appraisals.html.

Kang, Sonia K., Katherine A. DeCelles, András Tilcsik, and Sora Jun. "Whitened Résumés: Race and Self-Presentation in the Labor Market." *Administrative Science Quarterly* 61 (2016): 469–502.

Katz, Jackson. "I Draw a Line Down the Middle of a Chalkboard…" Goodreads Quotable Quotes, accessed June 15, 2023. https://www.goodreads.com/quotes/905315-i-draw-a-line-down-the-middle-of-a-chalkboard.

Katz, Michael B. *The Undeserving Poor: America's Enduring Confrontation with Poverty.* Second Edition. New York: Oxford University Press, 2013.

Katznelson, Ira. *When Affirmative Action Was White: An Untold History of Racial Inequality in Twentieth-Century America.* New York: W.W. Norton & Company, 2005.

Keating, Dan, and Kevin Uhrmacher. "In Urban Areas, Police Are Consistently Much Whiter than the People They Serve." *Washington Post*, June 4, 2020. https://www.washingtonpost.com/nation/2020/06/04/urban-areas-polie-are-consistently-much-whiter-than-people-they-serve/.

Kenney, Tanasia. "8 Times the U.S. Government Gave White People Handouts to Get Ahead." *Atlanta Black Star*, June 23, 2016. https://atlantablackstar.com/2016/06/23/8-times-u-s-government-gave-white-people-handuts-to-get-ahead/.

Keyes, Starr E. "Addressing Educational Inequity of Black Students by Demolishing the School-to-Prison Pipeline." *Multicultural Learning and Teaching* 17 (2022): 123–141.

Killermann, Sam. "Heterosexual Privilege Checklist." Accessed December 1, 2018. https://projecthumanities.asu.edu/heterosexual-privilege-checklist.

Kim, Jennifer Young-Jin, Caryn J. Block, and Duoc Nguyen. "What's Visible Is My Race, What's Invisible Is My Contribution: Understanding the Effects of Race and Color-Blind Racial Attitudes on the Perceived Impact of Microaggressions toward Asians in the Workplace." *Journal of Vocational Behavior* 113 (2019): 75–87.

Kimport, Katrina. "More than a Physical Burden: Women's Mental and Emotional Work in Preventing Pregnancy." *The Journal of Sex Research* 55 (2018): 1096–1105.

King, Erica Y. "Black Men Get Longer Prison Sentences than White Men for the Same Crime: Study." *ABC News*, November 17, 2017. https://abcnews.go.com/Politics/black-men-sentenced-time-white-men-crime-study/story?id=51203491.

Klain, Hannah, Kevin Morris, Max Feldman, and Rebecca Ayala. "Waiting to Vote: Racial Disparities in Election Day Experiences." Brennan Center for Justice, 2020. https://www.brennancenter.org/our-work/research-reports/waiting-vote.

Klein, Ezra. "Transcript: Ezra Klein Interviews Tressie McMillan Cottom." *New York Times*, April 13, 2021. https://www.nytimes.com/2021/04/13/podcasts/ezra-klein-podcast-tressie-mcmillan-cottom-transcript.html.

Klein, Shayla. "Rape Is One of the Most Underreported Crimes—Here's Why." 59News, August 3, 2022. https://www.wvnstv.com/news/rape-is-one-of-the-most-underreported-crimes-heres-why/.

Kline, Patrick M., Evan K. Rose, and Christopher R. Walters. "Systemic Discrimination among Large U.S. Employers." National Bureau of Economic Research Working Paper 29053, July 2021. https://www.nber.org/system/files/working_papers/w29053/w29053.pdf.

Kochhar, Rakesh. "The Enduring Grip of the Gender Pay Gap." Pew Research Center, March 1, 2023. https://www.pewresearch.org/social-trends/2023/03/01/the-enduring-grip-of-the-gender-pay-gap/.

Kodros, John K., Michelle L. Bell, Francesca Dominici, Christian L'Orange, Krystal J. Godri Polllitt, Scott Weichenthal, Xiao Wu, and John Volckens. "Unequal Airborne Exposure to Toxic Metals Associated with Race, Ethnicity, and Segregation in the USA." *Nature Communications* 13 (2022). https://doi.org/10.1038/s41467-022-33372-z.

Kohut, Maria. "Why Do Doctors Underdiagnose These 3 Conditions in Women?" *Medical News Today*, March 8, 2019. https://www.medicalnewstoday.com/articles/324659.

Korver-Glenn, Elizabeth. *Race Brokers: Housing Markets and Segregation in 21st Century Urban America*. New York: Oxford University Press, 2021.

Kovera, Margaret B. "Racial Disparities in the Criminal Justice System: Prevalence, Causes, and a Search for Solutions." *Journal of Social Issues* 75 (2019): 1139–1164.

Krysan, Maria, and Kyle Crowder. *Cycle of Segregation: Social Processes and Residential Stratification.* New York: Russell Sage Foundation, 2017.

Laguardia, Francesca F. "Pain that Only She Must Bear: On the Invisibility of Women in Judicial Abortion Rhetoric." *Journal of Law and the Biosciences* 9 (2022). https://doi.org/10.1093/jlb/lsac003.

Lamont, Michèle. *Seeing Others: How Recognition Works—and How It Can Heal a Divided World.* New York: One Signal Publishers, 2023.

Lane, Haley M., Rachel Morello-Frosch, Julian D. Marshall, and Joshua S. Apte. "Historical Redlining Is Associated with Present-Day Air Pollution Disparities in U.S. Cities." *Environmental Science and Technology Letters*, February 22, 2022. https://pubs.acs.org/doi/pdf/10.1021/acs.estlett.1c01012.

Lasic, Gillan. "10 Ways We Can Actually End Rape." POP!, July 23, 2018. https://pop.inquirer.net/55220/10-ways-we-can-actually-end-rape.

Lauzen, Martha M. "Boxed In: Women on Screen and Behind the Scenes on Broadcast and Streaming Television in 2021–2022." Center for the Study of Women in Television and Film, 2022. https://womenintvfilm.sdsu.edu/wp-content/uploads/2023/01/2022-celluloid-ceiling-report.pdf.

Lauzen, Martha M. "The Celluloid Ceiling: Employment of Behind-the-Scenes Women on Top Grossing U.S. Films in 2022." Center for the Study of Women in Television and Film, 2023a. https://womenintvfilm.sdsu.edu/wp-content/uploads/2023/02/2022-celluloid-ceiling-report.pdf.

Lauzen, Martha M. "It's a Man's (Celluloid) World: Portrayals of Female Characters in the Top Grossing U.S. Films of 2022." Center for the Study of Women in Television and Film, 2023b. https://womenintvfilm.sdsu.edu/wp-content/uploads/2023/03/2022-its-a-mans-celluloid-world-report-rev.pdf.

Lauzen, Martha M. "Streaming Women: Representation and Employment in Original U.S. Films Released by Streaming Services in 2022." Center for the Study of Women in Television and Film, 2023c. https://womenintvfilm.sdsu.edu/wp-content/uploads/2023/05/2022-Original-Streaming-Films-Report.pdf.

Lee, Alexandra. "Where You Live Matters: Access to Key Amenities Is Worse in Communities of Color." Zillow Research, June 23, 2021. https://www.zillow.com/research/nfha-where-you-live-matters-29661/.

Lee, Jennifer J., and Janice M. McCabe. 2021. "Who Speaks and Who Listens: Revisiting the Chilly Climate in College Classrooms." *Gender & Society* 35 (2021): 32–60.

Lee, Trymaine. "A Vast Wealth Gap, Driven by Segregation, Redlining, Evictions and Exclusion, Separates Black and White America." *New York Times*, August 14, 2019. https://www.nytimes.com/interactive/2019/08/14/magazine/racial-wealth-gap.html.

Lenthang, Marlene, Melissa Chan, Antonio Planas, and Corky Siemaszko. "What We Know about the Five Memphis Police Officers Charged with Beating Tyre Nichols to Death." *NBC News*, January 27, 2023. https://www.nbcnews.com/news/us-news/what-we-know-about-memphis-police-officers-tyre-nichols-death-rcna67861.

Lepage, Brooke, and Jasmine Tucker. "A Window into the Wage Gap: What's Behind It and How to Close It." National Women's Law Center, January 2023. https://nwlc.org/resource/wage-gap-explainer/.

Lewis, Amanda E., and John B. Diamond. *Despite the Best Intentions: How Racial Inequality Thrives in Good Schools.* New York: Oxford University Press, 2015.

Lewis, J. David, and Andew J. Weigert. "Social Atomism, Holism, and Trust." *Sociological Quarterly* 26 (1985): 455–471.

LGBTQ+ Bar. "LGBTQ+ 'Panic' Defense." Accessed June 12, 2023. https://lgbtqbar. org/programs/advocacy/gay-trans-panic-defense/.

Liptak, Adam, and Abbie VanSickle. "Supreme Court Backs Web Designer Opposed to Same-Sex Marriage." *New York Times*, June 30, 2023. https://www.nytimes. com/2023/06/30/us/supreme-court-same-sex-marriage.html.

Littlejohn, Krystale E. *Just Get on the Pill: The Uneven Burden of Reproductive Politics*. Oakland: University of California Press, 2021.

Livingston, Robert. *The Conversation: How Seeking and Speaking the Truth about Racism Can Radically Transform Individuals and Corporations*. New York: Currency, 2021.

Lloyd, E. Paige, Gina A. Paganini, and Leanne ten Brinke. "Gender Stereotypes Explain Disparities in Pain Care and Inform Equitable Policies." *Policy Insights from the Behavioral and Brain Sciences* 7 (2020): 198–204.

Lukes, Steven. *Power: A Radical View: The Original Text with Two Major New Chapters*. Second Edition. New York: Palgrave Macmillan, 2005.

Maddow, Rachel. "Rachel Maddow > Quotes > Quotable Quote." Goodreads.com, accessed August 9, 2022. https://www.goodreads.com/quotes/7214148-the-thing-about-rights-is-they-re-not-actually-supposed-to.

Mahowald, Lindsay, Sharita Gruberg, and John Halpin. "The State of the LGBTQ Community in 2020: A National Public Opinion Study." Center for American Progress, 2020. https://www.americanprogress.org/issues/lgbtq-rights/reports/2020/ 10/06/491052/state-lgbtq-community-2020/.

Mai-Duc, Christine. "Cleveland Office who Killed Tamir Rice Had Been Deemed 'Unfit for Duty." *Los Angeles Times*, December 3, 2014. https://www.latimes.com/ nation/nationnow/la-na-nn-cleveland-tamir-rice-timothy-loehmann-20141203-story.html.

Manjani, Samiksha. "To the Food Police in My Life." The Women's Center at UMBC, February 15, 2019. https://womenscenteratumbc.wordpress.com/2019/02/15/to-the-food-police-in-my-life/.

Manne, Kate. *Down Girl: The Logic of Misogyny*. New York: Oxford University Press, 2018.

Manne, Kate. *Entitled: How Male Privilege Hurts Women*. New York: Crown, 2020.

Manning, Kate. "Antiabortion Laws Are Forced-Birth Laws. Here's What That Looks Like." *Washington Post*, May 31, 2022. https://www.washingtonpost.com/opinions/ 2022/05/31/antiabortion-laws-are-forced-birth-laws/.

Mapping Police Violence. "Mapping Police Violence." Updated March 31, 2023. https:// mappingpoliceviolence.org.

Marco, Tony, and Lauren DelValle. "A Group of Black Women Say a Golf Course Called the Cops on Them for Playing Too Slow." CNN, April 25, 2018. https://www.cnn. com/2018/04/25/us/black-women-golfers-pennsylvania-trnd/index.html.

McCabe, Katharine. "Criminalization of Care: Drug Testing Pregnant Patients." *Journal of Health and Social Behavior* 63 (2022): 162–176.

McGhee, Heather. *The Sum of Us: What Racism Costs Everyone and How We Can Prosper Together*. New York: OneWorld, 2021.

McGregor, Alyson J. *Sex Matters: How Male-Centric Medicine Endangers Women's Health and What We Can Do about It*. London, UK: Quercus Editions, 2020.

McIntosh, Peggy. "White Privilege: Unpacking the Invisible Knapsack." 1990. racialequitytools.org/resourcefiles/mcintosh.pdf.

McKown, Clark, and Rhona S. Weinstein. "Teacher Expectations, Classroom Context, and the Achievement Gap." *Journal of School Psychology* 46 (2008): 235–261.

McNamarah, Chan Tov. "White Caller Crime: Racialized Police Communication and Existing While Black." *Michigan Journal of Race and Law* 24 (2019): 335–415.

Medwed, Daniel S. "Black Deaths Matter: The Race-of-Victim Effect and Capital Punishment." *Brooklyn Law Review* 86 (2021): 957–973.

Mellman, Mark. "The Systemic Racism in Voting." *The Hill*, May 26, 2021. https://thehill.com/opinion/campaign/555430-mellman-the-systemic-racism-in-voting.

Menendian, Stephen, Arthur Gailes, and Samir Gambhir. "The Roots of Structural Racism: Twenty-First Century Racial Residential Segregation in the United States." Othering and Belonging Institute, University of California Berkeley, 2021. https://belonging.berkeley.edu/roots-structural-racism.

Merkin, Stacie, and Veronyka James. "Perpetrating the Myth: Exploring Media Accounts of Rape Myths on 'Women's' Networks." *Deviant Behavior* 41 (2020): 1176–1191.

Merton, Robert. "The Self-Fulfilling Prophecy." *The Antioch Review* 8 (1948): 193–210.

Mesic, Aldina, et al. "The Relationship between Structural Racism and Black-White Disparities in Fatal Police Shootings at the State Level." *Journal of the National Medical Association* 110 (2018): 106–116.

Milkman, Katherine L., Modupe Akinola, and Dolly Chugh. "What Happens Before? A Field Experiment Exploring How Pay and Representation Differentially Shape Bias on the Pathway into Organizations." *Journal of Applied Psychology* 100 (2015): 1678–1712.

Miller, Jake. "Insensitivity, or Worse, Discrimination, Takes a Significant Toll on the Health of LGBTQ Individuals." *Harvard Medicine* 93 (2020): 26–30.

Mills, C. Wright. *The Sociological Imagination*. Fortieth Anniversary Edition. New York: Oxford University Press, 2000.

Mishel, Emma. "Discrimination against Queer Women in the U.S. Workforce: A Résumé Audit Study." *Socius: Sociological Research for a Dynamic World* 2 (2016): 1–13.

Misir, Prem. *COVID-19 and Health System Segregation in the US: Racial Health Disparities and Systemic Racism*. Cham, Switzerland: Springer, 2022.

Molinari, Susan, and Beth Brooke. "Opinion: Women Are More Likely to Die or Be Injured in Car Crashes. There's a Simple Reason Why." *Washington Post*, December 21, 2021. https://www.washingtonpost.com/opinions/2021/12/21/female-crash-test-dummies-nhtsa/.

Moody-Ramirez, Mia, and Hazel Cole. "Victim Blaming in Twitter Users' Framing of Eric Garner and Michael Brown." *Journal of Black Studies* 49 (2018): 383–407.

Morris, Edward W., and Brea L. Perry. "Girls Behaving Badly? Race, Gender, and Subjective Evaluation in the Discipline of African American Girls." *Sociology of Education* 90 (2017): 127–148.

Morris, Edward W., and Brea L. Perry. "The Punishment Gap: School Suspension and Racial Disparities in Achievement." *Social Problems* 63 (2016): 68–86.

Movement Advancement Project. "Bans on Best Practice Medical Care for Transgender Youth." Movement Advancement Project, 2023a. https://www.lgbtmap.org/equality-maps/healthcare/youth_medical_care_bans.

Movement Advancement Project. "Equality Maps: LGBTQ Curricular Laws." Movement Advancement Project, 2023b. https://www.lgbtmap.org/equality_maps/curricular_laws.

Movement Advancement Project. "Equality Maps: Religious Exemption Laws." Movement Advancement Project, 2023c. https://www.lgbtmap.org/equality-maps/religious_exemption_laws.

Movement Advancement Project. "LGBTQ Policy Spotlight: Bans on Medical Care for Transgender People." April, 2023d. https://www.mapresearch.org/2023-medical-care-bans-report.

Movement Advancement Project. "Under Fire: Banning Medical Care and Legal Recognition for Transgender People." September, 2023e. https://www.mapresearch.org/under-fire-report.

Movement Advancement Project. "Under Fire: Erasing LGBTQ People from Schools and Public Life." March, 2023f. https://www.mapresearch.org/under-fire-report.

Movement Advancement Project. "Under Fire: Erecting Systematic and Structural Barriers to Make Change Harder." June, 2023g. https://www.mapresearch.org/under-fire-report.

Moyano, Nieves, and María del Mar Sánchez-Fuentes. "Homophobic Bullying at Schools: A Systematic Review of Research, Prevalence, School-Related Predictors and Consequences." *Aggression and Violent Behavior* 53 (2020). https://doi.org/10.1016/j.avb.2020.101441.

Mullen, Shannon, Lisa Robyn Kruse, Andrew J. Goudsward, and Austin Bogues. "Crack vs. Heroin: An Unfair System Arrested Millions of Blacks, Urged Compassion for Whites." *Asbury Park Press*, June 17, 2019. https://www.eveningsun.com/in-depth/news/local/public-safety/2019/12/02/crack-heroin-race-arrests-blacks-whites/2524961002/.

Murdock-Perriera, Lisel Alice, and Quentin Charles Sedlacek. "Questioning Pygmalion in the Twenty-First Century: The Formation, Transmission, and Attributional Influence of Teacher Expectancies." *Social Psychology of Education* 21 (2018): 691–707.

Musto, Michela. "Brilliant or Bad: The Gendered Social Construction of Exceptionalism in Early Adolescence." *American Sociological Review* 84 (2019): 369–393.

Nardone, Anthony, Joey Chiang, and Jason Corburn. "Historic Redlining and Urban Health Today in U.S. Cities." *Environmental Justice* 13 (2020): 109–119.

Nasir, Na'ilah Suad, Cyndy R. Snyder, Nirah Shah, and Kihana Miraya Ross. "Racial Storylines and Implications for Learning." *Human Development* 55 (2012): 285–301.

Netherland, Julie, and Helena B. Hansen. "The War on Drugs that Wasn't: Wasted Whiteness, 'Dirty Doctors,' and Race in Media Coverage of Prescription Opioid Misuse." *Culture, Medicine & Psychiatry* 40 (2016): 664–686.

New York Times Editorial Board. "End Legacy College Admissions." *New York Times*, September 7, 2019. https://www.nytimes.com/2019/09/07/opinion/sunday/end-legacy-college-admissions.html.

New York Times Editorial Board. "The Supreme Court Turns 'Equal Protection' Upside Down." June 30, 2023. https://www.nytimes.com/2023/06/30/opinion/editorials/supreme-court-affirmative-action-decision.html.

Newman, David M. *Identities and Inequalities: Exploring the Intersections of Race, Class, Gender and Sexuality*. Fourth Edition. New York: McGraw-Hill, 2022.

Niedringhaus, Cassa. "Boulder Council Grills Police Chief, Community Speaks Out about Officers Confronting Black Man Picking Up Trash." *Denver Post*, March 5, 2019. https://www.denverpost.com/2019/03/05/boulder-council-officers-black-man-picking-up-trash/.

Niemann, Yolanda Flores, Gabriella Gutiérrez y Muhs, Yolanda Flores Niemann, and Carmen G. Gonzalez, eds. *Presumed Incompetent II; Race, Class, Power, and Resistance of Women in Academia*. Logan: Utah State University Press, 2020.

Nunley, John M., Adam Pugh, Nicholas Romero, and Richard Alan Seals, Jr. "An Examination of Racial Discrimination in the Labor Market for Recent College Graduates: Estimates from the Field." Auburn University Department of Economics Working Paper 2014–06, 2014. https://cla.auburn.edu/econwp/archives/2014/2014-06.pdf.

O'Neal, Eryn Nicole. "'Victim Is Not Credible': The Influence of Rape Culture on Police Perceptions of Sexual Assault Complainants." *Justice Quarterly* 36 (2019): 127–160.

Ogles, Jacob. "Ron DeSantis Signs 'Right to Discriminate' Law that Could Be Used against LGBTQ+ Patients." *The Advocate*, May 13, 2023. https://www.advocate.com/politics/ron-desantis-discriminate-law-lgbtq.

Opotow, Susan. "Moral Exclusion and Injustice: An Introduction." *Journal of Social Issues* 46 (1990): 1–20.

Opotow, Susan. "How This Was Possible: Interpreting the Holocaust." *Journal of Social Issues* 67 (2011): 205–224.

Opotow, Susan, Janet Gerson, and Sarah Woodside. "From Moral Exclusion to Moral Inclusion: Theory for Teaching Peace." *Theory into Practice* 44 (2005): 303–318.

"Ordination of Women." Wikipedia, accessed December 28, 2022. https://en.wikipedia.org/wiki/Ordination_of_women.

Owens, Ann. "Unequal Opportunity: School and Neighborhood Segregation in the USA." *Race and Social Problems* 12 (2020): 29–41.

Owens, Ann, and Jennifer Candipan. "Social and Spatial Inequalities of Educational Opportunity: A Portrait of Schools Serving High- and Low-Income Neighborhoods in US Metropolitan Areas." *Urban Studies* 56 (2019): 3178–3197.

Owens, Jayanti. "Double Jeopardy: Teacher Biases, Racialized Organizations, and the Production of Racial/Ethnic Disparities in School Discipline." *American Sociological Review* 87 (2022): 1007–1048.

Ozier, Elise M., Valerie Jones Taylor, and Mary C. Murphy. "The Cognitive Effects of Experiencing and Observing Subtle Racial Discrimination." *Journal of Social Issues* 75 (2019): 1087–1115.

Padgaonkar, Namita T., Paul J. Frick, Laurence Steinberg, and Elizabeth Cauffman. "Exploring Disproportionate Minority Contact in the Juvenile Justice System Over the Year Following First Arrest." *Journal of Research on Adolescence* 31 (2020): 317–334.

Pager, Devah, Bruce Western, and Bart Bonikowski. "Discrimination in a Low-Wage Labor Market: A Field Experiment." *American Sociological Review* 74 (2009): 777–799.

Patterson, Orlando. "Making Sense of Culture." *Annual Review of Sociology* 40 (2014): 1–30.

Paul, Harpreet Kaur. "Climate Change: IPCC Report Reveals How Inequality Makes Impacts Worse—and What to Do about It." *The Conversation*, March 2, 2022. https://theconversation.com/climate-change-ipcc-report-reveals-how-inequality-makes-impacts-worse-and-what-to-do-about-it-178049.

Pearman, Francis A., II, F. Chris Curran, Benjamin Fisher, and Joseph Gardella. "Are Achievement Gaps Related to Discipline Gaps? Evidence from National Data." *AERA Open* 5 (2019): 1–18.

PEN America. "Banned in the USA: State Laws Supercharge Book Suppression in Schools." *PEN America*, 2023. https://pen.org/report/banned-in-the-usa-state-laws-supercharge-book-suppression-in-schools.

Percy, Jen. "What People Misunderstand about Rape." *New York Times*, August 22, 2023. https://www.nytimes.com/2023/08/22/magazine/immobility-rape-trauma-freeze.html.

Perry, Andre, Jonathan Rockwell, and David Harshbarger. *The Devaluation of Assets in Black Neighborhoods: The Case of Residential Property*. Washington, DC: Brookings Institute Metropolitan Policy Program, 2018.

Peters, Rebecca T. *Trust Women: A Progressive Christian Argument for Reproductive Justice*. Boston: Beacon Press, 2018.

Pheterson, Gail. "Alliances between Women: Overcoming Internalized Oppression and Internalized Domination." *Signs: Journal of Women in Culture and Society* 12 (1986): 146–160.

Phillips, Scott, and Justin Marceau. "Whom the State Kills." *Harvard Civil Rights—Civil Liberties Law Review*, 2020. https://harvardcrcl.org/wp-content/uploads/sites/10/2020/07/07.30.2020-Phillips-Marceau-For-Website.pdf.

Pierson, Emma, et al. "A Large-Scale Analysis of Racial Disparities in Police Stops across the United States." *Nature Human Behavior* 4 (2020): 736–745.

Pittman, Cassi. " 'Shopping while Black': Black Consumers' Management of Racial Stigma and Racial Profiling in Retail Settings." *Journal of Consumer Culture* 20 (2020): 3–22.

Pollitt, Katha. *Pro: Reclaiming Abortion Rights*. New York: Picador, 2014.

Portillo, Shannon, Dominic Bearfield, and Norma M. Riccucci. "The Disenfranchisement of Voters of Color: Redux." *Public Integrity* 23 (2020): 111–128.

Pyke, Karen D. "What Is Internalized Racial Oppression and Why Don't We Study It? Acknowledging Racism's Hidden Injuries." *Sociological Perspectives* 53 (2010): 551–572.

Quadlin, Natasha. "The Mark of a Woman's Record: Gender and Academic Performance in Hiring." *American Sociological Review* 83 (2018): 331–360.

Quillian, Lincoln. "Does Segregation Create Winners and Losers? Residential Segregation and Inequality in Educational Attainment." *Social Problems* 61 (2014): 402–426.

Quillian, Lincoln, John J. Lee, and Brandon Honoré. "Racial Discrimination in the U.S. Housing and Mortgage Lending Markets: A Quantitative Review of Trends, 1976–2016." *Race and Social Problems* 12 (2020): 13–28.

Quillian, Lincoln, John J. Lee, and Mariana Oliver. "Evidence from Field Experiments in Hiring Shows Substantial Additional Racial Discrimination after the Callback." *Social Forces* 99 (2020): 732–759.

Quillian, Lincoln, and Arnfinn H. Midtbøen. "Comparative Perspectives on Racial Discrimination in Hiring: The Rise of Field Experiments." *Annual Review of Sociology* 47 (2021): 391–415.

Quillian, Lincoln, Devah Pager, Ole Hexel, and Arnfinn H. Midtbøen. "Meta-Analysis of Field Experiments Shows No Change in Racial Discrimination in Hiring Over Time." *Proceedings of the National Academy of Sciences* 114 (2017): 10870–10875.

Raikes, Jeff, and Linda Darling-Hammond. "Why Our Education Funding Systems Are Derailing the American Dream." Learning Policy Institute, February 18, 2019. https://learningpolicyinstitute.org/blog/why-our-education-funding-systems-are-derailing-american-dream.

Ramey, David M. "The Social Structure of Criminalized and Medicalized School Discipline." *Sociology of Education* 88 (2015): 181–201.

"The Rape of Mr. Smith, 2012: With New & Improved Victim-Blaming!" Kyriolexy, September 1, 2012. https://speakingon.wordpress.com/2012/09/01/the-rape-of-mr-smith-2012/.

Ray, Victor. "A Theory of Racialized Organizations." *American Sociological Review* 84 (2019): 26–53.

Ray, Victor. *On Critical Race Theory: Why It Matters and Why You Should Care.* New York: Random House, 2022.

Real, Julian. "Male Privilege Checklist." Accessed December 1, 2018 https://projecthumanities.asu.edu/male-privilege-checklist.

Reflective Democracy Campaign. "Abortion Bans and Minority Rule." Women Donors Network, May 2022. https://wholeads.us/wp-content/uploads/2022/05/rdc-briefingmemo-2022may-abortionbans.pdf.

Reflective Democracy Campaign. "Confronting the Demographics of Power: America's Sheriffs." Women Donors Network, June 2020. https://wholeads.us/wp-content/uploads/2020/06/reflectivedemocracy-americassheriffs-06.04.2020.pdf.

Reid, Jonathan C., and Miltonette O. Craig. "Is It a Rally or a Riot? Racialized Media Framing of 2020 Protests in the United States." *Journal of Ethnicity in Criminal Justice* 19 (2021): 291–310.

Reiman, Jeffrey, and Paul Leighton. *The Rich Get Richer and the Poor Get Prison: Thinking Critically about Class and Criminal Justice.* Twelfth Edition. New York: Routledge, 2020.

Richardson, Jason, Bruce C. Mitchell, Jad Edlebi, Helen C. S. Meier, and Emily Lynch. "The Lasting Impact of Historic 'Redlining' on Neighborhood Health: Higher Prevalence of COVID-19 Risk Factors." National Community Reinvestment Coalition, September 10, 2020. https://ncrc.org/holc-health/.

Ridgeway, Cecilia L., Rachel M. Korn, and Joan C. Williams. "Documenting the Routine Burden of Devalued Difference in the Professional Workplace." *Gender & Society* 36 (2022): 627–651.

Rivera, Lauren A. *Pedigree: How Elite Students Get Elite Jobs.* Princeton, NJ: Princeton University Press, 2015.

Roithmayr, Daria. *Reproducing Racism: How Everyday Choices Lock in White Advantage.* New York: New York University Press, 2014.

Rooney, Emma. "The Effects of Sexual Objectification on Women's Mental Health." *Applied Psychology Opus*, 2021. https://wp.nyu.edu/steinhardt-appsych_opus/the-effects-of-sexual-objectification-on-womens-mental-health/.

Rosner, Helen. "The Long American History of 'Missing White Woman Syndrome'." *The New Yorker*, October 8, 2021. https://www.newyorker.com/q-and-a/the-long-american-history-of-missing-white-woman-syndrome.

Rothstein, Richard. *The Color of Law: A Forgotten History of How Our Government Segregated America.* New York: Liveright Publishing, 2017.

Rothstein, Richard, and Leah Rothstein. *Just Action: How to Challenge Segregation Enacted under the Color of Law.* New York: Liveright Publishing Corporation, 2023.

Rugh, Jacob S. "Why Black and Latino Home Ownership Matter to the Color Line and Multiracial Democracy." *Race and Social Problems* 12 (2020): 57–76.

Russo, Omar T. "How to Get Away with Murder: The 'Gay Panic' Defense." *Touro Law Review* 35 (2019). https://digitalcommons.tourolaw.edu/lawreview/vol35/iss2/9/.

Salam, Maya. "What Is the Equal Rights Amendment, and Why Are We Talking about It Now?" *New York Times*, February 22, 2019. https://www.nytimes.com/2019/02/22/us/equal-rights-amendment-what-is-it.html.

Samulowitz, Anke, Ida Gremyr, Erik Eriksson, and Gunnel Hensing. "'Brave Men' and 'Emotional Women': A Theory-Guided Literature Review on Gender Bias in Health Care and Gendered Norms towards Patients with Chronic Pain." *Pain Research and Management* February 25, 2018, Article ID 6358624. https://doi.org/10.1155/2018/6358624.

Sanger, Carol. *About Abortion: Terminating Pregnancy in Twenty-First-Century America*. Cambridge, MA: Harvard University Press, 2017.

Schaeffer, Katherine. "The Changing Face of Congress in 8 Charts." *Pew Research Center*, February 7, 2023. https://www.pewresearch.org/short-reads/2023/02/07/the-changing-face-of-congress/.

Schilt, Kristen. *Just One of the Guys? Transgender Men and the Persistence of Gender Inequality*. Chicago: University of Chicago Press, 2010.

Schmidt, Brie. "What Is the Average Weight for a Woman in the US?" *The List*, June 9, 2022. https://www.thelist.com/890274/what-is-the-average-weight-for-a-woman-in-the-us/.

Schwalbe, Michael. *Making a Difference: Using Sociology to Create a Better World*. New York: Oxford University Press, 2020.

Schwalbe, Michael. *Rigging the Game: How Inequality Is Reproduced in Everyday Life*. Second Edition. New York: Oxford University Press, 2015.

Schwalbe, Michael. *The Sociologically Examined Life: Pieces of the Conversation*. Fifth Edition. New York: Oxford University Press, 2018.

Schwartz, Sarah. "Map: Where Critical Race Theory Is under Attack." *EducationWeek*, updated May 5, 2023. https://www.edweek.org/policy-politics/map-where-critical-race-theory-is-under-attack/2021/06.

Schwegman, David. "Rental Market Discrimination against Same-Sex Couples: Evidence from a Pairwise-Matched Email Correspondence Test." *Housing Policy Debate* 29 (2019): 250–272.

Scientific American Editorial Staff. "Why We Must Protect Voting Rights." *Scientific American*, April 1, 2022. https://www.scientificamerican.com/article/why-we-must-protect-voting-rights/.

Seale, Elizabeth. *Understanding Poverty: A Relational Approach*. Hoboken, NJ: Polity Press, 2023.

The Sentencing Project. "The Color of Justice: Racial and Ethnic Disparity in State Prisons." The Sentencing Project, 2021a. The-Color-of-Justice-Racial-and-Ethnic-Disparities-in-State-Prisons.pdf.

The Sentencing Project. "Racial Disparities in Youth Incarceration Persist." The Sentencing Project, 2021b. Racial-Disparities-in-Youth-Incarceration-Persist.pdf.

Serano, Julia. "He's Unmarked, She's Marked." In *Believe Me: How Trusting Women Can Change the World*, edited by Jessica Valenti and Jaclyn Friedman, 51–63. New York: Seal Press, 2020.

Settles, Isis S., NiCole T. Buchanan, and Kristie Dotson. "Scrutinized but Not Recognized: (In)visibility and Hypervisibility Experiences of Faculty of Color." *Journal of Vocational Behavior* 113 (2019): 62–74.

Settles, Isis S., Martinique K. Jones, NiCole T. Buchanan, and Kristie Dotson. "Epistemic Exclusion: Scholar(ly) Devaluation that Marginalizes Faculty of Color." *Journal of Diversity in Higher Education* 14 (2021): 493–507.

Shaw, Jessica, Rebecca Campbell, Debi Cain, and Hannah Feeney. "Beyond Surveys and Scales: How Rape Myths Manifest in Sexual Assault Police Records." *Psychology of Violence* 7 (2017): 602–614.

Shin, Annys, Nick Kirkpatrick, and Anne Branigin. "Anti-Trans Bills Have Doubled Since 2022. Our Map Shows Where States Stand." *Washington Post*, May 19, 2023. https://www.washingtonpost.com/dc-md-va/2023/04/17/anti-trans-bills-map/.

Siegel, Rachel. "Nordstrom Rack Apologizes after Calling the Police on Three Black Teens Who Were Shopping for Prom." *Washington Post*, May 9, 2018. https://www.washingtonpost.com/news/business/wp/2018/05/08/nordstrom-rack-called-the-police-on-three-black-teens-who-were-shopping-for-prom/?utm_term=.b9d11943ac05.

Sieghart, Mary Ann. *The Authority Gap: Why Women Are Still Taken Less Seriously than Men and What We Can Do about It*. New York: W.W. Norton & Company, 2021.

Sima, Richard. "Racism Takes a Toll on the Brain, Research Shows." *Washington Post*, February 16, 2023. https://www.washingtonpost.com/wellness/2023/02/16/racism-brain-mental-health-impact/.

Simons, Ronald L., Man-Kit Lei, Steven R. H. Beach, Ashley B. Barr, Leslie G. Simons, Frederick X. Gibbons, and Robert A. Philibert. "Discrimination, Segregation, and Chronic Inflammation: Testing the Weathering Explanation for the Poor Health of Black Americans." *Developmental Psychology* 54 (2018):1993–2006.

Singhal, Astha, Yu-Yu Tien, and Renee Y. Hsia. "Racial-Ethnic Disparities in Opioid Prescriptions at Emergency Department Visits for Conditions Commonly Associated with Prescription Drug Abuse." *PLOS One* 11 (2016): e0159224. Doi: 10.1371/journal.pone.0159224.

Singletary, Michelle. "Being Black Lowers the Value of My Home: The Legacy of Redlining." *Washington Post*, October 23, 2020. https://www.washingtonpost.com/business/2020/10/23/redlining-black-wealth/.

Singletary, Michelle. "Shopping while Black. African Americans Continue to Face Retail Racism." *Washington Post*, May 17, 2018. https://www.washingtonpost.com/news/get-there/wp/2018/05/17/shopping-while-black-african-americans-continue-to-face-retail-racism/?utm_term=.6db02f5c2e5c.

Slakoff, Danielle C., and Pauline K. Brennan. "The Differential Representation of Latina and Black Female Victims in Front-Page News Stories: A Qualitative Document Analysis." *Feminist Criminology* 14 (2019): 488–516.

Slakoff, Danielle C., and Henry F. Fradella. "Media Messages Surrounding Missing Women and Girls: The 'Missing White Woman Syndrome" and Other Factors that Influence Newsworthiness." *Criminology, Criminal Justice, Law & Society* 20 (2019): 80–102.

Smiley, CalvinJohn, and David Fakunle. "From 'Brute' to 'Thug:' The Demonization and Criminalization of Unarmed Black Male Victims in America." *Journal of Human Behavior in the Social Environment* 26 (2016): 350–366.

Smith, Jordan. "Oklahoma Lawmakers Want Men to Approve All Abortions." *The Intercept*, February 13, 2017. https://theintercept.com/2017/02/13/oklahoma-lawmakers-want-men-to-approve-all-abortions/.

Smith, Stacy L., Katherine Pieper, and Sam Wheeler. "Inclusion in the Director's Chair: Analysis of Director Gender and Race/Ethnicity across the 1,600 Top Films from 2007 to 2022." Annenberg Inclusion Initiative, January 2023. https://assets.uscannenberg.org/docs/aii-inclusion-directors-2023.pdf.

Smolkowski, Keith, Erik J. Girvan, Kent McIntosh, Rhonda N. T. Nese, and Robert H. Horner. "Vulnerable Decision Points for Disproportionate Office Discipline Referrals: Comparisons of Discipline for African American and White Elementary School Students." *Behavioral Disorders* 41 (2016): 178–195.

Solnit, Rebecca. *Whose Story Is This? Old Conflicts, New Chapters*. Chicago, IL: Haymarket Books, 2019.

Sommers, Zach. "Missing White Woman Syndrome: An Empirical Analysis of Race and Gender Disparities in Online News Coverage of Missing Persons." *The Journal of Criminal Law & Criminology* 106 (2017): 275–314.

Stacey, Lawrence, Rin Reczek, and Ryan Spiker. "Toward a Holistic Demographic Profile of Sexual and Gender Minority Well-Being." *Demography* 59 (2022): 1403–1430.

Steele, Claude M. *Whistling Vivaldi: How Stereotypes Affect Us and What We Can Do.* New York: Norton, 2010.

Stevenson, Bryan. *Just Mercy: A Story of Justice and Redemption.* New York: OneWorld, 2014.

St. George, Suzanne, and Cassia Spohn. "Liberating Discretion: The Effect of Rape Myth Factors on Prosecutors' Decisions to Charge Suspects in Penetrative and Non-Penetrative Sex Offenses." *Justice Quarterly* 35 (2018): 1280–1308.

Stuber, Jenny M. *Exploring Inequality: A Sociological Approach.* Second Edition. Los Angeles, CA: Sage Publications, 2022.

Sue, Derald Wing. *Microaggressions in Everyday Life: Race, Gender, and Sexual Orientation.* Hoboken, NJ: John Wiley & Sons, 2010.

Sun, Hua, and Lei Gao. "Lending Practices to Same-Sex Borrowers." *Proceedings of the National Academy of Sciences* 116 (2019): 9293–9302.

Susaneck, Adam P. "American Road Deaths Show an Alarming Racial Gap." *New York Times*, April 26, 2023. https://www.nytimes.com/interactive/2023/04/26/opinion/road-deaths-racial-gap.html.

Swidler, Ann. "Culture in Action: Symbols and Strategies." *American Sociological Review* 51 (1986): 273–286.

Tasca, Melinda, Nancy Rodriguez, Cassia Spohn, and Mary P. Ross. "Police Decision Making in Sexual Assault Cases: Predictors of Suspect Identification and Arrest." *Journal of Interpersonal Violence* 28 (2012): 1157–1177.

Tatum, Beverly Daniel. *Why Are All the Black Kids Sitting Together in the Cafeteria? And Other Conversations about Race.* Twentieth Anniversary Edition, Revised and Updated. New York: Basic Books, 2017.

Tavris, Carol. *The Mismeasure of Woman: Why Women Are Not the Better Sex, the Inferior Sex, or the Opposite Sex.* New York: Touchstone, 1992.

Taylor, Jessica. *Why Women Are Blamed for Everything: Exposing the Culture of Victim-Blaming.* London: Constable, 2020.

Taylor, Keeanga-Yamahtta. *Race for Profit: How Banks and the Real Estate Industry Undermined Black Homeownership.* Chapel Hill, NC: University of North Carolina Press, 2019.

"Ted Bundy." Wikipedia, accessed November 6, 2023. https://en.wikipedia.org/wiki/Ted_Bundy.

Tessum, Christopher W., David A. Paolella, Sarah E. Chambliss, Joshua S. Apte, Jason D. Hill, and Julian D. Marshall. "PM2.5 Polluters Disproportionately and Systemically Affect People of Color in the United States." *Science Advances* 7 (2021). https://doi.org/10.1126/sciadv.abf4491.

Thomas, John C., and Jonathan Kopel. "Male Victims of Sexual Assault: A Review of the Literature." *Behavioral Sciences* 13 (2023): 304–325.

Thomas, William I., and Dorothy S. Thomas. *The Child in America: Behavior Problems and Programs.* New York: Knopf, 1928.

Tilly, Charles. *Durable Inequality.* Berkeley, CA: University of California Press, 1998.

Traister, Rebecca. "Let's Just Say It: Women Matter More than Fetuses Do." *The New Republic*, November 11, 2014. https://newrepublic.com/article/120167/womens-abortion-rights-trump-fetuses-rights.

Traister, Rebecca. "The Necessity of Hope." *The Cut,* June 24, 2022. https://www.thecut.com/2022/06/rebecca-traister-on-the-necessity-of-hope.html.

Trevor Project. "The Trevor Project 2022 National Survey on LGBTQ Youth Mental Health." Trevor Project, 2022. https://www.thetrevorproject.org/survey-2022/assets/static/trevor01_2022survey_final.pdf.

Tuerkheimer, Deborah. *Credible: Why We Doubt Accusers and Protect Abusers.* New York: HarperCollins, 2021.

Udis-Kessler, Amanda. *Abundant Lives: A Progressive Christian Ethic of Flourishing.* Cleveland, OH: Pilgrim Press, 2024.

Udis-Kessler, Amanda. *Queer Inclusion in the United Methodist Church.* New York: Routledge, 2008.

Umberson, Debra. "Black Deaths Matter: Race, Relationship Loss, and Effects on Survivors." *Journal of Health and Social Behavior* 58 (2017): 405–420.

United States Census Bureau. "Race and Ethnicity in the United States: 2010 Census and 2020 Census." US Census Bureau, 2021. https://www.census.gov/library/visualizations/interactive/race-and-ethnicity-in-the-united-state-2010-and-2020-census.html.

United States Federal Bureau of Investigation. "2019 Crime in the United States: Expanded Homicide Data Table 6." Accessed June 15, 2023. https://ucr.fbi.gov/crime-in-the-u.s/2019/crime-in-the-u.s.-2019/tables/expanded-homicide-data-table-6.xls.

United States Sentencing Commission. "Quick Facts: Sexual Abuse Offenders." U.S. Sentencing Commission, 2022. https://www.ussc.gov/sites/default/files/pdf/research-and-publications/quick-facts/Sexual_Abuse_FY22.pdf.

University of California San Diego Center on Gender Equity and Health/Stop Street Harassment. "Measuring #MeToo: A National Study on Sexual Harassment and Assault." UCSD Center on Gender Equity and Health/Stop Street Harassment, April 2019. https://promundoglobal.org/wp-content/uploads/2019/04/2019-MeToo-National-Sexual-Harassment-and-Assault-Report.pdf.

Valenti, Jessica. "Anti-Abortion Lawmakers Have No Idea How Women's Bodies Work." *Medium,* May 15, 2019. https://medium.com/s/jessica-valenti-anti-abortion-lawmakers-have-no-idea-how-womens-bodies-work-3ebea9fd6015.

Van Cleve, Nicole Gonzalez. *Crook County: Racism and Injustice in America's Largest Criminal Court.* Stanford, CA: Stanford University Press, 2016.

Venema, Rachel M. "Police Officer Schema of Sexual Assault Reports: Real Rape, Ambiguous Cases, and False Reports." *Journal of Interpersonal Violence* 3 (2016): 872–899.

Wang, Shengnan, Christine M. Rubie-Davies, and Kane Meissel. "A Systematic Review of the Teacher Expectation Literature over the Past 30 Years." *Educational Research and Evaluation* 24 (2018): 124–179.

Washington, Harriet A. *A Terrible Thing to Waste: Environmental Racism and Its Assault on the American Mind.* New York: Little, Brown Spark, 2019.

Washington Post. "Fatal Force: 1,083 People Have Been Shot and Killed by Police in the Past 12 Months." *Washington Post,* May 25, 2023. https://www.washingtonpost.com/graphics/investigations/police-shootings-database/.

Watson, Katie. *The Scarlet A: The Ethics, Law, and Politics of Ordinary Abortion.* New York: Oxford University Press, 2018.

Weiser, Dana A. "Confronting Myths about Sexual Assault: A Feminist Analysis of the False Report Literature." *Family Relations* 66 (2017): 46–60.

Westerfeld, Adrienne. "Watch a Never-Before-Aired James Baldwin Interview from 1979." *Esquire*, June 15, 2021. https://www.esquire.com/entertainment/books/a36727428/james-baldwin-1979-abc-interview-buried-surfaced/.

What We Know. "What Does the Scholarly Research Say about the Effects of Discrimination on the Health of LGBT People?" Cornell University Public Policy Research Portal, 2019. LGBT-Discrimination-Printable-Findings-121319.pdf.

Williams, Joan C., Matina Multhaup, Su Li, and Rachel Korn. "You Can't Change What You Can't See: Interrupting Racial & Gender Bias in the Legal Profession." American Bar Association Commission on Women in the Profession/Minority Corporate Counsel Association, 2018. https://www.americanbar.org/content/dam/aba/administrative/women/you-cant-change-what-you-cant-see-print.pdf.

Willingham, Alexandra J. "Researchers Studied Nearly 100 Million Traffic Stops and Found Black Motorists Are More Likely to Be Pulled Over." *CNN*, March 21, 2019. https://www.cnn.com/2019/03/21/us/police-stops-race-stanford-study-trnd/index.html.

Wills, Lawrence M. *Not God's People: Insiders and Outsiders in the Biblical World*. Lanham, MD: Rowman & Littlefield, 2008.

Wilson, Bev. "Urban Heat Management and the Legacy of Redlining." *Journal of the American Planning Association* 86 (2020): 443–457.

Wing, Nick. "When the Media Treats White Suspects and Killers Better than Black Victims." *Huffington Post*, December 6, 2017. https://www.huffpost.com/entry/media-black-victims_n_5673291.

Winter, Jessica. "What Should a Queer Children's Book Do?" *The New Yorker*, July 11, 2022. https://www.newyorker.com/news/annals-of-education/lgbt-books-kids-ban.

Withers, Erik T. 2017. "Whiteness and Culture." *Sociology Compass*, 2017. https://doi.org/10.1111/soc4.12464.

"Women CEOs of the S&P 500." Catalyst, February 2, 2023. https://www.catalyst.org/research/women-ceos-of-the-sp-500/.

"Women in the Workplace 2021." LeanIn.org/McKinsey & Company, 2021. https://www.mckinsey.com/~/media/mckinsey/featured%20insights/diversity%20and%20inclusion/women%20in%20the%20workplace%202021/women-in-the-workplace-2021.pdf.

"Women in the Workplace 2022." LeanIn.org/McKinsey & Company, 2022. https://www.mckinsey.com/~/media/mckinsey/featured%20insights/diversity%20and%20inclusion/women%20in%20the%20workplace%202022/women-in-the-workplace-2022.pdf.

Wong, Jaclyn S. *Equal Partners? How Dual-Professional Couples Make Career, Relationship, and Family Decisions*. Oakland: University of California Press, 2023.

Woodruff, Katie. "Coverage of Abortion in Select U.S. Newspapers." *Women's Health Issues* 29 (2019): 80–86.

Wootson, Cleve R., Jr. "A Black Woman Was Accused of Stealing—So This Victoria's Secret Kicked Out All Black Customers." *Washington Post*, December 11, 2016. https://www.washingtonpost.com/news/post-nation/wp/2016/12/11/a-black-woman-was-accused-of-stealing-so-this-victorias-secret-kicked-out-all-black-customers/?utm_term=.4f70d58b46cc.

World Bank. "Population—Female (% of Total Population)—United States." World Bank, 2022. https://data.worldbank.org/indicator/SP.POP.TOTL.FE.ZS?locations=US.

Wright, Jennifer. "When Women Rush to Defend Men Accused of Sexual Assault." Harpers Bazaar, October 25, 2017. https://www.harpersbazaar.com/culture/politics/a13090746/women-defend-men-sexual-assault/.

Wu, Xiao, Rachel C. Nethery, M. Benjamin Sabath, Danielle Braun, and Francesca Dominici. "Air Pollution and COVID-19 Mortality in the United States: Strengths and Limitations of an Ecological Regression Analysis." Science Advances 6 (2020). https://doi.org/10.1126/sciadv.abd4049.

Zarya, Valentina. "We Talk about Women Being Raped, Not Men Raping Women." Fortune, October 18, 2017. https://www.jacksonkatz.com/news/talk-women-raped-not-men-raping-women/.

Zeiders, Katharine H., Antoinette M. Landor, Melissa Flores, and Alaysia Brown. "Microaggressions and Diurnal Cortisol: Examining within-Person Associations among African-American and Latino Young Adults." Journal of Adolescent Health 63 (2018): 482–488.

Zerubavel, Eviatar. Taken for Granted: The Remarkable Power of the Unremarkable. Princeton, NJ: Princeton University Press, 2018.

Zhang, Lanlan, Elizabeth A. Reynolds Losin, Yoni K. Ashar, Leonie Koban, and Tor D. Wager. "Gender Biases in Estimation of Others' Pain." The Journal of Pain 22 (2021): 1048–1059.

Zhavoronkova, Marina, Rose Khatter, and Mathew Brady. "Occupational Segregation in America." Center for American Progress, March 29, 2022. https://www.americanprogress.org/article/occupational-segregation-in-america/.

Zhong, Raymond, and Nadia Popovich. "How Air Pollution across America Reflects Racist Policy from the 1930s." New York Times, March 9, 2022. https://www.nytimes.com/2022/03/09/climate/redlining-racism-air-pollution.html.

INDEX

www.ingramcontent.com/pod-product-compliance
Lightning Source LLC
Chambersburg PA
CBHW030648270326
41929CB00007B/268